Mons

An Artillery Battle

David Hutchison

Helion & Company

Helion & Company Limited
Unit 8 Amherst Business Centre
Budbrooke Road
Warwick
CV34 5WE
England
Tel. 01926 499 619
Fax 0121 711 4075
Email: info@helion.co.uk
Website: www.helion.co.uk
Twitter: @helionbooks
Visit our blog http://blog.helion.co.uk/

Published by Helion & Company 2018
Designed and typeset by Mach 3 Solutions Ltd (www.mach3solutions.co.uk)
Cover designed by Paul Hewitt, Battlefield Design (www.battlefield-design.co.uk)
Printed by Hobbs the Printers, Totton, Hampshire

Text © David Hutchison 2018
Photographs open source
Maps drawn by George Anderson© Helion & Company 2018

Front cover: 'L' Battery, RHA in action, Retreat from Mons, 1 September 1914 by Fortunino Matania.

Every reasonable effort has been made to trace copyright holders and to obtain their permission for the use of copyright material. The author and publisher apologize for any errors or omissions in this work and would be grateful if notified of any corrections that should be incorporated in future reprints or editions of this book.

ISBN 978-1-912390-73-1

British Library Cataloguing-in-Publication Data
A catalogue record for this book is available from the British Library.

All rights reserved. No part of this publication may be reproduced, stored in a retrieval system, or transmitted, in any form, or by any means, electronic, mechanical, photocopying, recording or otherwise, without the express written consent of Helion & Company Limited.

For details of other military history titles published by Helion & Company Limited contact the above address or visit our website: http://www.helion.co.uk.

We always welcome receipt of book proposals from prospective authors.

Contents

List of illustrations	vi
List of Maps	vii
Summary of the Battle	ix
Introduction	13
I.1 Gunners	13
I.2 The Artillery	14
I.3 Guns of the British Army	15
I.4 7.7 cm Feldkanone neuer Art	17
I.5 Artillery Tactical Development	20
I.6 Field Service Regulations 1912	22
I.7 Tactical Deployment at divisional level	25
I.8 Senior Command	29
1 The First Twenty Days of August 1914	31
1.1 Mobilisation	31
1.2 The Move to France	34
1.3 The Move towards Belgium	35
1.4 Events in Belgium and France	36
1.5 The German Armies	37
1.6 The British Concentration	38
2 The 21st & 22nd of August 1914	43
2.1 Advance of the British Expeditionary Force	43
2.2 Arrival of General Smith Dorrien	44
2.3 The British plan, as envisaged by I Corps for 23 August	48
2.4 The British plan, as envisaged by II Corps for 23 August	49
2.5 Geography	50
2.6 General Smith-Dorrien's Reconnaissance	51
2.7 5th Division Reconnaissance of the Frontline	51
2.8 3rd Division Reconnaissance of the Frontline	53
2.9 The British Plan as envisaged by GHQ for 23 August	54
2.10 Reaction to Events: I Corps	55
2.11 Summary of Plans for 23 August on evening of 22 August	61

3	The Day of Battle – 23 August 1914	62
	3.1 I Corps Artillery	62
	3.2 The Salient	63
	3.3 The Conference of the Generals	64
	3.4 Planning a Fighting Withdrawal	67
	3.5 The Immediate Consequences of the Meetings	68
	3.6 5th Division Artillery, II Corps	69
	3.7 3rd Division Artillery, II Corps	72
	3.8 Summary of II Corps Artillery Dispositions	74
	3.9 The German Army and its Artillery	74
	3.10 The British Artillery in the Salient, 3rd Division	77
	3.11 The 4th (Guards) Brigade	82
	3.12 General Haig's Account of I Corps Dispositions	84
	3.13 British Artillery along the Canal, 5th Division	85
	3.14 I Corps Artillery	89
	3.15 First Request for Assistance by II Corps	91
	3.16 2nd Division Artillery Dispositions	94
	3.17 The Salient in late afternoon	95
	3.18 I Corps Artillery in Action	96
	3.19 Second Request for Assistance by II Corps	99
	3.20 II Corps Retirement to Second Positions	103
	3.21 I Corps on the evening of 23 August	104
	3.22 GHQ Reaction to the events of 23 August	106
4	Second Day of Battle – 24 August 1914	107
	4.1 GHQ Orders a Withdrawal	107
	4.2 GHQ Orders to the left flank	108
	4.3 German Intentions on 24 August	109
	4.4 Withdrawal of I Corps	111
	4.5 II Corps Prepares for Withdrawal	115
	4.6 First German Infantry Advance	116
	4.7 Rear-guard of 3rd Division	119
	4.8 Second German Infantry Advance	120
	4.9 Third German Infantry Advance	124
	4.10 Left Wing of the BEF	125
	4.11 The Retirement of the 3rd Division Howitzers	126
5	Consequences of Mons	128
	5.1 Aftermath	128
	5.2 Artillery Tactics at Mons	128
	5.3 Impact of Field Service Regulations	131
	5.4 The Generals	133

5.5 Potential Lessons of the Battle	137
5.6 Postscript	142

Appendices
I	British Artillery Organisation, 1914	143
II	BEF Orders of Battle, August 1914	145
III	German Army General Structure, 1914	149
IV	Lecture on Co-operation between Artillery and Infantry, August 1913	151

Bibliography	157
Index	163

List of illustrations

18-pounder Field Gun.	16
4.5-inch howitzer.	16
15 cm (5.9 inch) schwere Feldhaubitze 13.	18
7.7 cm Feldkanone.	19
Field Marshal Sir John French.	39
Lieutenant General Sir Douglas Haig.	41
Lieutenant-General Sir Horace Smith-Dorrien.	45
British 18-pounder battery on the move.	52
Brigadier General Henry Horne.	62
Artist's impression of the German assault on Nimy bridge.	75
2nd Grenadier Guards, 4th (Guards) Brigade on the march, August 1914.	83
General Alexander von Kluck.	110
Major General Hubert Hamilton.	115
Major General Sir Edmund Allenby.	125
Mons and Le Cateau, a German cartoon commentary: "The 'dear' cousin from England:" I came; I saw; I conquered. (*Kladderadatsch*, 6 September 1914)	134
BEF prisoners, 1914.	140

List of Maps

In colour section

All maps are schematic and designed to clarify points made in the text. The exact position of villages roads railways and formation/units are shown diagramatically for the sake of clarity. Modern maps should not be utilised to research the battle. Too much has changed in the century since the battle occurred, including the Mons Canal line. Sheet 4, North West Europe, 1:250,000, Geographical Section, War Office, Apr. 1918, revised edition, is a useful reference.

	Map	Page
	Times of arrival of British artillery units in Northern France, August 1914.	i
1.	The advance of the British Expeditionary Force to Northern France from 17 August.	ii
2.	The concentration areas of the five divisions of the BEF in Northern France, showing railheads.	iii
3a.	I and II Corps start their advance into Belgium on 21 August.	iv
3b.	I and II Corps continue the advance into Belgium on 22 August.	iv
4.	Artillery and Infantry positions at Mons on the evening of 22 August.	v
5.	German and British Army movements on the afternoon and evening of 22 August.	vi
6.	Actual or planned artillery positions for 1st, 2nd and 3rd Divisions at 3 am on 23 August.	vii
7.	3rd Division Infantry in the Mons salient in early hours of 23 August.	viii
8.	I and II Corps Artillery in transit at noon on 23 August, and construction of II Corps 'second position'.	ix
9.	3rd Division Artillery in the Mons salient at midday on 23 August.	x
10.	II Corps retirement to 'second positions' from the Mons salient and Conde Canal on 23 August; the gap at Paturages.	xi

11. Construction of the 'Haig' defence line at Harveng, south of Mons, by the 2nd Division, from 5 p.m. on 23 August. — xii
12. I Corps artillery dispositions at 6 p.m. on 23 August. — xiii
13. 'Second position' lines at 3 a.m. on 24 August. I Corps reinforcements occupy the gap at Paturages at 2.30 a.m. — xiv
14. Rear-guard artillery positions in first hours of the retreat, morning of 24 August. — xv
15. Staff officer sketch of 3rd Division artillery positions in early hours of 24 August. — xvi

Summary of the Battle

Statements in **bold type** are those that contradict or, at least, significantly depart from the narrative provided in Brigadier General J.E. Edmonds, *History of the Great War: Military Operations, France and Belgium 1914*, Vol. I (1922, revised 1933, reprinted 1996) Imperial War Museum and Battery Press Inc. References to substantiate these revisions are in the text.

The Battle of Mons took place on 23 August 1914 because the British Expeditionary Force advanced to support the left flank of the French Armies just as the German Armies swung south following their westward sweep through Belgium.

Field Marshal French ordered a three-day advance into Belgium on the 20th, starting the next day. Unfortunately, **this was before his army was concentrated, with the result that his lead Corps had almost no artillery on the first or second day of the advance, and no divisional ammunition reserves on the day of battle.** His plan of advance over the three days allowed a huge gap to open between the two halves of his force. He arranged no British cavalry screen to its north and west.

II Corps was unhappy with their advance in defiance of British Army doctrine on many counts; but had no effective leadership, due to the sudden death of their Commander, Lieutenant General Grierson, **and the hospitalisation, following a car accident, of their artillery commander. Lieutenant General Haig, of I Corps, was also unhappy, and 'varied' his instructions, under powers given him in British Field Service Regulations, to advance further than ordered,** thus partially closing the gap between the two Corps on the morning of the 22nd.

On the evening of the 21st, General Smith-Dorrien arrived, and **pointed out the tactical flaws in the planned advance of II Corps.** French responded by immediately ordering the majority of his cavalry across to the west flank; and adjusting II Corps' billets for the 22nd, to a more defensible, but longer, line. **The dispositions for II Corps were now so extended, that, by definition, an offensive advance from this line was inadvisable under British tactical doctrine.** The next day, French ordered his I Corps to perform two days' advance in one, to enable the two forces to regain contact, with the further intention of allowing II Corps to retract the right of its extended line and concentrate for offensive action.

General Haig of I Corps, fully informed, by the afternoon of the 22nd, of the disorganised retreat of the French forces on his right, cancelled the advance of his

2nd Division at the last minute (to their considerable discomfort), but failed to stop the advance of his 1st Division, which had reacted more quickly to the GHQ order. He wanted his Corps on a line east of Bavai, in anticipation of the withdrawal of II Corps to a line west of Bavai. He confidently expected French to order this retirement, in compliance with British tactical doctrine.

Smith-Dorrien, aware of the exposed nature of his positions, **did not commit any of his artillery forward, planning, from the moment he arrived,** an outpost, rear-guard battle on the Mons canal, whilst simultaneously preparing a defence line, supported by all his artillery, south of Mons. This was **a 'variance' on the offensive intentions of Field Marshal French** who saw the canal line, as the battle line. The proposed advance for the 23rd was cancelled at **5 p.m. (not 10 p.m.)** on the 22nd, but no order to fall back was forthcoming.

Haig waited in vain for the order for II Corps to withdraw, and his staff made no firm arrangements for the 2nd Division to take over the line east and south of Mons by 6 a.m., as ordered by GHQ and expected by II Corps. Realising at midnight how far out of position his 2nd Division was, he ordered it onto the road **so hurriedly, that some units went without breakfast, further eroding their effectiveness.**

French met his Corps commanders at 6 a.m. on the day of the battle. He did not reconnoitre the ground, or inspect the dispositions of his two Corps. **He was misled by both his commanders as to their preparedness and intentions.** General Allenby of the Cavalry Division, **who was still smarting from a public rebuke that he had overstated German strength the day before**, and whose intelligence was, anyway, at least 12 hours out of date, **gave advice** which supported his decision to fight. **Field Marshal French left General Murray, his Chief of Staff, to discuss a retreat with his two Corps commanders, if, and when, it became necessary; and he, at least of GHQ staff, was made aware of General Smith-Dorrien's battle plan.**

Smith-Dorrien fought the battle he had always intended; astonishingly successfully, **but only because of defects in the German light artillery ammunition, which was non-lethal to a remarkable degree.** During the two days of battle, only four British batteries had guns in the front line with the infantry, and never a whole battery. **It was army doctrine generally not to advance guns into the front line in battle. That morning, Haig, anticipating the total defeat of the 3rd Division in the face of the German assault, cancelled the advance of the 4th (Guards) Brigade of his 2nd Division well short of the line he had been ordered by GHQ to take up in their support.**

II Corps was aware of dangerous gaps, either side of the 3rd Division at Mons, that on the right, unfilled by I Corps, and that on the left at Paturages. **I Corps ignored pleas for help during the afternoon, believing that II Corps was terminally compromised. I Corps staff ordered the 1st Division to prepare for an urgent withdrawal and ordered two brigades of the 2nd Division to the tiny hamlet of Harveng, a few miles south of Mons to dig and man a defence line south of Mons in anticipation of a German breakthrough. It took most of the afternoon to sort out the resulting confusion.** The gap on the right, which should have been filled by I Corps at 6 a.m., was partially filled at 7 p.m. The gap at Paturages on the left was not filled on the 23rd. I Corps, despite promises to do so, did not release the necessary troops till 10 p.m., for fear of a significant breach in 3rd Division lines. The gap was filled at 2.30 a.m. on the 24th. There was no effective liaison between I and II Corps on the first day of battle.

Brigadier General Horne, Artillery Commander of I Corps, determined I Corps positions on the right flank. He placed his artillery on a line to which the infantry subsequently conformed, their fire preventing any enemy infantry attacks developing on the I Corps front during the 23rd. **He commandeered artillery from the unnecessary defence of Harveng, placing them on this line;** and he commanded a well-coordinated rear-guard on the morning of the 24th, involving units from both I and II Corps. I Corps suffered **at least 60 (not 40) casualties** on 23 August.

The withdrawal from the defence line south of the canal on the 24th, was carried out professionally, always with artillery cover from behind. The only major error was on the left flank, where **General Allenby, as with his commander in chief, did not understand the II Corps tactical plan,** and also lost touch with the left flank of the 5th Division. He fell back too far and too fast with his 19th (Independent) Infantry Brigade, thus opening a gap for an encirclement attempt by the German right wing in the first hours of the Retreat. **Field Marshal French was not directly responsible for this error.**

The post-war accounts given by both Field Marshal French and General Smith-Dorrien are consistent with the narrative in what they do say. General Haig's account in his I Corps diary, written up after the event, contains so many serious errors of fact, that it is almost valueless as a narrative. It serves only to illuminate how he was trying to protect his personal reputation. All three accounts leave much unsaid.

Introduction

In the twenty years before 1914, all the continental armies had modernised their artillery. The energy and inventiveness of the latter stages of the industrial revolution did not confine itself to peaceful applications. By a series of steps, guns became more powerful, more accurate, and more rapid firing.

The stimulus for the British Army to modernise their artillery arm was the South African War (1899-1902). The artillery had not performed well, for a number of reasons. This book will not discuss in detail all the twists and turns of artillery tactical thinking between 1902 and 1912. To understand the battle of Mons, it is simply necessary to understand the ordnance available, the level of organisation achieved, and the resulting preparedness for war, which the artillery had reached in the summer of 1914.

I.1 Gunners

The British Army in 1914 was a professional one of about 250,000 regulars. Approximately half of the Army was based overseas, the majority in India, where regular infantry battalions made up 25 percent of the huge Indian Army.

This regular army was supported in Britain by the Territorial Force, which had 14 infantry, and 14 cavalry, divisions, both with their own artillery; and by reservists. There were three forms of reserves. The Army Reserve of retired soldiers, who were paid a retainer and attended 12 training days annually, numbered 145,000 men. The Special Reserve had another 64,000 men who had had an initial six months full-time training and three or four weeks training per year thereafter. In addition, a register was kept of 215,000 other men who had had military experience, but no reserve obligations. At least on paper, this came to over 600,000 men, potentially available for mobilisation. Only a small proportion of these were gunners, but those in, or recently retired from, the army were of high quality.[1]

---

1 The National Archives (TNA) WO 95/1527: 61st Battery, VIII Brigade RFA, 6 August 1914.

The officers of the Regular Army were professionals. An academy had been set up at Woolwich Arsenal in East London for the training of young officers for the artillery and engineers as early as 1720. By the 1880s the Royal Military Academy ('the shop') was performing the same role for the artillery and engineers as Sandhurst Royal Military Academy did for infantry and cavalry officers. Potential officers had to pass a tough entry examination at about 18 years old, and then attend a year of technical and practical training, before they were commissioned into the Army. They formed the new annual intake to join a corps of officers who were in the profession for life.

I.2 The Artillery

See Appendix I for a full description of the structure of the artillery in 1914. It will be assumed during the course of this book that the composition of batteries and brigades is known to the reader. The following does not go into detail, but briefly:

The majority of the young artillery officers, who graduated from Woolwich, were commissioned into the largest artillery regiment, the Royal Field Artillery, which supported the infantry and was armed mainly with 18-pounder field guns. There were two other artillery regiments in the British army. The cavalry was supported by the 13-pounder guns of the Royal Horse Artillery. The Royal Garrison Artillery managed the heavy guns, 60 pounders, four guns to a division on mobilisation in 1914.

The smallest independent unit of the Field Artillery was the battery of six guns, with an attached wagon line. In 1914, but not invariably later in the war, there were three batteries to a brigade. Each brigade also included a horse-drawn Brigade Ammunition Column (BAC).

There were four such brigades in each infantry division of about 18,000 men. Three were equipped with the 18-pounder field gun, and one with the 4.5-inch howitzer. In manoeuvres, each field gun brigade might support an allocated infantry brigade, there being three to a division. The one howitzer brigade and the Royal Garrison Artillery battery of four heavy guns were divisional resources.

The four divisional artillery brigades were commanded by an artillery brigadier. Each of the three infantry brigades in the division was also commanded by a brigadier. This structure was robust, and designed to ensure that both a division, usually the largest unit in any given conflict, and an infantry brigade with an attached artillery brigade, could be self-sufficient and able to act independently.

Artillery units operated in five modes, as documented in their war diaries. The first was 'in billets', when they were resting. The second was 'on the march' to new billets or a new position. The third was 'in reserve' which meant they had reached a destination and were waiting for further orders. The fourth was 'in action', which meant manning a position, not firing, but ready to do so. The fifth was 'firing'. This last occupied a very small proportion of their time, but the military task was to get the right force into action at the right point at the right time.

This 'right force' included ammunition. A battery would exhaust its own supply of ammunition in half an hour of brisk firing.[2] The Brigade Ammunition Column had not much more; and relied on re-supply from a Divisional Ammunition Column (DAC).

I.3 Guns of the British Army

The British, at the turn of the century, had been to war against the Boers in South Africa. It had become immediately apparent that the artillery of the British Army was obsolete. Neither the BL 15 pounder 7 cwt, nor the BL 5-inch howitzer, was a match for the new continental quick firing guns, which the Boers had imported. These included the 155 mm (Long Tom) siege guns and 75 mm field guns, made by Creusot in France; and the 75 mm field guns and 120 mm howitzers, made by Krupp in Germany. (The Boers used many different guns, including older models).[3]

In consequence, an urgent working party, set up by the War Office, reviewed British Army equipment, and after thorough and collaborative research, a new 18 pounder field gun was designed with a modern recoil system at an acceptable weight to allow both mobility and effective fire power. The Mark 1 was accepted into service after successful trials in 1903. Over the following ten years, a number of incremental improvements to the sights and barrel followed (Mark 2). Thus, the Ordnance QF (quick-firing) 18 pounder was born and became the standard British field gun for the next twenty years, albeit with small modifications and improvements during the First War. An almost identical 13 pounder QF Horse Artillery Gun followed in 1904.

At the same time, and by the same process, the 5-inch Ordnance BL 60-pounder was accepted into use in 1905; the Ordnance QF 4.5-inch howitzer in 1910. The latter had a five-foot barrel and a 35-pound high explosive shell; and was issued to a quarter of artillery brigades in the army of 1914.

In 1910, the 9.2-inch BL Mark 1 Siege Howitzer was commissioned for siege work and its design approved. It was totally impractical for mobile warfare, weighing in at over three tons and requiring nine tons of earth to be shovelled into a front box to hold it steady when fired. The prototype did not reach France till late 1914.[4]

Other designs had been adopted by the Indian Army. One siege brigade, but only one, went to France from there, late in 1914, armed with the 6-inch BL Siege Howitzer. In Britain, there were many older guns in armouries around the country being used for territorial training, including a variety of coastal defence guns. Of

---

2   TNA WO 95/1510: 5th Division, p.45.
3   Maj Darrell Hall, 'Guns in South Africa 1899-1902, Part 3', *South African Military History Society Journal*, Vol. 2, No. 2, December 1971.
4   Ian Hogg & L.F. Thurston, *British Artillery Weapons and Ammunition 1914-1918* (Shepperton: Ian Allan Ltd, 1972), pp.58, 80, 102, 116.

18-pounder Field Gun.

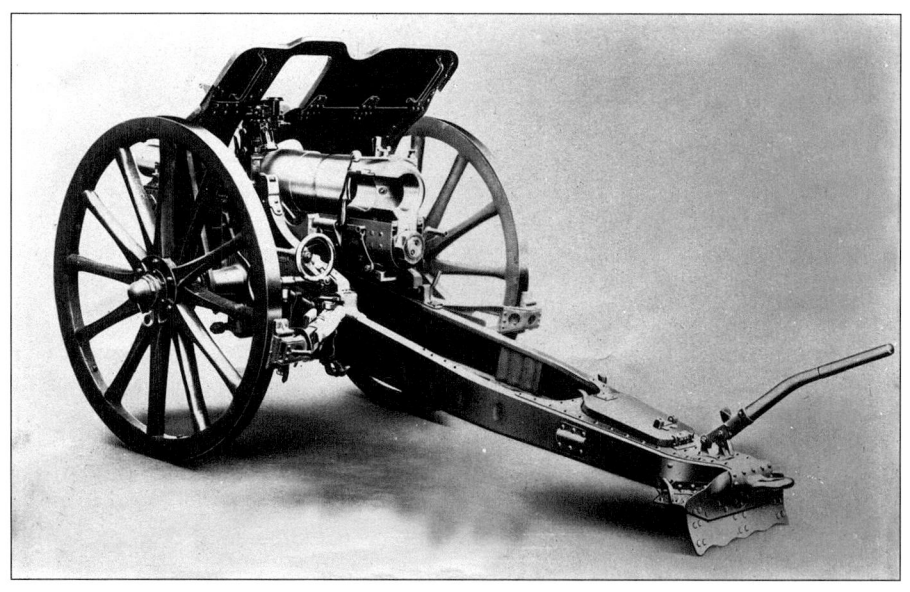

4.5-inch howitzer.

these, only the 4.7-inch QF Field Gun, adapted from a ship's gun in 1900, went briefly to France.[5]

The British had not been alone in keenly observing the effectiveness of the respective guns in the South African war of 1899. The French were impressed by the effectiveness of their Canon de 75 Modèle 1897, which is widely regarded as being the first modern artillery piece, firing fifteen rounds per minute and stabilized by a hydropneumatic recoil mechanism. They purchased large numbers for their army, though they also maintained obsolete guns for use in an emergency.[6]

The Germans opted to remain with their 7.7 cm Feldkanone 96 neuer Art, developed as the name suggests in 1896, but not tested in South Africa. It was lighter and more mobile than the French gun, which fitted in with German plans for mobile wars of aggression in Europe. It fired a fifteen-pound shell, comparable with the French field gun, but smaller than the eighteen-pound British projectile. It required some updating through the first decade of the twentieth century.

For effective fire power in the sieges the Germans envisaged, they had concentrated on the development of a range of howitzers, the lightest being the 10.5 cm Feldhaubitze 98/09, equivalent to the British 4.5 inch. They deployed a heavier howitzer, the 15 cm (5.9 inch) Schwere Feldhaubitze 1902, in the field. The shell for this gun weighed 93 pounds, much heavier than that of the British 60-pounder. They also had the 21 cm (8.3 inch) Morser 10, the 28 cm (11 inch) Haubwitz L12 and the massive 42 cm Kurze Marine-Kanone (Big Bertha), which fired a shell weighing 1700 pounds.[7]

For their light guns, the British and French used mainly shrapnel projectiles, and indeed the British Expeditionary Force did not take any field artillery high explosive shells with them to France.[8] The Germans however had opted for a universal shell, which served both shrapnel and high explosive functions by adjustment of a complicated fuse. These shells were difficult to manufacture in quantity.[9] This fact had profound consequences as they prepared for war in 1914.

I.4 7.7 cm Feldkanone neuer Art

In contrast to the British field gun, which had been introduced in 1903 and upgraded thereafter, the German Feldkanone was an old-style gun that had been improved since its introduction in 1896, but not completely re-designed. It was light and mobile,

---

5   Ibid., pp.111, 124, 161.
6   Spencer Tucker (ed.), *World War I: A Student Encyclopedia* (Santa Barbara, California: ABC-CLIO Inc., 2006), p.726.
7   Herbert Jäger, *German Artillery of World War One* (Marlborough: Crowood Press, 2001), pp. 27, 39.
8   Brig. Gen. J.E. Edmonds, *Military Operations France and Belgium 1914*, Vol. I (London: Macmillan, 1922), p. 10..
9   Jäger, *German Artillery of World War One*, p.194.

15 cm (5.9 inch) schwere Feldhaubitze 13.

and fired a universal shell that could be time-fused to deliver air-bursting shrapnel, or contact fused to deliver high explosive, this explosive being packed around the shrapnel bullets. Only the German (and Austro-Hungarian) artillery of all the continental armies had opted for this universal shell. Of necessity, it had a complicated fuse (KZ11), which was expensive to produce.

In comparison with the British 18-pound round, the Feldkanone 15-pound projectile had a lower muzzle velocity (1,525 and 1,615 feet per second respectively) and was loaded with lighter individual bullets (10 and 11 grams respectively). They also had fewer of them (294 to 375).[10] These shrapnel bullets were accelerated by an expelling charge at the base of the shell to achieve lethal velocity, or in other words a sufficient kinetic energy to kill; this being a factor of both weight and speed of the bullet when it hit the target. It is clear that the range of killing power of the German shrapnel would have been less than that of the British shrapnel. With fewer bullets and less weight, their lethal zone was smaller.

Knowing this, the German artillery concentrated on accuracy, and there is no doubt that German gunners were very proficient. All accounts, and there will be many instances at Mons, emphasise the accuracy of their fire.

10   Hogg & Thurston, *British Artillery*, p.237, 240

7.7 cm Feldkanone.

German pre-war Feldkanone shrapnel projectiles had a light pressed steel casing and contained 250 grams of TNT. However, in early 1914, when the German high command ordered a stockpiling of ammunition in anticipation of conflict:

> [M]ore could not be produced rapidly of the usual quality; the heavy presses necessary, and even steel, were lacking. In August 1914, a new type of shell was introduced: the 7.7 cm Kanonen-granate 14. Its development had been perfected by the Spring of 1914. It was a step back in every way. The shell body was cast in iron and had therefore to be thick enough to take the shock of firing and to produce large enough fragments on detonation. This reduced the interior volume so that the shell only contained 180 grams of explosive. And the explosive was no longer the powerful TNT, but at first a replacement of ammonium-nitrate-carbon explosives.[11]

These changes in specification were made without sufficient testing. The reduction in both weight and power of the high explosive charge rendered the shell almost useless in impact ground-bursting mode, particularly in damp farmland where the soil absorbed the explosion.

And the shell also proved useless in air-burst shrapnel mode. Without slow motion photography, the exact reason for this is impossible to identify, but either the complicated fuse failed to separate smoothly from the new casing, destabilising the projectile; or the brittle cast iron casing fractured on detonation of the expelling charge, dissipating the forward energy of the shrapnel bullets. A number of British reports comment that the air-bursts were too high to be effective, so there may have been a

11 Jäger, *German Artillery of World War One*, p.194.

human element as well. Whatever the reason, most of the shrapnel dropped without lethal effect.[12] A few men and horses were wounded, but it was a few. This new shell was withdrawn from use before the end of the year.

That the German light artillery shell was ineffective was quickly appreciated by both sides. General von Falkenhayn, Chief of the General Staff of the German Field Army observed after the campaign that our 'men felt uncomfortably conscious of the inferiority, in terms of both range and effectiveness, of our field gun.'[13] He initiated a review which led to improved projectiles in 1915, and a redesign of the 7.7 cm Feldkanone for 1916.

Colin Hutchison, an artillery subaltern with the 3rd Division put it more bluntly. 'The German guns are useless' he said.[14] 'Effect nil', states a British Cavalry Division report on 22 August.[15]

The War Office sponsored a booklet of front line tactical advice for training purposes in late 1914. Two unnamed British artillery officers are quoted, one saying of the German gun that 'their shrapnel is far inferior to that of the 18-pounder. This is admitted by all', the other that 'their shell is very indifferent and does very little damage, but their fire is very accurate.'[16] For reasons that are difficult to understand, the ineffectiveness of this 1914 German field artillery shell was forgotten by the end of the war; and has continued to be forgotten to the present day.

There is no doubt that being under their heavy and accurate fire was frightening. This alone made them weapons to be feared by conscript armies. It is difficult to find a First World War commentary which does not describe the German field artillery as highly effective in the mobile campaigns of 1914, on any front. It is possible that the Germans were using stocks of pre-war ammunition on some fronts, but this assertion so far as Mons is concerned is just wrong.

I.5 Artillery Tactical Development

Throughout the South African War, batteries were almost universally attached to the infantry, and indeed when General Kitchener took command, he abolished the post of General commanding the artillery on the grounds that it was superfluous. The defeat of a British army, with the loss of front line gunners, and thereby guns, to accurate

---

12   David Hutchison, 'The Effectiveness of German Field Artillery at Mons and during the Retreat in August 1914', *Journal for the Society of Army Historical Research*, No. 95 (2017), pp. 331-337.
13   Herman Cron, *Imperial German Army 1914-18* (Solihull: Helion & Company Ltd, 2001), p.135.
14   Colin Hutchison, Journals and letters, 1914. Ref. D Hutchison, *The Young Gunner: The Royal Field Artillery in the Great War* (Kibworth Beauchamp: Troubador Press 2016), p.13.
15   TNA WO 95/629/4: II Corps staff intelligence, 22 August 1914.
16   *Notes from the Front: Collated by the General Staff* (London: HMSO, 1914), pp.20, 22.

rifle fire at the Battle of Colenso in 1899 was a considerable shock to the army establishment. At the Battle of Paardeberg in 1900, an artillery plan, which subsequently succeeded, was initially vetoed in favour of a disastrous frontal attack which caused heavy infantry losses. Later in the war, it became almost impossible to concentrate the artillery for specific objectives, in the absence of an over-riding commander. There was a general feeling after the war that the artillery had been badly mishandled.

The introduction of new quick firing guns (with shields against rifle fire), developed as a consequence of the war, made it difficult to obtain consensus on how best to improve matters. The debate was not just a military one. Signallers to the artillery had been abolished in 1899 to save money, and the treasury refused to pay for the huge stocks of ammunition that would be required by proponents of heavy artillery firepower. The ebb and flow of debate was complicated by observations of artillery in action in the Russo-Japanese War (1904-05), and then by the French Army embracing a culture of ultra-aggressive élan, in which all arms of the attacking force advanced together. But it was of public interest and is well documented in the *Encyclopaedia Britannica* 1911 (see artillery entry) and in subsequent works on the subject.[17]

The problems of command were addressed in 1907 by the adoption of the divisional artillery command structure already described, as a consequence of the Haldane Reforms. (These far-reaching reforms were primarily designed to create the structure for an Expeditionary Force that could be quickly mobilised for a continental war, backed up by a well-trained home defence force, but they went further than this in rationalising and codifying the structure of the whole army. Sir Richard Haldane's reforms transformed the army into a modern fit-for-purpose force that was able to cope with the extraordinary demands put on it by the out-break of war. As Minister for War, he was by all accounts a brilliantly effective politician.)

Artillery at brigade level still worked very closely with their infantry counterparts, and the brigadier general commanding divisional artillery was at first absurdly underresourced, but by 1911, the structure was in place, though still evolving. The artillery brigadier was, at first, primarily an adviser to the commander of the division,[18] but the role fairly quickly evolved into one of true command.[19]

The reforms did not elevate the artillery into an offensive arm in its own right in the eyes of corps and army generals. The modern structure of the Royal Field Artillery was too new. Their job was to support the infantry and cavalry. This job description was totally accepted by the artillery officers at the time. It was the task of divisional generals of both infantry and cavalry to use the artillery as a support to their individual manoeuvres.

---

17 Marble, Sanders, *The Infantry cannot do with a gun less: The Place of the Artillery in the British Expeditionary Force, 1914-1918* (Gutenberg-E, 2013).
18 H. A. Bethell, *Modern Artillery in the Field: A Description of the Artillery of the Field Army, and the Principles and Methods of its Employment* (London: Macmillan, 1911), pp.224-8.
19 TNA WO/279/47, Army Manoeuvres 1912, pp.130, 147.

Of more importance to the Mons campaign than the intricacies of the various debates and reforms between 1900 and 1913, is the point it had reached in the summer of 1914.

Issues concerning ammunition had been decided, for better or for worse. The Treasury would not allow any significant stockpiling of ammunition, and its transport anyway was difficult in the mobile war envisaged. Commanders of artillery had to accept a low level of supply as a fact of life. The 18-pounders of the Royal Field Artillery would use shrapnel, on the grounds that their task was to kill enemy infantry. High explosive was not considered lethal enough.

The importance of inter-arm cooperation was a point on which all sides in the debate could agree. In 1909, a document was produced which not only standardised all basic procedures, from message taking to military manoeuvres, but also laid down an ethos for the army, one of aggression, cooperation and initiative. *Field Service Regulations* (1909) crystallised a seminal concept, and General Haig was one of those influential in ensuring that it was taken up by the whole army. It was updated in 1912.[20]

I.6 Field Service Regulations 1912

This document was the army rule-book. It is absolutely central to the Battle of Mons. The battle cannot be understood, without knowing its philosophy and some of its principal assertions. Unsurprisingly its contents were fully ingrained into the military lives of those who were in training from 1909 onward, perhaps less so in those who had trained before this date, and not at all in those who left the army before it came into operation.

The document is prescriptive in detail, and lays out, clearly and emphatically, procedures and organisational arrangements, dealing with all aspects of army life, from the issuing of major orders to the laying out of latrines. Firm guidelines are laid down in detail on the manoeuvres of different units in different situations, and it is made clear that deviance from best practice is to be severely discouraged.

But it is also astonishingly non-prescriptive when it comes to considering the uncertainty and confusion of war. In one crucial paragraph, two points of great philosophical and practical importance are made. The first is that a senior officer, divorced from the fray should issue only 'brief and very general instructions'. He should not attempt to micro-manage his juniors. As a corollary of this, his juniors should show initiative, using these 'brief and very general instructions' as a guide to intentions:

> It is necessary to train subordinates not only to work resolutely and intelligently in accordance with brief and very general instructions, but also to take on

---

20 War Office, *Field Service Regulations, 1909*, reprinted with amendments 1912 (London: HMSO, 1914).

themselves, whenever it be necessary, the responsibility of departing from, or of varying the orders they may have received.[21]

This could only work in a highly professional army, but the British Army was just that. It is impossible to overestimate the importance of this ethos. It means that operational orders were to some extent advisory, not totally prescriptive. Many of the errors which have crept in to accounts of the battle are because this point has not been recognised. From corps commanders down to second lieutenants, there are numerous examples of officers at Mons 'departing from or varying' their orders. It means that a senior officer might think he was using one tactical doctrine, but his subordinate might modify it to another, or that a staff officer might, in good faith, record that a certain move had been made, when it had not.

It seems out of character that Sir Douglas Haig, who was one of the main architects of the Field Service Regulations project, should have allowed a paragraph like this in to the document. All the rest of the document is rigidly prescriptive. One detects the hand of Smith-Dorrien or Grierson, of whom more anon.

Its importance in determining ethos is clear in the report of the 1912 manoeuvres. These army war games were designed to test the ability of senior generals in managing large bodies of men. That of 1912 was almost a dress rehearsal for the Mons campaign. Sir John French was the director. Haig and Grierson were the combatants; Smith-Dorrien was a senior umpire.

Sir John French, in his summing up of the exercise, does not even once mention the artillery. But he fully embraces the philosophy of the Field Regulations. 'The general applicability of these remarks must be considered in conjunction with Field Service Regulations', he says. And he goes on to endorse the idea of the senior general issuing 'brief and very general instructions' by praising General Grierson for 'wisely, and to a great extent necessarily, [appearing] to have given his divisional commanders a very free hand.'[22] Indeed, as one of Lieutenant General Grierson's staff officers recalled:

> Sir Peter Radcliffe later recalled that he was detailed to deliver orders to a Territorial unit, but on arrival found that the situation had changed completely. Taking the initiative, he ignored the orders and instructed the unit to undertake a completely different mission. Radcliffe stated that he would not have taken such a step if he "had not known that General Grierson would have backed me." In stark contrast, the official report on the manoeuvres criticized the fact that Haig's orders to Lomax left him "with little scope for the exercise of initiative".[23]

---

21 *Field Service Regulations*, 1912, p.28.
22 TNA WO/279/47 Army Manoeuvres 1912, p.53, 55.
23 Spencer Jones (ed.), *Stemming the Tide: Officers and Leadership in the British Expeditionary Force 1914* (Solihull, Helion & Company, 2013), Chapter 6.

Haig was criticised for not following his own regulations, and the assessors, led by Sir John French, took him to task for it.

Field Service Regulations summarise the role of the field artillery in one sentence as a universal premise: 'The object of artillery fire is to help the infantry maintain its mobility and offensive power.' This statement merely enshrined the role of the artillery within the British Army as envisaged and developed since 1907 and before. The artillery was not an arm of the Army. The Royal Field Artillery was a support to the infantry, and the Royal Horse Artillery was a support to the cavalry; and this support was commanded at sub-divisional level. Thus, orders from General Headquarters to Corps, or from Corps to Division contain no specific reference to artillery. They would issue 'brief and very general' instructions, and it was up to the division and other smaller units as to how the order was obeyed, incorporating the use of artillery into their plan. But Field Service Regulations had previously stated: 'Infantry depends on artillery to enable it to obtain superiority of fire and to close with the enemy.'[24]

This is as close as field regulations get to recognising the artillery as an essential arm in its own right. Few generals in the British Army would have totally accepted this statement. Infantry generals did not like the idea of 'depending' on guns, even if they did. 'Infantry would like the help of artillery in obtaining superiority of fire' probably sums up better how they felt.

General Smith-Dorrien was one who did believe it. He was an umpire to the 1912 manoeuvres, with Generals Grierson and Haig going head to head in simulated warfare. He observed that:

> The cooperation of infantry and artillery in the attack still leaves much to be desired. So long as attacks continue to be conducted at the pace usual at manoeuvres, it is difficult to provide any remedy for this fault.[25]

He was saying that infantry trained generals were rushing into attack without deploying their artillery in prior support. He went further. He said that the umpires should have judged more casualties to units caught in the fire of artillery; and goes on to criticise the artillery for not making better use of covered positions.[26] He was emphasising the effectiveness and necessity of good artillery deployment in infantry manoeuvres. They were prescient observations.

Field Service Regulations (1912) seldom refer directly to the artillery in the chapter on general manoeuvres. This deals with divisional and brigade movements, and the artillery is simply assumed to be in support. One major exception is in the section on advance against an organised enemy:

---

24 *Field Service Regulations*, 1912, p.14.
25 TNA WO/279/47: Army Manoeuvres 1912, pp.138.
26 Ibid., pp.138, 152.

> It is then essential ... that every force that takes the field against an organised enemy should be composed of all arms[27] ... As a rule, the divisional artillery will follow the leading brigade of the main body of its division. Artillery brigade and mounted brigade ammunition columns usually march in rear of the fighting troops of their own division or brigade, but it may be advisable to place one, or a portion of one, brigade ammunition column further forward in the order of march.[28]

These two paragraphs in the Regulations will be brought into sharp focus in time, but it is unusual for such explicit instructions on artillery deployment to be given. Usually, they are mentioned along with machine guns and mounted troops. This example pertains to outposts. Again, this section will be considered later in the run-up to Mons:

> Artillery may be usefully employed with outposts if they occupy the ground which the main body is to hold in case of attack; if there is limited ground over which the enemy must pass; or if it is important to prevent the enemy from occupying artillery positions within close field artillery range of the outposts ... Machine guns with outposts may be employed to sweep approaches.[29]

This seems to support the use of guns close up on the battlefield, but a later paragraph implies the opposite. 'Artillery will generally be protected by the distribution of the other arms', though there is a section describing designated escorts to be supplied if the guns should happen to be in the infantry line. In short, Field Service Regulations is not prescriptive on the issue.

The section on bombardment of fortresses, which is essentially what fortified trenches were, demonstrates little belief in the usefulness of artillery. 'By itself, bombardment should not succeed against a good garrison.'[30] Even the next section on siege operations emphasises that it is the infantry who will lead the whole process, and that the siege guns will conform to their needs, rather than vice versa.

I.7 Tactical Deployment at divisional level

So, *Field Service Regulations* (1912) do not go into fine detail on the deployment of guns in battle. But at divisional headquarters, and in artillery barracks, there was much debate. A lecture given in 1913 on the subject is reproduced in Appendix III. It

---

27 *Field Service Regulations*, 1912, p.14.
28 Ibid., p.51.
29 Ibid., p.102.
30 Ibid., p.163.

was kept for reference in the War Diary of the 5th Division and was thus presumably a guide to their tactical deployment. It is worth reading in its entirety, but very briefly, it starts with the universal premise, as given with only slightly different wording in the Field Regulations:

> Infantry has been, and always must be, the decisive arm, so it follows that the role of the artillery is to help the infantry maintain its mobility and offensive power by all the means at its disposal, and this must be the underlying principle of all artillery tactics.[31]

In retrospect, this underlying principle is arguable. In defence, artillery might well be the decisive arm. In a siege, which is essentially what trench warfare was, artillery might also be the decisive arm in the early stages. One of the surprises of the pre-war debate was how 'few noticed how much the trench lines of other battles mimicked sieges'.[32] But it was a fundamental premise all the same, and artillery tactics in 1914 must be assessed in its light.

The author then discusses the possible command pathways for controlling artillery during infantry movements. In the 1912 manoeuvres, the new artillery commanders kept very close control of their guns, hardly ever allowing them independence of divisional direction.[33] They loosened up in the light of experience and tactical debate.

The brigadier in charge of artillery had two choices, and there are examples of both in the Mons battle. The first is that he retained control himself. With knowledge of tactical objectives, he would site his guns for divisional protection. The infantry would then take up positions such that they were sheltered by those guns. This scenario was routinely followed in advancing to defence, when, with artillery positions selected, the infantry moved forward to entrench in front of them.

The second is that he ceded command of a specific artillery brigade to an infantry brigade, to be used in support of the objectives of that brigade. Now, the artillery brigade is commanded by the infantry brigadier. This was the common mode of use in attack or close defence. The artillery brigadier, in consultation with his divisional general, would make the decision as to when this transfer of responsibility became desirable. It was important for artillery brigade colonels to know who their commanding officers were, and command pathways were therefore strictly enforced. While the artillery brigade was ceded to an infantry brigade, the artillery brigade commander could, and would, disregard orders from other sources, however senior, until released from his allocated task by the infantry brigadier. More rarely a battery, or a section of a battery, might be ceded to the control of an infantry battalion, under a colonel.

---

31 TNA WO 95/1510: 5th Division, p.45.
32 Marble, *The Infantry cannot do with a gun less.*
33 TNA WO/279/47: Army Manoeuvres, 1912, pp.130, 147.

Sometimes, the artillery brigadier would select positions, and then transfer the artillery to infantry brigade command. Like all compromises, this ran the risk of failing to satisfy either party.

A further and complicating command structure was required when elements of more than one artillery brigade were working together on the same tactical task. In this scenario, it was desirable to have one artillery commander in control, and the senior officer took command of the 'group', if it was so designated by the artillery brigadier.

There will be many instances of these transfers of command in the following accounts, and it is one reason why the artillery war is difficult to follow. The artillery diaries concentrate on those units under direct command, recording much less detail on units allocated elsewhere. Transfers happen so seamlessly that it is not always clear when they have occurred.

It is an extraordinary testament to the professionalism of the army in general that such a flexible and pragmatic system worked. The artillery brigadier did not sit back and ignore his brigades so seconded. He would visit their positions and advise his colonels, liaising with his infantry counterpart. Personal relationships and trust were important.

Once in position, there was debate as to whether the battery or brigade of artillery, should be allocated a task, such as keeping the heads of the opposing infantry down, or allocated a zone, with instructions to engage any target of opportunity. Generally, the former was accepted practice in attack, and the latter in defence, but the importance of the distinction should not be underestimated. Rigid adherence to an inappropriate mode of management had severe consequences all through the war.

Cooperation with the forward infantry was regarded as of critical importance, and there are many good examples of this liaison at Mons. But this cooperation was not formalised. It fell under the requirement that all officers should show initiative. By and large, all the officers of a division knew each other. Units did not fight in isolation. They established contact on either side, and forward and back, clarifying their military task within the tactical plan. It was part of the job description, an integral part of their training. They were in a professional army and they fought as a team.

And then there was the vexing question of how close the guns should be to the infantry. This treatise argues against guns being placed in the infantry line. The reasons are clear. If close, gunners could be killed, rendering the guns useless; or horses could be killed, and limbers destroyed, so that guns were immobilised. In addition, ammunition resupply was almost impossible in the front line; the flat trajectory of fire required at close range limited the field of fire; and there was a risk of hitting friendly infantry in the back, particularly with shells that exploded prematurely, a not unusual occurrence. The author does however concede that some generals (and the French) considered it desirable to bolster the morale of the infantry, an argument he found faintly patronising, but which was a significant consideration in conscript armies.[34]

34 Marble, *The Infantry cannot do with a gun less.*

There are issues which are not covered in the lecture. One is the distinction between open, semi-covered and covered gun positions.[35] The terms are self-explanatory, referring to use of terrain. For obvious reasons, the gunners preferred covered positions, when only the observer, usually the commanding officer, was directly exposed to enemy fire. He would control the battery from an observation post (OP), usually, but not always, in front of the guns. Field guns usually fired from covered, or semi-covered positions. But they were also expected to use their mobility to fire from open positions with direct observation on vulnerable targets. This was particularly true for the Royal Horse Artillery.

Howitzer batteries, in contrast, almost never fired from open positions, usually targeting enemy batteries or constructed defences. They were trained to dig in and set up observation posts before opening fire. This could be a very slow process.

The lecture also deals with the effectiveness of artillery fire. It is asserted that a British field battery, with good observation of a road down which an enemy infantry column was marching, would expect, at 4000 yards, to cause casualties in one minute, and decimate the formation in two. He also says that any artillery unit exposed to enemy counter fire while on the move could expect to be at least partially immobilised due to horses being killed, and wagons smashed, in an equally short space of time.

The failure of the German light artillery ordnance was going to hand a priceless, and probably decisive, advantage to the British in the coming battle. There are many descriptions of British units of all arms retiring under close and accurate fire; and emerging completely unscathed.

Not only the guns were vulnerable, of course. Lieutenant General Ferguson of the 5th Division not only retained a copy of this lecture, he arranged practical exercises for his troops in Ireland in late 1913. Paraphrasing the journal of Lieutenant Rory McLeod of the 15th Brigade RFA:

> The general wished to find the best formations for infantry to advance and attack against artillery. Two brigades of artillery came into action with OP's forward. The infantry advanced, shaking down into lines as they approached the position. Every battery commander said that they offered splendid targets. It was suggested that they should form up in irregular 'blobs', and advance in 'worms' to take advantage of the ground. The infantry tried again, and the battery commanders said that they were much more difficult targets to hit.

General Ferguson also demanded that his batteries be able to shoot by sections (of two guns each, three to a battery) at different targets of opportunity.[36]

---

35 Bethell, *Modern Artillery in the Field*, p.271.
36 Royal Artillery Museum, Larkhill, MD/1150, Lieutenant (later Colonel) Roderick McLeod, Journal, 1913.

Neither infantry nor artillery tactics were set in stone. The best commanded divisions of the regular army learnt very fast how best to modify their tactics in the light of experience.

I.8 Senior Command

The line of promotion in the artillery effectively peaked at brigadier general, commanding the artillery of a division. The step from commanding the divisional artillery, as a brigadier general, to commanding an infantry division, as a major general, was a very big one, and put a block on promotion to all but the most talented. Infantry and cavalry brigadiers could get experience handling artillery when they had a brigade of artillery under their command, as would happen if they were lucky enough to gain an independent posting. But artillery officers seldom had such an opportunity to gain experience with infantry. Those artillery officers who were promoted to general rank beyond brigadier had usually distinguished themselves as colonial administrators or as academic soldiers. There were very few of them, and most took up an administrative role.

Field Marshal French, as an army commander, had a Major General of Royal Artillery on his staff; Corps commanders were supported by a brigadier general of artillery in 1914. But their role was purely advisory to divisions. It would be a brave man, of course, who ignored their advice. But the distinction is important. The brigadier general of divisional artillery was the man who bore the responsibility, and his primary job was to protect the infantry, or cavalry, of his division.

Major General W.F.L. Lindsay is listed in the Official History as Major General Royal Artillery for the BEF in August 1914, but it is difficult to understand what his role was, or indeed to know if he ever took up the post. He is not included in Field Marshal French's list of staff officers in his memoires, and there is no mention of him in any of the contemporary records examined. He had no discernible impact on events.

Promotion in the army was based on merit, but that is not to say that it was not affected both by experience in high status units, and by social attributes. It undoubtedly was.

Social standing was very important in the Great Britain of 1914. As a generalisation, the best connected young officers went in to the cavalry, often backed by considerable family money. The less well connected opted for the infantry, the more prestigious a regiment the better. Becoming a gunner or a sapper did not have the same social cachet. Sir John French was a cavalry officer as was Sir Douglas Haig; French's Chief of Staff and all the divisional generals were from the infantry. Sir James Grierson was the only significant figure who trained at Woolwich, passing out in 1878, but by 1882 he had started a career in international military studies, and apart from one year as a brigade major in 1891 spent the rest of his life in staff work.[37] Of the

---

37 Jones (ed.), *Stemming the Tide*, Chapter 6.

senior generals, Sir Horace Lockwood Smith-Dorrien had the greatest experience of all arms combat. He was from the infantry, and had fought in the Zulu war in 1879, in Sudan in 1885 and 1898, on the Indian Frontier in 1897, and in the South African War. 'His forthright views were not always in tune with the doctrinal outlook of the army as a whole,'[38] is an understatement he would have enjoyed.

Early training has a life-long impact. The cavalry was trained in aggressive reconnaissance for the army, and to set up battle for a decisive charge. The infantry had learnt from the very effective sniping of the Boers in South Africa and worked hard on marksmanship and mobility. Neither group fully embraced the artillery as a primary force in war. The generals of 1914 carried their experience to a continental war.

It was accepted that all generals needed to be able to weld their staff into a cohesive unit. Junior officers on the staff had a significant advisory role in their area of expertise; and were expected to use their special knowledge to influence the decisions their generals came to. Some generals were better than others at avoiding a hierarchical structure in their staff. The 1912 manoeuvres brought this factor into focus: 'General Haig is less tolerant of advice than his rival, and the value of his staff will therefore be more evident in the acts of General Grierson.'[39] Commanders of artillery on the staff came from a background of supporting, rather than initiating manoeuvres, and were not of the highest rank. Their voices were not always heard as loudly as perhaps they should have been by the senior command.

There were many other factors at work in the upper echelons of the British Army in these pre-war years and these have been explored in depth by a number of excellent biographies and general accounts. Inclusive cliques formed, with less senior generals pinning their coats to the patronage of more senior ones, and more senior ones working on royal and political connections to maintain their influence. Much of this was done under public scrutiny, and a bad review in the newspapers of the army exercises was not a happy experience. Comments that in private might have been absorbed as constructive criticism, when published, became personal insults.

No artillery generals, except arguably General Grierson, were of sufficient seniority, or had sufficiently good connections, to move into this senior circle. There was almost no challenge to the general concept that the artillery was, and should ever be, a divisional resource; and that it was the cavalry and infantry divisions that were the major army units to be manoeuvred by the very senior generals.

---

38 Ibid., Chapter 7.
39 Ibid., p. 146, ref. *Manchester Guardian*, 9 September 1912.

1

The First Twenty Days of August 1914

1.1 Mobilisation

On 28 July 1914, the British Army was put on alert for possible war with Germany. Events moved fast. Mobilisation was implemented on 4 August when news of the breaching of Belgian neutrality arrived in London. The reserves were called up. This process was rehearsed (every winter with random units), and there was a mobilisation plan of great sophistication in place. It worked remarkably smoothly.[1]

Five Regular army divisions, one of them cavalry, were brought up to full strength within days and moved by train from all parts of the British Isles to Southampton or ports in Ireland. Most of the infantry units were mobilised in three or four days as reservists brought the units up to strength with relative ease. The 4th (Guards) Infantry Brigade, based in London, describe the process in their war diary:

> London. Aug 4th. 5 p.m. Mobilisation orders received by telegram.
>
> 5th. Headquarters move from Horse Guards to Chelsea Barracks, and personnel and horses were complete by 6 p.m. Excellent draft horses supplied by GWR, and Carter Paterson; and quite good riding horses by Mrs Stubbs and Aerated Water Company.
>
> 6th. Draw mobilisation equipment at the Tower.
>
> 7th. 6 p.m. Mobilisation complete in all details except one or two articles of saddlery.[2]

All units started at peace-time manning levels. Men unfit for overseas service had to be replaced, and all units brought up to strength. The 8th Infantry Brigade of the

---

1 Edmonds, *Military Operations France and Belgium 1914*, Vol. I, p.31.
2 TNA WO 95/1341: 4th (Guards) Infantry Brigade, 7 August 1914. Times provided throughout this volume are Greenwich Mean time. In August, sunrise was before 6 a.m., and sunset before 8 p.m., with a further hour of light, during dawn and dusk.

3rd Division, at Devonport, took a day longer to mobilise, reporting that their four battalions comprised between 48 and 77 percent reservists.[3]

Artillery units generally took longer to achieve readiness, but most reported they were mobilised and ready to move within ten days.[4] The artillery brigades attached to the 3rd Division were based at Bulford Camp on Salisbury Plain in Wiltshire. Like the infantry, the 23rd, 30th (Howitzer), 40th and 43rd Brigades RFA were not on a war footing, and they had to be brought up to full strength from a standing start. Those in the 5th Division were in Ireland and on a higher manning level.[5] In both places, there was frantic activity, as men were reshuffled, fresh horses obtained and kit renewed. Few units documented their difficulties in their war diaries, but of those who did at Bulford the following entries are typical:

> Considerable delay was experienced in obtaining neck collars for heavy draft horses, and the pattern supplied was too large and of inferior workmanship.[6]
>
> 13th August: Except for the non-arrival of some 60 purchased horses, mobilisation would have been complete two days earlier.[7]

Approximately 120,000 horses were requisitioned for the army in just twelve days.[8] A brigade ammunition column mobilising in Ireland recorded that 'practically every horse which came to the column required to be shod, some came without shoes.'[9]

The better equipped, and better manned, brigades in Ireland completed mobilisation quicker than those in England, but it was a struggle for both:

> 6th: All marking, and issue of equipment finished. The battery suffered badly from promotions, losing two sergeants and the majority of the battery staff.
>
> 7th: Reservists commenced to join. The gunners are good; the drivers indifferent, bad horsemen and unaccustomed to riding and driving for some years.[10]

According to a young subaltern, Colin Hutchison, in the 130th (howitzer) Battery, 30th Brigade the reservists who streamed in to Bulford were:

> [F]or the most part fairly old men, most of them with South African war medals, but they proved very useful in the way they influenced the younger and less experienced members of the battery. …Both my No 1's left me, promoted to Sergeant

---

3   TNA WO 95/1416: 8th Infantry Brigade, 8 August 1914.
4   TNA WO 95/1390: 3rd Division Artillery, August 1914.
5   TNA WO 95/1532: 123rd Batt, XXVIII Brigade RFA, 11 August 1914.
6   TNA WO 95/1399: XXIII Brigade RFA, 5-17 August 1914.
7   TNA WO 95/1401: XLII Brigade RFA, 13 August 1914.
8   Edmonds, *Military Operations France and Belgium 1914*, Vol. I, p.31.
9   TNA WO 95/1532: 123rd Batt, XXVIII Brigade RFA, 11 August 1914.
10 TNA WO 95/1527: 61st Batt, VIII Brigade RFA, 6 August 1914.

Majors. This was rather a handicap as we had to work with two new men who did not know much about gun drill. [Number 1's were gun captains. Unsurprisingly, there was not instant cohesion. At the same time, all the men were sent for inoculation, a relatively crude process in 1914.]

Another 60 or 70 of our men were taken down and inoculated this afternoon, so that if we start within two days it will be a sorry battery during the journey, as these Tommies will imagine they are going to die. It's rather rotten work with half the battery laid up through the inoculation.

Our first full parade with our fresh horses and men, all with brand new equipment and harness was an impressive sight, rather spoilt by several of the horses refusing to move with the rest of their teams, and by one horse rearing and falling over backward. However, after about an hour, they were all induced to move, and we went for a short march along the Tidworth Road, returning shortly afterwards intact.[11]

The same process was being followed by the 1st and 2nd Divisions' artillery who were based at Aldershot. Together these two divisions made up I Corps. The 3rd and 5th Divisions made up II Corps, and the two corps, along with a cavalry division would form the first wave of the British Expeditionary Force to France.

Mobilisation took place against a background of fervent patriotism and the process affected every man in the army from top to bottom. I Corps, under Lieutenant General Haig, had a general staff which had been together as a unit for some time. II Corps, under Lieutenant General Grierson, had to put together a general staff from scratch. Both reached France on the 15th, but officers were still joining II Corps Headquarters on the 13th, just hours before embarkation.[12]

General Grierson was very unimpressed with the arrangements made, or rather not made, at Havre to accommodate him. Field Marshal French, who was commanding the British Expeditionary Force (BEF), and the staff of his General Headquarters (GHQ), had already commandeered the best hotel:

> On arrival at 2 p.m. the 15th instant of the ship conveying myself, Sir Douglas Haig and the Headquarters Staffs of the two armies, neither the Base Commandant or any of his staff who could give information as to the arrangements for accommodation were present. …He appears to be a man quite unacquainted with the duties of his office, and completely devoid of that mental activity which might make up for that deficiency in knowledge.[13]

---

11   Hutchison, *The Young Gunner*, pp.2-3.
12   TNA WO 95/630: II Corps War Diary, 13 August 1914.
13   Ibid., 16 August 1914.

The poor man only had about 50,000 men to disembark and get into billets in the area. Irascible generals he could do without, but he was replaced.[14]

At Southampton and the Irish ports, enough shipping was laid on to move 70,000 men with all their horses and equipment, mainly to Havre and Rouen, but some to Boulogne, most under naval escort for the voyage. Simultaneously the supplies needed to keep the army going sailed from Avonmouth, Newhaven and Liverpool.[15]

1.2 The Move to France

Despite the difficulties, in ten days, all the 3rd Division artillery brigades, along with the 48th Heavy Battery and the Divisional Ammunition Column, were reported 'mobilised'. The brigadier general and his staff entrained at Amesbury station for Southampton and on to France on 14 August.

The 3rd Division artillery brigades, and the divisional ammunition column followed, the final brigade not arriving in Rouen, via Havre in France until 21 August. Almost all the artillery followed the same route, although a small number of brigades went to France through Boulogne. They were all a long way from Belgium. Colin Hutchison was one of a number of officers who wrote an account of the journey:

> The train journey to Southampton was accomplished without incident. Every village on the way had its crowd of children and civilians who waved to us and cheered. At Southampton, we embarked in one of the Irish Mail boats that had every convenience for loading a limited number of animals. We sailed about 8 p.m. and were convoyed across by a destroyer arriving off the mouth of the Seine in the early hours of the morning. We lay at anchor there until we were able to get up the Seine, as we were to disembark at Rouen. Our transport was of light draught and twin screw and consequently able to negotiate all the twists and turns of the Seine with the greatest of ease.
>
> We arrived at Rouen soon after noon [on 20 August] but had to lie in the middle of the Seine for two or three hours until there was room at the wharf. Disembarkation was affected without much trouble, though considerable difficulty was encountered before a man could be obtained to work a crane for us. ... The march through Rouen was a triumphal succession; ...We marched to our camp situated in some meadows about a mile and a half south of Rouen.[16]

---

14 Ibid., 16 August 1914.
15 Edmonds, *Military Operations France and Belgium 1914*, Vol. I, pp.31-32.
16 Hutchison, *The Young Gunner*, p.5.

The Cavalry Division, with units on the outbreak of war at Colchester, Norwich and York gathered at Aldershot, also embarked with all their horses through Southampton to Havre and Rouen. Their advance party also arrived on 14 August.[17]

It was enough of a logistical problem getting the infantry, artillery and cavalry with all their horses, wagons and guns from all over England, Scotland and Wales to Southampton. But then the French transport system had to cope with moving 70,000 men, with all their horses and equipment, from the Channel ports up towards Belgium, at the same time as managing its own much greater mobilisation.

1.3 The Move towards Belgium (Maps 1 & 2)

From Havre and Rouen, this meant the railway, each battery or troop of cavalry requiring one very long train.

> The train journey was a long one, and the timetable was not rigidly kept. We had great difficulty in getting our horses watered satisfactorily. At Amiens, we were supposed to have a full 15 minutes' halt and a great effort was made to get the horses watered. No notice was taken of the frantic whistles of railway officials as it was important that the horses should get water and the men's rations be distributed. The train began to move, but the whole battery was still off the train. As it began to gather momentum, we succeeded in getting most of the men aboard, but 10 or 11 were left behind. Some of these men we never saw again, but some seven or eight re-joined us after various experiences as infantrymen etc.[18]

This is important. The adjutant of every brigade kept close tabs on the strength of his unit for pay and ration purposes, but this loss of men is not mentioned in the war diary. All units would have experienced similar problems. The 5th Infantry Brigade diary incorporates a table for the numbers from each battalion who fell out on one particular march, but it was not filled in – just a pencilled note – 'no records'.

The 3rd Infantry Brigade is gloriously unsympathetic to those who did fall out on another march but describes the likely scale of the problem. '9 – 12 men per Bn fell out owing to feet, exhaustion, etc; most of these came in eventually. They had to, as there was no vehicle to pick them up.'[19]

When casualties came to be calculated, many units would have been short of their full complement. Some of the absentees possibly joined the missing list on the day of battle, the adjutant happy to balance his records.

---

17   TNA WO 95/1096: 1st Cavalry Division, 14 August 1914.
18   Hutchison, *The Young Gunner*, p.6.
19   TNA WO 95/1274: 3rd Infantry Brigade, 21 August 1914.

The British Expeditionary Force had been allocated a pear-shaped area in Northern France, which was about 25 miles long and 20 miles deep, situated about 10 miles south of the Belgian border. This area had been decided on in mid-August, in accordance with a pre-war plan agreed with the French.[20] It was on the left flank of the five French armies that were mobilising to positions on the French border all along the eastern half of their border with Belgium, facing north, and then along the German border to Switzerland, facing east.

Each of the four British divisions was allocated a base headquarters round which to rally. The 3rd and 5th Divisions of II Corps were to the north, lined out east of Landrecies, a major rail-head. The 1st and 2nd Divisions of I Corps were similarly lined out east of Bohain and Wassigny, about 18 miles further south and slightly west. The Cavalry Division was north of both divisions, headquartered south-east of Maubeuge and already scouting forwards north and east, as far as Binche. Of course, there had been a lot of action by the time the last few units of the first five divisions of the British Expeditionary Force arrived in Havre and Rouen.

1.4 Events in Belgium and France[21] (Map 2)

Only a (very) brief summary is required. French would have had even less information on German movements than this. Belgium had been invaded on 5 August. The Belgian Army fought a desperate rear-guard action, destroying all bridges and heroically defending their great fortress at Liège which defended vital railway junctions and the crossing of the River Meuse. Liège was not completely occupied until the 16th, thus delaying the westward advance of the First and Second German Armies. They did not reach Brussels till the 20th and only on the 22nd were they in a position to start wheeling south to approach the border with France. Despite a significant shortage of artillery, the weak Belgian Army had disrupted the German advance, and still held Namur, which was under siege.

The importance of this lack of artillery was painfully obvious at the time. The Germans attempted first to capture Liège with a swift infantry assault. This was repulsed with heavy losses. Further attacks supported by light artillery made some gains, but on August 12, the Germans brought up their heavy guns. This was the beginning of the end. The huge 380-millimetre (15 in) coastal mortars and the 420-millimetre (17 in) siege howitzers made short work of the defenses, and the last fort surrendered on the 16th.

The Belgians had not prepared for war in the same way that the continental superpowers had done. Their army was weak, their system of reserve call-up underdeveloped, and even their strongest forts incomplete. But the speed with which these forts

---

20 Edmonds, *Military Operations France and Belgium 1914*, Vol. I, p. 36.
21 Ibid., pp.31-48.

were systematically destroyed by the German heavy guns was noted by all parties. It was a new factor in warfare.

The bulk of the Belgian army fell back to the north, concentrating at Antwerp. This proved a distraction to both sides as the French and British attempted to support their efforts to defend the city, and the Germans diverted troops to hold them in the north of the country.

The French had not been inactive as they watched the first two huge German armies move in to Belgium with the obvious intention of attacking them from the north. General Joffre had initially followed the pre-war plan, which was to attack on his extreme right, and some units of his First Army crossed the border into Alsace-Lorraine as early as 6 August. But he was soon altering his dispositions to instruct his armies on either flank to take up defensive positions, while he prepared the Third and Fourth Armies for an attack due north into Belgian territory behind the advancing German armies, who were moving due west.

The small British Expeditionary Force, coming up on his left flank, was not a particularly significant element in his plans, given the huge size of the continental armies which had been mobilised by both France and Germany.

1.5 The German Armies[22]

The British Expeditionary Force were not aware of it in mid-August, but the full force of the German First Army was advancing through Belgium. This army had more than seven corps, 320,000 men. The British had only two, 70,000 men.

From west to east, II, IV, III and IX corps made up the forward echelons of the First Army, and so about 140,000 men, supported by additional cavalry, were moving forward, unaware of the British position, with the intention of out-flanking the French Fifth Army east of Maubeuge. Two Reserve Corps and six Landwehr regiments were behind them. The composition of the armed forces of the German Empire is briefly summarised in Appendix II. It will be seen that a very high proportion of the army were conscripts.

Like the British, each corps had two divisions and the two armies were similar in composition, if with slightly different command structures. Both had twelve infantry battalions per division, and there was parity, in field artillery, at one battery per battalion. Both armies also had one field howitzer battery for every three field gun batteries.

But the German forces also had eight 15cm (5.9 inch) schwere Feldhaubitze 13 (field howitzers) per division, in two batteries of four guns each, commanded at corps level. Each of these guns fired a shell weighing 93 pounds. The British had only four

---

22   R. Reiley, *The Organization of the German Army, August 1914* <http://www.worldwar1.com/sfgarmy.htm>.

smaller 60 Pounder guns per division, commanded at that level. The British would not only be vastly out-numbered, but also heavily out-gunned.

The ethos of the German armed forces was as aggressive as that of the British. 'The manual of the field artillery contained the regulation that individual batteries had to follow the infantry attack to the closest possible quarters', and they did. In peace-time manoeuvres prior to the war, the guns practiced advancing beside a solid phalanx of infantry till they got close to the enemy line, then threw their guns round in a violent U-turn to point their muzzles at the enemy line and come into action, targeting not only enemy infantry, but also the enemy field gun batteries it was assumed would be in sight. Emphasis was placed on keeping the guns of each battery close to each other. Field howitzer batteries were held back to attack those field fortifications which held up the attacking front line of infantry and field guns.[23] Like the British howitzers, they were slower to come into action, and generally less responsive to events on the battlefield.

It must be remembered that these tactical generalisations apply only to the very first hours of the war. All sides learnt very fast from experience. Both the infantry and the forward German field artillery batteries at Mons lost very heavily to rifle fire and machine gun fire when they applied these tactics. The guns were also very vulnerable to counter-battery fire when the British field guns spotted them. The batteries soon learnt to hold back, spread out and dig in.

But the German army ethos put less emphasis on independent action and initiative than the British. The leadership was more formal and less consultative, with more layers of responsibility.[24] They were a formidable adversary nonetheless.

1.6 The British Concentration (Map 2)

Field Marshal French, commanding the British Expeditionary Force, had to bring himself up to speed very quickly. He had been given command of the army, but the politicians in London had no real idea what they had let themselves in for. At mobilisation, the army was intended for Belgium with a view to fighting alongside them.

Events moved very fast, and by the time he arrived in France, Field Marshal French found himself very much a junior partner in the alliance with France. He was ordered by Lord Kitchener, Secretary of State for War, to be aggressive, to conserve his army at all costs, to liaise closely with the French, but not take orders from them; and to report his every move to England.[25] In short, they were every commanding officer's nightmare. Success would be claimed by the politicians; failure would be his fault alone. He spoke almost no French and he played the bluff soldier in his political manoeuvrings.

---

23 Cron, *Imperial German Army 1914-18*, p. 138.
24 Ibid., pp. 301-305.
25 Edmonds, *Military Operations France and Belgium*, Vol. I, Appendix 8, p. 499.

"Politics are not matters for soldiers to dabble in" he wrote in 1912 in the Army Review',[26] (in another context), which was disingenuous, but he may even have believed it.

Arriving in France on the evening of the 14th, he embarked on a whirlwind tour, which took him first to Paris to meet the French Minister of War, then to Vitry-le-Francois, General Joffre's headquarters a hundred miles further east, and finally up to Rethel, fifty miles north on the Aisne, headquarters of the French 5th Army to see General Lanrezac, with whom General Joffre had asked that he principally liaise.[27] They did not get on. Neither was bilingual, and both were unimpressed by the other. General Lanrezac's Fifth Army consisted of five corps and a cavalry division, and while General Lanrezac regarded the British mainly as a left flank guard, Field Marshal French was determined, as ordered, to maintain British autonomy, albeit he wanted to borrow the French cavalry as an initial screen for his arriving force. It was not a successful meeting.

Field Marshal Sir John French.

On the 17th, as he was heading back the fifty miles to his General Headquarters (GHQ) at Le Cateau, General Grierson, his friend and the commander of II Corps, dropped dead in the train carrying him to the front. French had no opportunity to cope emotionally with this shocking disaster. He had to liaise with London on political matters, absorb hourly military updates of very varying reliability on French, German and British dispositions, and develop his plan of campaign.

General Grierson's death was not only a personal grief to Field Marshal French. It was a loss to the army as a whole. As French wrote in his book *1914*:

> [S]ince 1906 ... he had taken a leading part in the preparation of the army for war ... He had been British military attaché in Berlin for some years and had thus acquired an immense knowledge of the German Army. An excellent linguist, he spoke French with ease and fluency, ... his military acquirements were brilliant, and in every respect thoroughly up to date. Apart from the real affection I felt for him, I regarded his death as a great calamity in the conduct of the campaign.[28]

---

26   Jones (ed.), *Stemming the Tide*, p. 36.
27   Edmonds, *Military Operations France and Belgium*, Vol. I, p.44.
28   Sir John French, *1914* (London: Constable, 1919), ch.3.

It is all too likely that the shock of his good friend's sudden death significantly impaired French's powers of concentration for a few days.

On the 20th, the arrival of the British Expeditionary Force artillery was still in its early stages. As already described, some units were still arriving at Rouen on that day. All the railheads in northern France were south and east of Maubeuge on the Belgian border, and not all units arrived at the most convenient railhead. Some had a long march to billets. The transport of artillery, with all their wagons and horses, was a slow job. And once they did arrive, inevitably there were occasional mishaps. That day, the ammunition column of one brigade (the 40th) was taken 20 miles out of its way by an erring guide.[29] The next day, an advance party of a battery lost two men killed by the sentries of another unit's wagon line.[30] Generally, however, it was being smoothly accomplished.

But on the 20th, Field Marshal French was under heavy pressure from the French to advance his Force to their support. He issued Operation Order 5 which gives a detailed itinerary of advance for his two corps over three days.[31] They were to move out of Northern France, and fifteen miles into Belgium, at dawn on the 21st. Naturally, the orders do not mention the artillery at all. No mention would be expected.

'The concentration was virtually complete on the 20th', says the Official history.[32] This statement is simply not true, and the Battle of Mons cannot be understood unless the lack of preparedness of the British Expeditionary Force is understood. (Even Lord Kitchener in England was under the impression that the concentration of the army was complete on the 21st, stating as such in a press release, which left much else unsaid, on the 26th.[33]) None of the five divisions had completed their concentration.

The Cavalry Division, which had been almost the first to arrive, still lacked '2 squadrons and two field ambulances'.[34] The four infantry divisions were far worse off. All were awaiting the arrival of significant units, including most of their artillery. An entry in the General Staff diary, dated the 20th, states:

> I and II Corps completed concentration except for some important units – (list not available) e.g. The Field Ambulance of II Corps, Divisional Ammunition Columns of II Corps expected.[35]

This was completely misleading. Leaving aside the engineers, signallers and medical units who had not arrived, the most serious deficiency was in the artillery. None of the four divisions had an ammunition column, which also carried small arms ammunition

---

29 TNA WO 95/1390: 3 Division Artillery, 20 August 1914.
30 RAM MD/1150: McLeod, Journal, 21 August 1914.
31 TNA WO 95/1/2: General Staff, Operation Order No 5, 20 August 1914.
32 Edmonds, *Military Operations France and Belgium 1914*, Vol. I, p. 50.
33 TNA WO 159/23: Creedy papers, 26 August 1914.
34 TNA WO 95/1096: 1st Cavalry Division, 20 August 1914.
35 TNA WO 95/1/2: General Staff, 20 August 1914.

for the infantry; in addition, the 1st and 2nd Divisions both lacked one brigade of artillery, the 3rd and 5th Divisions lacked three, each marching with only one brigade, that of the 3rd Division without its ammunition column. Only the 1st Division had its heavy battery.

I Corps artillery was better prepared, as a generality, arriving earlier in Northern France. Yet II Corps was the forward division, which would advance further from the railheads at an earlier stage. What Major General Lindsay, Commander of Royal Artillery (CRA) on the General Staff, (if he was in post,) was doing, is difficult to ascertain. His one task was to ensure adequate artillery cover for the Force, and he failed utterly. In the absence of all the Divisional Ammunition Columns on the day of advance, even those artillery brigades who marched with their own ammunition columns carried only enough ammunition for an hour's continuous firing. Without the brigade column, it was half an hour. A table at the beginning of the colour section documents the arrival time at a railhead of every artillery unit and ammunition column, together with the length of time it took each unit to catch up with their division. Some of these units actually missed the battle on the 23rd.

Field Service Regulations go into considerable detail on the organisation and billeting arrangements of a concentration and are very clear on the organisation of the subsequent advance of each division. To reiterate:

> It is then essential … that every force that takes the field against an organised enemy should be composed of all arms.[36] … As a rule, the divisional artillery will follow the leading brigade of the main body of its division. Artillery brigade and mounted brigade ammunition columns usually march in rear of the fighting troops of their own division or brigade, but it may be advisable to place one, or a portion of one, brigade ammunition column further forward in the order of march.[37]

General Haig, commanding I Corps, was both aware of, and relatively unconcerned by his deficiencies. Even units arriving late on the 21st did not have that far to march to catch up. He composed detailed notes, on the 20th, during a meeting with his staff to discuss the proposed advance and did not once mention the artillery.[38]

Lieutenant General Sir Douglas Haig.

36   *Field Service Regulations*, 1912, p.14.
37   Ibid., p.51.
38   NLS, Acc.3155/98, Douglas Haig Papers, 20 August 1914, pp. 69-70, 79.

It was a different matter for II Corps. They advanced on the 21st as ordered. The terse entry in the 3rd Division war diary communicates their anxiety. 'Division (less 23rd, 42nd and 30th FA Bdes, Amm Col 40th Bde FA, and Div Amm Col not yet detrained) marched as per operation order.'[39]

As late as the evening of the 22nd, the 3rd Division artillery was asking GHQ where their howitzers and ammunition column were and being assured (erroneously) that they would be at Bavai that night.[40] The 5th Division entry is more plaintive. 'No record at present available of arrival of remainder of division in area of concentration, but concentration was not complete when division moved.'[41]

II Corps headquarters had problems. Major General Charles Ferguson of the 5th Division had stepped up to temporarily command the Corps on the death of General Grierson; and Brigadier General Short, Commander of Corps Artillery, had been hospitalised in France following a car accident on the 16th.[42] It is not clear when, or if, he returned to duty.

Major General Ferguson, so much junior to the generals at GHQ, had little choice but to comply. But it is difficult to envisage Lieutenant General Grierson being persuaded to move with most of his artillery still at Rouen. Corps intelligence staff were briefed on the 18th. At least ten front line German army corps were known to have either crossed the Meuse or been involved in fighting at the Belgian forts of Liège and Namur. At least another four reserve Corps were also known to be in Belgium.[43] From Liège to Mons is about 75 miles (90 if travelling via Brussels); from Namur to Mons less than 40 miles.

The position of German forces was not known on 20 August, but none were thought to be within striking range. The British evidence of this came from forward reconnaissance by the Cavalry Division, who had that day reconnoitred forward (in compliance with Field Service Regulations[44]) as far as Binche with no enemy contact,[45] supported by a report on the 19th from the first patrol of the Royal Flying Corps, which saw nothing (on a cloudy day when both planes got spectacularly lost) as far as Brussels.[46]

But the 20th was the day of the French Fifth Army advance, and Field Marshal French did not want to be seen by them as a laggard. He ordered the advance and turned a blind eye to any objections.

---

39 TNA WO 95/1375: 3rd Division, 21 August 1914.
40 TNA WO 95/1390: 3rd Division Artillery, 22 August 1914.
41 TNA WO 95/1521: 5th Division, 21 August 1914.
42 TNA WO 95/630: II Corps staff, 16 August 1914.
43 TNA WO 95/629: II Corps Intelligence, 18 August 1914.
44 *Field Service Regulations*, 1912, p.114.
45 TNA WO 95/1138: 5th Cavalry Brigade, 20 August 1914.
46 John Terraine, *Mons: The Retreat to Victory* (London: Batsford, 1960), p.61.

2

The 21st & 22nd of August 1914

2.1 Advance of the British Expeditionary Force (Maps 3a & 3b)

All of Field Marshal French's corps and division commanders had to have been aware of this dangerous departure from advice on major troop movements as laid down in Field Service Regulations. Only half the artillery was marching with the infantry; and the army in general had only negative information on the movements of the enemy.

Operation Order No. 5 instructed II Corps to lead the way north, advancing about 12 miles on the first day to Bavai on the frontier, and another 10 miles on the second day to just south of Mons. I Corps was to advance a mere 8 miles, on the first day, and another 7 miles the next, billeting on the 22nd south of Maubeuge still in France. No British cavalry was allocated to the left wing of the army in this manoeuvre for any of the three days. The two corps would be 14 miles apart on the evening of the 22nd.

General Haig of II Corps wrote up the campaign, and for the 21st, he wrote:

> I and my staff are rather anxious about our position. We are advancing against a difficult position (Charleroi-Mons), a boggy valley, many coal pits and greatly intersected country. Briefly a country in which the enemy could hold us with a few troop; meanwhile his great masses are marching as fast as possible round our left flank, and as far as we know are unopposed.[1]

By this account, he was already pessimistic about the plan of campaign, and fearing encirclement. He visited 3rd Division headquarters that day, at about 6 p.m., to personally advise them that there were 'German cavalry west and south west of Mons'.[2] He went on to record that:

---

1   Duff Cooper, *Haig* (London, Faber & Faber, 1935), p.141.
2   TNA WO 95/1375: 3rd Division, 21 August 1914, p.30.

> [A]eroplanes reported that all the roads running west from Brussels to Ath and Tournai were thickly covered with masses of German troops of all arms marching very rapidly westwards. This was indeed an alarming situation.[3]

This 'diary' is retrospective, presumably from notes. He could not have written three or four pages of dense fair copy for each day at the time. This reconnaissance report, attributed by him to that day, may have been received later. All quotes from his papers should be treated with caution.

For the second day of the advance (the 22nd), General Haig ordered his 3rd Infantry Brigade of the 1st Division, with two brigades of artillery, to advance significantly further than planned to Fort des Sars three miles north of Maubeuge.[4] By 10 a.m. on the 22nd, this reduced the distance between the vanguard of I Corps, and the right wing of II Corps by four miles. Any variance of Operation Order No. 5 can be cited as evidence of his concern.

II Corps in front, and I Corps behind, were not just to advance north. On the third day of advance, the 23rd, II corps was to advance north and slightly east of Mons, wheeling to face north-east, I Corps also advancing and wheeling, the left flank of I Corps joining up with the right flank of II Corps just east of Mons, also facing north-east.[5] II Corps advancing far and fast would still be without significant elements of artillery, including their howitzers and divisional ammunition column at the conclusion of this manoeuvre; and they would be without a protective screen of British cavalry cover to their north-west.

This wheeling manoeuvre was based on two assumptions. The first was that the French Fifth Army would remain in position to the east level with the advancing and wheeling British Army. The second was that the German armies were still to the east.

Both assumptions proved to be wrong. By the 21st, the German 1st and 2nd Armies were starting to wheel south and, on making contact with the French Fifth Army, it was forced back nine miles. The British Expeditionary Force would no longer be in line with the French. And worse, the German 1st Army had moved further west than expected and was now due north of the British Forces.

2.2 Arrival of General Smith Dorrien

Lieutenant General Smith-Dorrien had been sent by the War Office to take over command of II Corps on the death of Lieutenant General Grierson. He was not French's choice of replacement. General Kitchener, Secretary of State for War, had

---

3   NLS Acc.3155/98: Haig Papers, 21 August 1914, wrongly attributed in Duff Cooper, *Haig*, p.143 to 23 August 1914.
4   TNA WO 95/1274: 3rd Infantry Brigade, 21 August 1914.
5   TNA WO 95/1/2: General Staff, Operation order No. 5, 20 August 1914.

told him as such.⁶ He arrived on the 21st, during the first day of the Force's advance into Belgium. He had very little time to get to grips with the situation.

Operation order No. 5, which had been issued by GHQ on the 20th, required his Corps to be on a line between 'Mons (exclusive) and Thulin' on the evening of the 22nd with outposts for 'local protection', not necessarily on the canal.⁷ All the British cavalry would be on his right – to the east. A further advance was scheduled for the 23rd, as previously described.

Smith-Dorrien, by his own account in a book not written till 1924, arrived at Amiens at 8 a.m. on the 21st, and entrained for Landrecies. From there, he was taken by car to II Corps Headquarters at Bavai, arriving at 4 p.m.⁸ and briefed by his staff. He went to Le Cateau to meet French that evening. His book,

Lieutenant-General Sir Horace Smith-Dorrien.

written many years later, needs to be read with caution. He says in the preface that he had never spoken publicly about the events of 1914, and for a definitive account of the campaign, he refers his reader to the Official History, by which he says he is content to be judged. He glosses over important events in his narrative, and his only target is Field Marshal French, who had sacked him ignominiously in 1915. His tone throughout is gently ironic. Smith-Dorrien tells of their first meeting in France. Apparently, he was received 'gruffly' by French,⁹ but their meeting needs to be judged on results, not tone:

> He received me pleasantly, and explained the situation as far as he could, for the fog of war was peculiarly dense at that time. I gleaned however that we were to move on the morrow to the general line of the Mons – Conde canal, the I Corps on my right, my Corps on the left, the latter's position to be along the line of the canal from Mons westwards, but that it was only to be a preliminary step to a further move forward which would take the form of a slight right-wheel into Belgium, the British Army forming the outer flank, pivoting on the French 5th

---

6   Sir Horace Lockwood Smith-Dorrien, *Memories of Forty-Eight Years' Service* (New York: Dutton, 1925), p.375.
7   TNA WO 95/1/2: General Staff, Operation order No. 5, 20 August 1914.
8   TNA WO 95/630: II Corps staff, 21 August 1914.
9   Ian Becket & Stephen Corvi, *Haig's Generals* (Barnsley: Pen & Sword, 2006), p. 192.

Army.[10] [Presumably, he then brought up the subject of his missing artillery.] ... the French were so insistent on our moving forward to cover their left flank that, although short of guns, field hospitals and Engineer Units, the C-in-C decided to go without them, as the news of the enemy was that they had left Brussels and were advancing west and south of that town.[11]

Smith-Dorrien gently ticks off the points of strategic concern. His 'C-in-C' was planning an offensive wheeling advance, without guns, engineers or medical units, with only half his army, across the presumed line of the advancing enemy. There was no British flank guard in place. General Smith-Dorrien had had experience of judging the performance of senior generals as umpire to the 1912 army manoeuvres. His account says no more, except that he got back to his headquarters at 11 p.m. and slept. He does however refer to an incident on the road when an artillery advance party was shot at, and a man killed. This accident befell the 15th Brigade RFA,[12] which de-trained at 7.20 p.m., confirming his approximate timing. He likes to use anecdotes to deflect attention from serious decision making.

The 'news of the enemy' General Smith-Dorrien refers to is available in Corps records. There were four sources of reconnaissance evidence. Reports from the cavalry, reports from the French, reports from Belgian civilians, including phone messages, and aerial observation. In the early evening of the 21st, it was known that at least fourteen German corps had been in Belgium for some days, and that a German cavalry patrol had reconnoitred the canal west of Mons that afternoon.[13] Field Marshal French and General Haig had been briefed at General Allenby's Cavalry Division headquarters at Givry that afternoon.[14] They were told that 'a column of all arms', (probably a cavalry division, with Jäger infantry attached), had reached Soignies, about ten miles north-east of Mons; that '7000 cavalry (were) moving from direction of Nivelles', which was only 18 miles north-east of Mons; and that the French reported contact with infantry four miles south of Nivelles.[15]

It is almost certain that General Smith-Dorrien queried Field Marshal French's decision to wheel his corps east without firm knowledge of the enemy line of southward advance, and without cavalry ahead of him and to his left. He would also have feared being outflanked by the German infantry to his east.

During the course of, or immediately after, this meeting, steps were taken by GHQ to improve II Corps protection. French issued Operation Order No. 6, timed at 11.55 p.m. The first part of this order advised II Corps to advance as planned on the 22nd, but to move its outposts forward to occupy Mons, to line the canal from in front of

10 Smith-Dorrien, *Memories of Forty-Eight Years' Service*, p. 376.
11 Ibid., p.379.
12 RAM MD/1150: McLeod, Journal, 21 August 1914.
13 TNA WO 95/629: II Corps Intelligence, 18 August 1914.
14 TNA WO 95/588/4: I Corps Staff, 21 August 1914.
15 TNA WO 95/1096: 1st Cavalry Division, 21 August 1914.

Thulin to Nimy; and to extend the line of its right flank seven miles to the southeast, as far as Givry.[16] Note the reference to 'outposts'. In Operation Order No. 6, and in every subsequent order that emanates from it, it is 'outposts' that are to take up forward positions. Field Regulations are very clear on the subject of outposts. 'Not a man or horse more than is absolutely necessary should be employed.'[17]

It is almost certain that these significant changes in dispositions were ordered as a direct result of the meeting between General Smith-Dorrien and Field Marshal French. The orders were received by II Corps at 2 a.m. and passed on to the divisions by 4.30 a.m.[18] At about 8 a.m. on the 22nd, 'verbal orders' were issued to the leading infantry brigades, revising their destinations, 'news of the enemy advance on Mons' having been received.[19]

General Smith-Dorrien judged it wise to employ two thirds of the 3rd Division on outpost duty in the Mons salient, leaving almost no resources to occupy the seven miles down to Givry. Just one battalion, the 2nd Royal Irish Rifles, of the 7th Infantry Brigade, covered three miles between Harmignies and Givry. (Major General Lomax, of the 1st Division, discovered only one platoon at Givry, when he reconnoitred forward on receipt of his orders to advance, later that day.[20]) General Smith-Dorrien also posted two thirds of his 5th Division on the canal line.

GHQ makes no comment on the weight of troops posted on the outpost line; indeed, French implied in subsequent orders that this was his intention from the start, and maybe it was. But Field Regulations state:

> If the frontage occupied in battle is so great as to reduce the force kept in hand for the ultimate assumption of the offensive much below half the total force available, the position may be considered as too extended to be held with a view to decisive action.[21]

In other words, in conventional military theory, the line that General Smith-Dorrien's II Corps had now taken up, was far too long to be used in expectation of an offensive victory. The advance planned for the 23rd in French's orders of the 20th was looking increasingly inadvisable. It could now be reasonably asked why II Corps was up in this position at all.

The second part of Operation Order No. 6 required the Cavalry Division, commanded by Lieutenant General Allenby, to move from the right flank of II Corps to its left flank, a distance of about fifteen miles, starting once II Corps was safely on

---

16 TNA WO 95/1/2: General Staff, Operation order No. 6, 21 August 1914.
17 *Field Service Regulations*, 1912, p. 99.
18 TNA WO 95/630: II Corps staff, 22 August 1914.
19 TNA WO 95/1425: 9th Infantry Brigade, 22 August 1914.
20 TNA WO 95/1274: 3rd Infantry Brigade, 22 August 1914.
21 Field Service Regulations, 1912, p.141.

the canal line. Their supplementary order started with a sharp reprimand; and it was copied to II Corps:

> The information which you have acquired and conveyed to the C-in-C appears to be somewhat exaggerated. It is probable that only mounted troops, perhaps supported by Jager Battalions are in your immediate neighbourhood.[22]

Allenby had forwarded French cavalry reports of infantry and artillery concentrations, described by them as forward elements of an infantry corps.[23] They may or may not have been a cavalry division, but the reprimand would have stung. He was being publicly rebuked and advised to report only what GHQ wanted to hear.

The independent 5th Cavalry Brigade, in touch with French cavalry, would, by the afternoon of the 22nd, be the only British cavalry screening the right of II Corps. (In the early hours of the 23rd, they were transferred to the command of General Haig of I Corps, under GHQ orders, and ordered to report direct to him, instead of General Allenby.[24])

GHQ did nothing at this stage about the dangerous degree of separation between the two corps. The left flank of I Corps was over 12 miles from Givry, which was the right flank of II Corps. General Haig had already planned to advance his 3rd Infantry Brigade of the 1st Division to north of Maubeuge, which was closer to Givry, but this was his right flank, not his left. (Separation of forces was not an unrecognised problem. General Grierson was criticised during the 1912 army manoeuvres for allowing it to happen.[25])

With the cavalry in place, Smith-Dorrien could feel more relaxed about his left flank. But his II Corps was very exposed, occupying a front extending more than 20 miles; and there was still an intention to perform the final stage of the advance, a wheel to the east, on the 23rd.

2.3 The British plan, as envisaged by I Corps for 23 August (Map 4)

The movements of I Corps were not addressed in Operation Order 6, which was issued in the early hours of the 22nd, though they were clearly affected by the change of plan. It must have given General Haig food for thought. There is a hand-written note in his private papers, allegedly written at 2 p.m. on the 22nd, at 'Fort des Sart' (sic). It is strange he spelt 'Sars' wrong, and the timing is also problematic, as will become clear

---

22 TNA WO 95/1/2: General Staff, 21 August p.29.
23 TNA WO 95/1096: 1st Cavalry Division, 21 August 1914.
24 TNA WO 95/1138: 5 Cavalry Brigade, 23 August 1914.
25 TNA WO 27/508: Reports by the Inspector General of Forces, 1912, p. 4 quoted in Jones, (ed.), *Stemming the Tide*, Chapter 6, p.147.

when his movements that afternoon are addressed. It details positions that he thought his corps should take up in the event of an attack on II Corps, advocating a line with his right at Fort des Sars, just north of Maubeuge, and his left due south of Mons, this line facing due east.[26] If this note is contemporary, it gives an insight into his defensive tactical thinking, being a considerable variance on the positions GHQ had detailed in Operation Order No. 5. There is no evidence he discussed this idea with French.

2.4 The British plan, as envisaged by II Corps for 23 August (Map 4)

General Smith-Dorrien, aware of the weight of German forces approaching Mons, ordered his divisions to occupy the new outpost line in strength. He advanced two infantry brigades of his 3rd Division to take up position in the Mons salient, with their third brigade in reserve behind them; and two infantry brigades of the 5th Division up to the canal, west of Mons, similarly supported by a reserve brigade. This manoeuvre was completed by midday on the 22nd:

> The morning of the 22nd saw us moving and…in accordance with our orders we took up a line of outposts extending from Pommeroeul (five miles east of Condé) round the north side of Mons to Nimy and thence to Givry … Our news of the enemy was very vague, but the general opinion was that considerable German forces were moving towards us and that contact on the morrow was almost a certainty.[27]

The 15th Infantry Brigade, the reserve brigade of the 5th Division, records a similar summary, late on the 22nd:

> Situation broadly; V Division outposts, 13th and 14th Inf Bds, Mariette to canal crossing south of Pommeroeul, (continued to Elouge by Norfolks). III Division outposts east of Mariette. 1st Army Corps coming up behind us, position unknown. French in touch on both flanks.[28]

Both accounts state that the front line was held by outposts. Field Service Regulations give clear advice. 'Artillery may be usefully employed with outposts if they occupy the ground which the main body is to hold in case of attack…'[29]

---

26 NLS Acc.3155/98: Douglas Haig papers, August 1914, pp. 80-81.
27 Smith-Dorrien, *Memories of Forty-Eight Years' Service*, p.380.
28 TNA WO 95/1566: 15th Infantry Brigade, 22 August 1914.
29 Field Service Regulations, 1912, p.102.

In other words, if an outpost was offensive, and to be firmly held against enemy attack, the guns should be up with the infantry, preparing to engage in counter battery fire. The Official History says that 'the general policy followed was to push batteries or sections of batteries up to the infantry for close defence.'[30]

The Official History was published in 1923, and written by Brigadier General Edmonds, who, in 1914, went forward to observe the battle, having just arrived in France as Chief of Staff of the 4th Division. His account implies that he believed at the time that the outposts on the canal were to be held offensively. But outposts were posted either offensively, to be firmly held; or, defensively, to give warning of attack and to fall back to the cover of the main force when endangered. In the latter scenario, guns would not be required. GHQ ordered outposts at the canal, and although offensive intent is implied, nowhere is it explicitly stated. A precise interpretation of Operation Order No. 6 gave General Smith-Dorrien a choice.

2.5 Geography (Maps 4 & 6)

For soldiers trained to manoeuvres in open countryside, the terrain along the canal was a nightmare. From north to south along the east-west length of the canal, the geography was as follows. Two miles north of the canal, dense woodland hid the German approach. The land was then open, roads across it leading to a number of hamlets close to the canal. Between these hamlets both north and south of the canal and along its whole length, the low ground was criss-crossed with waterways between plantations of young willow for basket making:

> West of Mons, the line of the canal is straight, and the actual borders are clear; the ground on both sides of it is cut by a net-work of artificial water-courses, chequered by osier beds, for a breadth of a mile or more. But the opening up of the coal measures has turned much of the country immediately south of this watery land into the hideous confusion of a mining district … practically one huge unsightly village, traversed by a vast number of devious cobbled roads, which lead from no particular starting point to no particular destination, and broken by pit-heads and great slag heaps, often over a hundred feet high.[31]

Within Mons, at the eastern end, there were wired off allotments where it was not built up. The coal mining strip was about two miles wide, and heavily built up. This not only made life difficult for the troops moving through, but it makes accounts of the battle difficult since there is a plethora of named cross roads which merge one with another from one mile to the next with ill-defined boundaries. Two units might

---

30 Edmonds, *Military Operations France and Belgium 1914*, Vol. I, p.75.
31 Ibid., p.71.

be going to the same place but use different names for their destination. Out to the west, north of Dour, the land was flat and open, cut by numerous ditches, including the River Haine, a significant waterway.

For five miles south-east of Mons, the country was relatively defensible to the east. There was a chalk ridge, which started on the outskirts of Mons as a hill, call Bois la Haut, heavily wooded and with a hospital at the northern end. Two miles south-east of this was another hill, named by the army, Hill 93, and then the ridge dropped down to Harmignies on the Mons to Givry road.

2.6 General Smith-Dorrien's Reconnaissance (Map 4)

General Smith-Dorrien, in his diary that day, wrote that 'the Mons salient …is almost an impossible one to defend, but I gather it is not expected to be treated as a defensive position.'[32] His memoirs, published in 1924, further elaborate:

> That afternoon I motored round the outposts and visited the positions as far as I had time, for the distances were very great. In my hasty survey, I had come to a conclusion that, from a fighting point of view, our position was a very difficult one. The ground on the enemy's side of the canal commanded it from comparatively short ranges, and was densely wooded, giving them the advantage of a covered approach. Any idea of fighting a serious action on the outpost line was therefore out of the question, although such a thing in any case would have been impossible in view of the enormous extension of the Corps, covering as it did 21 miles with only two divisions.
>
> … on our right was the salient town of Mons, open to fire from north east and west and quite indefensible… I came to the conclusion that our only hope, if attacked in force, would be to hold a less extended position in rear on which the outposts could fall back.[33]

This was not written with hindsight. He is confirming, in more detail, what he wrote in his diary that day, and what his dispositions imply. He had decided on defensive outposts. No artillery would be deployed forward.

2.7 5th Division Reconnaissance of the Frontline

During the afternoon of the 22nd, Brigadier General Headlam, commanding the 5th divisional artillery, was up at the canal at St Ghislain with Brigadier General

---

32 IWM: Smith-Dorrien papers, 87/47/10, Diary, 22 August 1914.
33 Smith-Dorrien, *Memories of Forty-Eight Years' Service*, p.384.

British 18-pounder battery on the move.

Cuthbert of the 13th Infantry Brigade.[34] One battery of the 27th Brigade RFA, the 120th, attached to the 13th Infantry, had gone up to the canal along one of the few passible roads. General Cuthbert recorded his opinion: 'ground most unsuited for anything in the nature of artillery cooperation'.[35]

General Headlam also assessed the defensive possibilities. He entirely concurred. Access to the canal along its whole length was by tortuous narrow tracks, impeded by mine workings and high slag heaps, many of them hot. And at the canal:

> [T]he ground was found quite unsuitable for artillery, consisting of water meadows intersected by ditches lined by trees, so that view and movement were alike almost impossible, and the presence of guns was therefore likely only to provide an embarrassment to the infantry.[36]

The 5th Division war diary was apparently destroyed at Le Cateau and written up during the Retreat to cover the lost pages. It does seem unlikely that such a blunt assessment was in the original. On the afternoon of the 22nd, they were scheduled to advance the next morning. Advance without artillery support was not an option.

General Headlam nearly ordered the battery back, but they wanted to stay and, since they were already there, he agreed that 'if necessary', they could post a section forward. Needless to say, as soon as he left, they did so, digging in two sections, of two guns each, on the south bank of the canal.[37] But he sent no more guns forward.

34 TNA WO 95/1521: 5th Division Artillery, 22 August 1914.
35 TNA WO 95/1548: 13th Infantry Brigade, 22 August 1914.
36 TNA WO 95/1521: 5th Division Artillery, 22 August 1914.
37 TNA WO 95/152: 120th Batt, XXVII Brigade RFA, 22 August 1914.

Headlam only had two brigades (six batteries) of field artillery, the 27th and 15th, at his disposal. Both were at Dour, three miles back from the canal, and the latter was exhausted after a very long march from a railhead. All the rest of his artillery was still in transit, most of it expected to billet at Bavai overnight, and therefore not available for many hours.

The East Surrey Regiment, 14th Brigade, on the left of the 5th Division line, covering the bridges at Herbieres, was expecting artillery support. At dawn on the morning of the 23rd, 'clearing of foreground over the canal commenced, tools for this purpose not arriving the previous night.'[38] This was to improve their field of fire. No guns arrived.

2.8 3rd Division Reconnaissance of the Frontline (Map 4)

Brigadier General Wing of 3rd divisional artillery also reconnoitred forward, though the entry in his war diary is much less forthcoming. He too would have been aware of the plan for a major offensive advance at dawn the next morning. His brief untimed entry merely says that 'positions were selected with a view to delaying or preventing enemy's advance.'[39]

General Wing had all three of his field artillery brigades, and his heavy battery, in touch with the infantry, billeted overnight within three miles of Mons. Two of them, and his heavy battery, had had very long marches in the last 24 hours. There is no evidence that any of these three artillery brigades reconnoitred front line positions in the salient. The 40th Brigade RFA did scout Bois la Haut, wooded high ground two miles back from the outpost line, but did not, as might be expected, select positions.

It was obvious by now that a German attack would fall on Mons the next morning. General Smith-Dorrien and his artillery brigadiers had seen for themselves that the outpost line was unsuitable for artillery deployment. With both Divisional Ammunition Columns still on the train from Rouen, ammunition supplies must also have been a consideration.

As early as 7.15 p.m., the brigade major of the 9th Infantry Brigade had prepared 'secret' and 'confidential' instructions for a retirement from the canal line in the event of heavy enemy attack, detailing fall-back positions to be covered by the 23rd Brigade RFA. Such preparations were required under Field Service Regulations, 'Orders for a possible retreat should always be thought out beforehand, in case of need.'[40] Nevertheless, it is significant that there were no plans to bolster the front-line infantry under attack with artillery.[41] This must have been a divisional decision, based on advice from corps.

---

38 TNA WO 95/1563: 1st East Surrey Regiment, 23 August 1914.
39 TNA WO 95/1390: 3rf Division Artillery, 22 August 1914.
40 *Field Service Regulations*, 1912, p.32.
41 TNA WO 95/1425: 9th Infantry Brigade, 22 August 1914, p.52.

54   Mons: An Artillery Battle

This was not Field Marshal French's expectation. He still hoped for an advance the next morning. General Smith-Dorrien had started preparations for a defensive battle. His available artillery was close to where he wanted it. They made no move.

2.9 The British Plan as envisaged by GHQ for 23 August (Map 5)

At about 1 p.m. on 22 August, GHQ sent an order (OA57) to I Corps Headquarters at Maubeuge. The corps was instructed to continue its advance into the positions planned for the finish of their march on the 23rd, i.e. two days march in one.[42] The Cavalry Division move was about to start, and would uncover the right flank of II Corps. If II Corps was to wheel east the next day, it was now desirable to have I Corps up to wheel on. This could perhaps have been foreseen. But, the initial disturbing reports from the French on their right rendered the move more urgent. The timing of this order was unfortunate for two reasons. Most of I Corps had arrived at their billets between midday and 1 p.m.[43] It took about two and a half hours to unpack, feed and water the horses, feed the men, and get them settled; and the same length of time to mobilise from billets into a line of march. Also, General Haig had just left his headquarters, and was unavailable to action the order.

The initial disturbing reports from the French became a torrent. French asserts in his memoires, that he knew later that afternoon of the retreat of the French army on his right in the face of German attack; and was reliably informed by the French that three German Corps were converging on II Corps from the north, one being at Ath, which is north-west of Mons.[44] If this was the case, there was every reason for him to consider ordering the immediate withdrawal of II Corps, and to cancel the advance of I Corps he had just ordered.

He did react, but not to order withdrawal. At 5 p.m., II Corps received two messages (OA62) in one from GHQ:

> Orders from GHQ for II Corps to remain tomorrow in positions occupied overnight. I Corps to take over at 6 a.m. tomorrow that portion of the outpost line which lies east of Mons.[45]

French was opting for delay, awaiting further information. He both cancelled the left-wheel advance of II Corps, scheduled for the 23rd, and addressed General Smith-Dorrien's concerns about his very long front. He had already ordered I Corps forward and believed them to be on the move. He rejected the option of a dangerous

---

42   TNA WO 95/1/2: General Staff, 22 August 1914.
43   TNA WO 95/1274: 3rd Infantry Brigade, 22 August 1914.
44   French, *1914*, ch.4.
45   TNA WO 95/630: II Corps staff, 22 August 1914.

counter-order, cancelling their advance, but refined their final positions, with a view to shortening II Corps lines, and, in the process free up 3rd Division battalions to create an offensive reserve. This crucial order (OA62) from GHQ, cancelling II Corps scheduled advance on the 23rd, is not mentioned in the Official History; and the account states that the advance was not cancelled till 10 p.m.[46] This makes no sort of sense in view of the known German positions much earlier in the day.

Brigadier General Spears, then 'only a subaltern', was liaising between GHQ and the French, being, as he observed, 'much intimidated by having to deal with such important people.' His much-quoted anecdote, telling of him sitting ashen faced at GHQ, well after 7 p.m., watching hearty generals working on optimistic plans to advance, in ignorance of the French retreat which he was reporting, either has to be brought forward, or rendered less dramatic. His account, written (in 1930), long after the events, is not totally credible.[47]

Telephone lines had, that day, been laid by the signallers from the new II Corps headquarters at Sars-la-Bruyère to their divisional headquarters, but some had to be re-laid the next day because they did not work.[48] It may have been quite late when the divisions got this news, perhaps as late as 10 p.m. None of the senior units of II Corps record the time they received the cancellation order. This was one of those occasions when some blurring of the chronology was not disadvantageous. They had been working for some hours on the assumption that it would not take place.

2.10 Reaction to Events: I Corps (Maps 4 & 5)

The first GHQ order (OA57), received at 1.30 p.m., ordered I Corps to immediately continue its advance deep into Belgium. They were to take up a line centred on Harmignies, Vellereille-le-Sec, Rouveroy and Peissant, facing north-east.[49] General Haig was not at I Corps Headquarters. He had just set off for Beaumont, 18 miles east, to visit General de Mas-Latrie, commanding the French 18th Army Corps.[50] Therefore, his staff at Maubeuge received the order during his absence. They summoned the two divisional commanders at 3 p.m. to Maubeuge to action the order.[51] Both sets of officers attended and were given their instruction to prepare for an immediate advance. The 1st Division prepared to leave at 6 p.m., the 2nd Division at 7 p.m. As already described, the order was most unfortunately timed. All brigades had just finished billeting.

---

46 Edmonds, *Military Operations France and Belgium 1914*, Vol. I, p.68.
47 E.L. Spears, *Liaison 1914: A Narrative of the Great Retreat* (London, Heinemann, 1930), pp.135, 149.
48 TNA WO95/646: II Corps Signal Co. RE, 23 August 1914.
49 TNA WO 95/588/4: I Corps staff, 22 August 1914.
50 NLS, Acc. 3155/98: Douglas Haig Papers, August 1914, p.82.
51 TNA WO 95/1283: 2nd Division, 22 August 1914.

General Haig states that he did not receive order OA57 'until 3.22 p.m.'.[52] That time is scrawled on a copy of the order, in addition to the time 1.30 p.m. recorded by his staff.[53] But by his own account, he was out of touch with his staff for hours, while he visited not only General de Mas-Latrie, but also a French divisional headquarters, being briefed on the unfolding disaster of their retreat in the face of heavy German attacks. When Haig arrived back at his headquarters, he tried desperately to cancel the advance. The vanguard 3rd Infantry Brigade of the 1st Division got the message too late:

> Just after the troops had started to act on this order, Brigadier Horne came up to us from Sir Douglas saying he did not want us to move on after all, but it was then too late; besides all the rest of the division from the S of Maubeuge was on the move to come up to where we were…[54]

This unit, with two brigades of artillery, was billeted north of Maubeuge; and their advance, once activated, was relatively easy. The whole division arrived at their destinations between 9 p.m. and 3 a.m. the next morning.[55]

The 2nd Division was situated further west, south and east of Bavai, their forward brigades, at least, having arrived in billets before noon.[56] All three infantry brigades had scheduled their further advance to start at 7 p.m., but shortly before their departure, it was cancelled. The order to the 5th Brigade at 7 p.m. was brusque. 'Under instructions just come from I Corps, 2nd Division movement from billets postponed till early tomorrow. Orders follow later.'[57]

Again, the timing was most unfortunate. The brigades were on the point of departure. They now had to return to billets and unpack once more. 'These various orders gave the troops a certain amount of fatigue, though no doubt necessitated by the changing situation,' says the divisional diary.[58] Criticism, even an understated criticism, of an order in a war diary is very unusual. It would take another two hours to get the men back into billets for the night.

Haig had, that same afternoon, received reports from the 5th Cavalry Brigade, as the Cavalry Division moved to the western flank of II Corps. They were reporting to his 1st Division by midday,[59] and their subsequent reports were very disconcerting:

---

52 TNA WO 95/588/4: I Corps staff, 22 August 1914.
53 TNA WO 95/588/1: I Corps Staff, A27, 22 August 1914, p.13.
54 TNA WO 95/1274: 3rd Infantry Brigade, 22 August 1914.
55 TNA WO 95/588/3: I Corps dispatches, 1 Division at Mons 22 August 1914.
56 TNA WO 95/1352: 6 Inf Bde & WO 95/1342, 2 Batt Gren. Gds. 22 August 1914.
57 TNA WO 95/1283: 2nd Division, 22 August 1914.
58 Ibid.: 22 August 1914.
59 TNA WO 95/1274: 3rd Infantry Brigade, 22 August 1914.

Patrols sent out reported (a) hostile bodies (of all arms) advancing generally from the north, (b) French troops retiring over the Sambre, this by liaison with 10th Hussars, at Thuin. French Cavalry Division (Cuirassiers) retired through us this morning. The bridges at Péronnes were attacked by artillery and infantry in considerable numbers.[60]

Péronnes is situated only eight miles east, and south, of Mons. The 5th Cavalry Brigade abandoned their defence of these bridges at 1.30 p.m., when they were ordered west into the space left by the withdrawal of the Cavalry Division.[61] By 2.25 p.m., the cavalry knew that German forces had advanced another mile to the south-east and were at Bray.[62] Bray was only four miles due north of the right flank of the position the 1st Division was coming up to occupy, and less than three miles from Vellereille-le-Sec, which the 2nd Division was to occupy. It is not clear at what time I Corps, or more specifically General Haig, received these subsequent reports. He issued the cancellation orders to both his divisions after 6 p.m.

The Official History states that the 2nd Division did not advance because of reports that the Germans had billeted for the night; and that General Haig therefore saw no need to comply with the order that evening.[63] No diaries record the billeting of any German troops, and why this should be a reason for cancelling an advance is not obvious. Rather the reverse. General Haig's account in I Corps war diary observed:

> Some time was inevitably lost in communicating with the 2nd Division, which was consequently unable to comply with the order, and billeted for the night as already arranged.[64]

This is simply not true. His staff had used their initiative in his absence and had arranged the advance of both divisions. All the 2nd Division brigades were well-prepared to advance at 7 p.m. General Haig cancelled their advance (and tried to cancel the 1st Division advance), against clear GHQ orders. The question is why?

Haig, that afternoon, had a right to think that he was better informed on German and French dispositions than GHQ. If the Germans continued their advance east from Bray, they would arrive at Vellereille-le-Sec well before the 2nd Division. Even if they did not immediately advance, the threat of a German advance from this direction could only increase with time. General Haig now knew the full scale of the envelopment threat to the right flank of II Corps. It was obvious to him that II Corps should

---

60 TNA WO 95/1138: 5 Cavalry Brigade, 22 August 1914.
61 Ibid., 22 August 1914.
62 TNA WO 95/629: II Corps intelligence summary, 22 August 1914.
63 Edmonds, *Military Operations France and Belgium*, Vol. I, p.64.
64 TNA WO 95/588/4: I Corps Staff, 22 August 1914.

be ordered to retire. There was nothing to gain, and everything to lose by leaving it up at Mons.

True, if II Corps was to stay up at Mons, it needed his support on its right flank, and it needed it as soon as possible. But surely when GHQ became aware of this threat, II Corps would be pulled back. As has already been described, British military doctrine ruled that II Corps at Mons was defending a line too long to offer an offensive threat, even without the risk of envelopment to their right wing. It seems likely that it never occurred to Haig that French would leave II Corps so exposed, once he understood the tactical position. Smith-Dorrien would have concurred with this assessment. He says, albeit ironically, that he was, that night, racking his 'brains as to what the object of our remaining so isolated was.'[65]

Haig's assessment was theoretically correct. And if II Corps was recalled, his 2nd Division was ideally placed where it was, lined out to the east of Bavai. His 1st Division, even after its advance, was in no danger of envelopment. It could very easily drop back west a few miles to regain touch with the 2nd Division. II Corps could fall back to the west of Bavai, where much of their artillery was billeted overnight. The whole Force could regain touch and present a united front. It was a seemingly perfect solution to the problems of both concentration and contact.

But inexplicably and with disastrous consequences, Haig informed neither French, nor Smith-Dorrien, what he was doing, and perhaps as importantly why, even though feedback was required under Field Service Regulations. 'Should a subordinate find it necessary to depart from an order, he should immediately inform the issuer of it, and the commanders of any neighbouring units likely to be affected by it.'[66] Of necessity, in ignoring OA57, the first order to advance, he had also, at least initially, to ignore OA62, which gave details of the help he was to give II Corps in the salient. His staff, at least, probably received this at about 5 p.m., the time it arrived at II Corps. Nor, on receipt of this second order, did he tell GHQ that his 2nd Division had not advanced. He told them that the order 'was not received [?] till late [6 p.m.? See message files] and involved a night march.'[67] GHQ wondered what he was up to. The entry could imply that a night march was intended, and at that stage it possibly was. But the question marks were fully justified. GHQ did not realise that the 2nd Division was not going to advance.

The reference to a night march reveals another fear, which is echoed by the 3rd Brigade in the vanguard of the 1st Division:

> From our point of view, it seemed a pity to move as we had a very good defensive position, and now the Bde is getting into its new position …in the dark, more or less mixed up with the 5th Cav Bde … and various other units. The Germans are

---

65 Smith-Dorrien, *Memories of Forty-Eight Years' Service*, p.381.
66 *Field Service Regulations*, 1912, p.32.
67 TNA WO 95/1/2: General Staff, 22 August 1914.

reported as near as Bonne Esperance, S of Binche. It is not pleasant to be so near them in the dark, out of touch with nearly everyone.[68]

General Haig now knew there were significant German forces at Péronnes. If, as his 2nd Division marched north-east in the dark, these German forces advanced south-west, between his 1st and 2nd Divisions, they might split his Corps in two, and include his 2nd Division in the envelopment of the 3rd Division.

The events of the next few hours are difficult to disentangle. It is likely that evening that Haig was beset by fears, and somewhat isolated. He had countermanded a perfectly reasonable show of initiative on the part of his Chief-of-Staff, acting in his absence. He had assumed total responsibility. There is in his papers a hand-written note, timed at 9 p.m., entitled 'orders for 23rd August'. 'Monro', commanding 2nd Division, 'to send as soon as light to hold line Givry to Mons; to dig in. – also push on detachments to take over outposts of 2nd Corps (Mons to Villers St Ghislain).'[69] This is hardly definitive about timing. Possibly he wrote it as a draft for his staff. There are further difficulties with it. It is the second of just four letters, copied out into a fresh note pad, on consecutive pages. Their position in General Haig's papers implies that they are contemporary. The first note, already referred to, gives details of positions that, perhaps in retrospect, he should have instructed the 2nd Division to take up that evening – on a line between Mons and Fort des Sars. It was allegedly written at Fort des Sart (sic), at 2 p.m., which is difficult to explain. He was on his way east from Maubeuge to visit the French generals at that time, and it is bizarre he misspelt the address. This second letter can also be interpreted as an order he should have given and did not. It is at least arguable that all four letters in this notepad were composed later when he was mulling over the campaign.

Half an hour after this second letter was allegedly written, his staff issued G63 to the 2nd Division. This was an order to advance, incorporating the revised final positions for the 2nd Division as ordered by GHQ OA62. It might be expected that this important order would have been signed by the Chief of Staff. It was not. The signature is illegible. It is possible to speculate that this order was sent on the initiative of a junior staff officer, without General Haig's knowledge. It is difficult otherwise to understand why he felt his 9 p.m. order important enough to choose to copy out into his personal papers. He must have written many notes during the day. At 9.30 p.m., G63 informed the 2nd Division that two battalions would be required to take over the eastern salient at Mons by 6 a.m.; that their attached artillery should take station on 'Bas la Haut' [sic]; and that one battalion should relieve a II Corps battalion at Harmignies. The 6 a.m. target arrival time is labelled AAA – meaning for urgent attention.[70]

---

68 TNA WO 95/1274: 3rd Infantry Brigade, 22 August 1914.
69 NLS, Acc.3155/98: Douglas Haig papers, August 1914, p.82.
70 TNA WO 95/588/1: I Corps Staff, G63, 22 August 1914, p.14.

Receipt of G63 is acknowledged by the 2nd Division, and 'orders issued', though no immediate action resulted. The 4th (Guards) Brigade was not formally notified of their revised destination, in a document labelled Operation Order No. 4, till after 2 a.m.[71] This was long past the time by which they would have had to set off in order to support the 3rd Division by 6 a.m. It was a seven-hour march.

G63 was an impossible order to obey. All three brigades of the 2nd Division had been on the march from 4 a.m. till midday, when they billeted. They had then immediately come out of billets and paraded; now they had just finished billeting again. Their 7 p.m. orders had postponed their advance until 'early tomorrow'. The 2nd division elected to obey those orders. It stayed where it was. It reverted to the timetable already set in GHQ orders (Operation order No. 5 issued on the 20th) for the morning of the 23rd.

It is difficult to be sure what General Haig thought the 2nd Division was doing. But at 00.30 a.m. on the morning of the 23rd, he suddenly realised they were very out of position. It is possible that a report from the 1st Division on enemy positions alerted him, or perhaps he only then learnt that they were not advancing following receipt of G63. Whatever the reason, he issued urgent orders for them to advance within the hour. The order has a ring of panic about it. It was simply impossible:

> Orders received to move at once. It is to be noticed that this order only resulted in a gain of one hour over operation order No 4, (sic) and that in many cases the men had to start without food.[72]
>
> At 12.30, orders were received to march at 1.30 a.m. This was found to be impossible, but the brigade was paraded ready to move off at 2.15 a.m. The actual hour of march was 3.10.[73]

This was the 5th Infantry Brigade. The 6th Brigade marched at 2.45 a.m., and it was not till 3 a.m. that the 1st Irish Guards, the lead battalion of the 4th (Guards) Brigade, set off to take up their position in the salient.[74] They would be far too late. Haig's attempt to second guess his Commander in Chief had failed; and worse, his actions that evening had tired his men and exasperated his officers. He had compounded his errors by failing, at any stage, to inform GHQ and II Corps that he had varied his orders.

The artillery, directed at corps level by Brigadier General Horne had already reacted to events, and well it was that they had. Their dispositions will be described presently.

---

71   TNA WO 95/1283: 2nd Division, 23 August 1914, p.44.
72   Ibid.: 23 August 1914.
73   TNA WO 95/1343: 5th Infantry Brigade, 23 August 1914.
74   TNA WO 95/1342: 1st Irish Guards, 23 August 1914.

2.11 Summary of Plans for 23 August on evening of 22 August (Map 4)

On the evening of the 22nd, Field Marshal French was still optimistic. He had cancelled the advance of II Corps scheduled for the 23rd, but, since he had already ordered I Corps forward, supplemented by French entreaties to remain in position, had decided to hold the line on the canal at Mons the next day. His Cavalry Division was in position on the left, and the independent 19th Infantry Brigade was shortly expected at Valenciennes – to be used to strengthen the left wing of II Corps. As far as he was concerned, I Corps would have reinforced the right flank of II Corps by dawn, allowing the latter to retract its line, and free up reserves for possible later offensive use.

Haig, the pessimistic tactician, saw no possible benefit in holding this line, and every reason for II Corps to be withdrawn. Expecting this withdrawal, he had 'varied' OA57, holding his 2nd Division on the eastern half of the logical fall-back line at Bavai, but failed to inform GHQ what he had done and why. His I Corps order and counter-order to the 2nd Division had rendered them unable to obey orders to march to the salient by 6 a.m. the next morning, in order to comply with OA62. His 2nd Division would be very late arriving on the battlefield. Neither II Corps, nor GHQ, had been informed of this delay.

General Smith-Dorrien, the pragmatist, knew II Corps was committed to the Mons positions, and was anticipating an attack. Like Haig, he was aware of the dangers of attempting to hold such a vulnerable salient position in the face of over-whelming numbers. He was 'varying' his orders to fight a battle of extraction, not confrontation. He was relying on the arrival of I Corps to take up positions to the east of Mons, to free up the reserves he required to bolster the centre of his line in the event of heavy attack.

3

The Day of Battle – 23 August 1914

3.1 I Corps Artillery (Map 6)

I Corps artillery, in marked contrast to II Corps, was almost collected. The 1st Division artillery had been complete with the exception of one field brigade and the divisional ammunition column on the 21st, but both had caught up by the evening of the 22nd. The 2nd Division howitzers and their heavy battery were in touch, albeit somewhat to the rear of their forward brigades. They also had half their ammunition column in touch. The second half would not reach them till the 23rd.

During the late evening of the 22nd, Brigadier General Horne, Haig's artillery commander at I Corps, went forward to ensure that the guns of the 1st Division were well placed to face the German line of advance as it was now projected. He met with Brigadier General Findlay, commanding 1st Division artillery at midnight and they agreed positions.

But Brigadier General Percival and the headquarters of the 2nd Division artillery were still six miles south and a touch east of Bavai.[1] They were dangerously out of position. General Percival hurried up, ahead of his guns, and met General Horne some three hours later, at about the time his guns were setting off. I Corps staff had already reconnoitred this line on the 21st, but Percival had not.[2] What they both saw was not reassuring:

Brigadier General Henry Horne.

---

1 TNA WO 95/1313: 2nd Division Artillery, 23 August 1914.
2 TNA WO 95/588/4: I Corps Staff, 21 August 1914.

Enemy observed in force to the north. Positions selected, arranged especially to bring our fire to bear on all ground over which enemy would have to advance to push home an attack.[3]

General Horne and his two junior brigadiers had a defensive mind-set, fully in tune with that of General Haig. They knew that the Germans were at least at Bray, to the east, and they could see them to the north. Their task was to protect the infantry who were advancing, and to resist a possible German advance from both these directions. The contours were relatively favourable, there being a low ridge running southeast from Mons. They selected covered positions, behind the line the infantry would take up. The guns would be on reverse slopes, firing with observers forward. These observers, on the ridge and looking over low flat ground, would have a good view of the approaches.

3.2 The Salient (Maps 6 & 7)

During the evening of the 22nd, II Corps asked GHQ whether they could evacuate the eastern flank of the salient as far south as Harmignies in anticipation of the arrival of the 2nd Division. (They had already pulled back the small 7th Infantry Brigade outpost at Givry.) At 11.40 p.m., GHQ responded that they were happy to leave 'it to discretion of 2nd Corps to withdraw right of outpost line to Harmignies,' in the light of the imminent, as they thought, arrival of the 2nd Division of I Corps to take over this section of the front line.[4] (General Haig had told neither GHQ, nor II Corps, that the advance of his 2nd Division had been delayed.) So, the 3rd Division ordered a withdrawal to coincide with the projected time of their arrival.

At 6 a.m., the 2nd Royal Irish Regiment of the 8th Infantry Brigade, was pulled back 'from their exposed positions' on the eastern flank of the salient to act as a reserve.[5] They had been digging in there since the previous evening but did not like the position. It was enfiladed from the north. But if this line was not held, the right flank of the Middlesex Regiment, in front of Obourg Bridge, was very insecure, and their retirement would be almost impossible if they were significantly outflanked.

The strategic high ground at Bois la Haut remained unoccupied in anticipation of the artillery reinforcements which were also expected to arrive with the 2nd Division.

The 2nd Royal Scots, who formed the right flank of the 8th Infantry Brigade, remained thinly spread up the road to Harmignies from Bois la Haut, awaiting relief. Also, at 6 a.m., the 7th Infantry Brigade, who made up the 3rd Division reserves took up the positions they had occupied the previous afternoon. Their forward battalion,

---

3 TNA WO 95/1313: 2nd Division Artillery, 23 August 1914.
4 TNA WO 95/630: II Corps Staff, 23 August 1914.
5 TNA WO 95/1416: 8th Infantry Brigade, 23 August 1914.

the 2nd Prince of Wales's Volunteers (South Lancashire Regiment), went back up to a position at Ciply, close south of Mons, and the 2nd Royal Irish Rifles were detached back along the railway to Harmignies to (again very thinly) cover behind the weak southern flank of the 8th Infantry Brigade, with the expectation that this would be bolstered by the arrival of the 2nd Division at any time after 6 a.m. They did not occupy the line from Harmignies to Givry leaving it to the 2nd Division. The remaining two battalions of the brigade remained in billets for the time being.[6]

3.3 The Conference of the Generals (Map 5)

General Smith-Dorrien had a sleepless night. His intelligence staff had advised him that at least two cavalry divisions and more than one German Corps were very close. They had also told him that German infantry were occupying a village only seven miles due east.[7] He was making dispositions considerably at variance with Field Marshal French's expectation that he would hold the enemy on the canal. As he said in his memoire, with deep, and presumably libel-proof, irony:

> [T]hat night I was happy in my mind, for official news of the enemy given me had indicated no great strength, and I fully expected that the Chief's expressed intention of moving forward again the next day would be carried out. I had been given no news of the somewhat serious happenings in the French Army on our right, which I learnt about years later, namely that it had been forced back … thus leaving us in a very vulnerable, indefensible and salient position. Had I known of this serious situation, I doubt much if my night's rest would have been as enjoyable as it proved to be – for I should have been racking my brains as to what the object of our remaining so isolated was.

Of course, he did know that the advance the next day had been cancelled, and that the French were falling back, but this is irony, and the point is made. French came up to his headquarters, at Sars-la-Bruyère, to be briefed at 6 a.m.:

> Nor was I disillusioned the next morning when about 6 a.m. the Chief appeared at my Headquarters, and addressing his Corps and Cavalry Division Commanders assembled there, told us (vide his despatch of 7 September) that little more than one, or at most two, enemy Corps with a cavalry Division were facing the BEF. So, it was evident that he too was in blissful ignorance of the real situation. Sir John was in excellent form and told us to be prepared to move forward, or to fight where we were, but to get ready for the latter by strengthening our outposts and

6   TNA WO 95/1413: 7th Infantry Brigade, 23 Aug 1914.
7   TNA WO 95/629: II Corps intelligence summary, 22 August 1914.

preparing the bridges over the canal for demolition. I took the opportunity of emphasising the weakness of my general line and the danger of holding on to the Mons salient, remarking that I was issuing orders for the preparation of a retired position south-west and clear of the town of Mons to cover, should a retirement become necessary, the advanced troops at Nimy and Oburg who would have to fall back behind Mons, as soon as things got so hot as to risk their being cut off. The Chief expressed himself in agreement and approved my action. He then went off to Valenciennes …[8]

Leaving aside how this should be interpreted, according to General Haig's diaries, and his account in I Corps records, this meeting took place at a nearby village at 10.30 a.m. He mentions only the dispositions of his divisions being decided at the meeting.[9] General Allenby of the Cavalry Division confirms attendance with both corps commanders at Sars-la-Bruyère at 6 a.m.[10] Field Marshal French confirms both the timing, and the presence of General Haig.[11] For General Haig to deny his well-documented presence at such an important meeting is bizarre.

French had much on his mind, even before he had to digest the unexpected reports of German forces to the north, and the sheer weight of the forces arraigned against him. General Kitchener had ordered him to attack, but also warned him not to risk the destruction of his army. He had told him to liaise closely with the French, but not to accept orders from them. He was being urged, on his honour, to stand his ground, if not advance, by General Lanrezac of 5th French Army, whom he neither liked nor trusted. He would have been very aware that General Smith-Dorrien's criticism of his tactical dispositions had forced him to make considerable adjustments the last time they met. They were not on easy terms.[12] He probably felt the need to reassert his authority, starting with an oration.

General Smith-Dorrien's account of the meeting, allowing for its ironic tone, is plausible. He would very likely have adopted an emollient stance, after his show of strength on the evening of the 21st. Indeed, being a charming man when he wanted to be, it is probable that he reassured French that he could hold the canal line against an enemy attack by equal numbers.

General Haig would not have felt comfortable. Both Field Marshal French and General Smith-Dorrien were assuming that his 2nd Division was arriving at the salient as they spoke. Having not told GHQ the night before that it had not advanced, he did not do so now. Perhaps he was holding on to the unrealistic hope that he had reacted in time for the orders to be obeyed. It was too late for him to point out

---

8   Smith-Dorrien, *Memories of Forty-Eight Years' Service*, pp.381-382.
9   TNA WO 95/588/4: I Corps Staff, 23 August 1914.
10 TNA WO 95/1096: Cavalry Division, 23 August 1914.
11 Sir John French, 1914, p.59.
12 Jones (ed.), *Stemming the Tide*, Chapter 7, p.158.

that a battle on the Mons canal was a tactical aberration about which he felt deeply pessimistic.

General Allenby too would have been ill at ease, having been publicly reprimanded for alarmist reporting by French's staff only a few hours before. There was much more than battle planning on the unspoken agenda that morning.

General Smith-Dorrien says that Field Marshal French ordered the canal line to be reinforced and held. According to Brigadier General Edmonds, (then Chief of Staff with the 4th Division and at the meeting), 'French said to Smith-Dorrien 'The British Army will give battle on the line of the Conde Canal.' When Smith Dorrien asked, "Do you mean take the offensive or stand on the defensive?"' (Since the troops on the canal were outposts, this was a very pertinent question.) French apparently retorted, 'Don't ask questions, do as you are told.'[13] He had never specifically ordered offensive outposts. General Smith-Dorrien had been given 'brief and very general instructions' and told to fight the battle as he saw fit. But there is no evidence that he mentioned his plan also to withdraw the 5th Division outposts to a second position where they could be supported by artillery.

The above anecdote perhaps reveals why he did not. The important decision as to whether the outposts on the canal were offensive or defensive was not even debated. It seems likely that this was the tone of the whole conference; that Field Marshal French issued general instructions as an oration; discouraged debate; and those present just had to listen. 'The 1st Corps was echeloned on the right and in rear of the 2nd. ... They all assured me that a quiet night had been passed and that their line was firmly taken up and held', says French in his memoir.

He goes on to say that: 'Allenby's bold and searching reconnaissance had not led me to believe that we were threatened by forces against which we could not make a bold and effective stand.'[14]

General Allenby had told him that 'from reports from the Scots Greys, the enemy's advance was slow, and no great push was made by them', implying the Germans were reluctant to fully engage.[15] But this was the day before, out on the right flank, describing elements of the German VII Corps of their 2nd Army, who were heading south, engaging the French. The Cavalry Division, now on the left flank, was not up to the hour with enemy movements.

As already described, Field Service Regulations required that 'orders for a possible retreat should always be thought out beforehand'.[16] So, having had his say, Field Marshal French asked his Chief-of-Staff, Lieutenant General Sir Archibald Murray, to draft 'full instructions as to arrangements which must be made if a retreat

---

13   Beckett & Corvi, *Haig's Generals*, p.193.
14   Sir John French, *1914*, p.61.
15   TNA WO 95/1096: Cavalry Division, 22 August 1914.
16   *Field Service Regulations*, p.32.

becomes necessary',[17] and left. It seems likely that General Allenby did too, which was unfortunate.

French travelled to Valenciennes, and spent time inspecting both French troops, and his own 19th Brigade, on their way up to support the left flank of the 5th Division. This was the action of a very tired man under excessive stress. He gave himself a routine task, which required no decisions; with the additional advantage that he could snatch some sleep in his car. But he might have remembered another Field Service Regulation. 'A commander, even of a large army, should rarely omit to reconnoitre personally'.[18]

3.4 Planning a Fighting Withdrawal

So, General Murray, General Smith-Dorrien and General Haig were left to discuss retreat scenarios. A secret memo, entitled 'General arrangements in case of attack', was distributed to II Corps staff that morning:

> The present line of the 2nd Corps from Harmignies through Bois-la-Haut – Nimy and line of canal to dividing point with Cavalry Division is to be held. Should the troops guarding these points be forced to retire, the bridges, (already ordered to be prepared for demolition) will be blown up, and the defensive position Harmignies Station – spur 3/4 of a mile north of Frameries – Bois de Boussu [a wood just north of Dour] will be taken up. All transport should now be parked to rear of fighting troops ready to move in any direction. [This withdrawal would leave no 3rd Division troops north of Harmignies station towards the salient.]
>
> In the event of it becoming apparent that our left flank is being turned … the 5th Division will probably be ordered to retire first … and entrench … from Bavai westwards. Similarly, one division of the 1st Army will be withdrawn to entrench east of Bavai. Eventually the 3rd Division and the remaining division of the 1st Corps will be withdrawn…General Haig wants the road from Genly – Riez de l'Erelle – Bavai but is not likely to get so much.
>
> Circumstances may, however, arise in which it will be necessary to retire the 3rd Division first instead of the 5th Division, or even necessitating the retirement of both divisions simultaneously. Administrative staff to consider the arrangements for retirement … in all three eventualities.[19]

One can almost hear General Smith-Dorrien dictating this resumé of the meeting with his irritable reference to General Haig's demand for the use of the main Mons

---

17 Sir John French, *1914*, p.61.
18 Field Service Regulations, p.117.
19 TNA WO 95/630: II Corps Staff, 23 August 1914, p.75.

to Bavai road, after Ciply, thereby implying that the 1st Division of I Corps was to be the one 'entrenching east of Bavai' in the event of this full retirement. The document confirms General Smith-Dorrien's 'second position', as it came to be known, from Harmignies in the east, to Dour in the west; and, further back, a line at Bavai, the eastern half of which General Haig's 2nd Division had occupied overnight.

The covering note to those officers who received this memo states that 'the retirement to the Bavai position, if it ever takes place, is to be a matter for General Headquarter orders'[20], which implies General Murray's participation in the decision-making. (When II Corps did achieve this second line that evening, General Smith-Dorrien informed GHQ, and asked for guidance as to when to activate the further retirement.)

General Smith-Dorrien, in his memoir, gives an account of the meeting with Field Marshal French. In it, he refers to French, both before and after the extracts quoted, as the 'C-in-C'.[21] Yet, solely for this section of the book, he calls him the 'Chief'. He writes that the 'Chief' was 'in agreement' with his plans. He has just agreed his strategy with French's Chief-of-Staff. Is Sir Horace, ten years later, playing word games? It seems not unlikely.

3.5 The Immediate Consequences of the Meetings

The consequences of these two meetings were profound. General Smith-Dorrien now felt there was no impediment to implementing his plan. By 7 a.m., II Corps staff was ordering the 3rd Division to urgently strengthen both the canal outpost line, and the 'second position' line, though without offering any extra resources to the former.

> A suitable defensive position to south of Mons should be selected and if possible prepared AAA. The southern exits to Mons should be barricaded AAA. This is to enable troops north of Mons to fall back in safety if necessity arises, but it must be understood that canal line and outpost line must be strengthened and held as long as possible.[22]

Neither he, nor General Hamilton, would have left Bois la Haut without artillery, in the light of this order, if they had known that the Second Division would not be taking it over. It is clear that they were still expecting I Corps reinforcements.

Field Marshal French (and probably General Allenby) thought that II Corps was preparing to hold a line on the canal. French's Chief of Staff, Sir Archibald Murray knew General Smith-Dorrien's intentions, and that he would hold his second position

---

20 Ibid., p.74.
21 Smith-Dorrien, *Memories of Forty-Eight Years' Service*, pp.379, 384, 387.
22 TNA WO 95/1375: 3rd Division, 23 August 1914.

unless ordered by GHQ to retire. He should have made French aware of the battle plan in the event of overwhelming strength, and maybe he tried so to do.

General Haig, in all of his related accounts, asserts the fiction that this conference took place later and elsewhere, but there is no doubt he was alarmed. He could foresee only disaster for II Corps. Significantly he now knew that General Smith-Dorrien intended to withdraw his right flank to Harmignies. He probably expected this to happen quickly, and the evidence suggests that he immediately changed his dispositions, of which more anon, as a consequence.

Unsurprisingly, Field Marshal French later disputed General Smith-Dorrien's version of the meeting. But as he neither picked up on General Haig's pessimism and delayed dispositions, nor stayed to discuss the possible retreat, he had only himself to blame. At 3.10 p.m., French dictated a letter to his liaison officer at French 5th Army Headquarters saying that his army would not be 'properly prepared to take offensive action till tomorrow morning.'[23] This is consistent with his understanding. He had been led to believe by General Smith-Dorrien that there would be no difficulty in holding the line (against equal numbers), while II Corps artillery was collected, and its right wing retracted; and by implication be prepared for an offensive the next day. But French was ignoring, or not receiving, credible reports that II Corps was being attacked by overwhelming numbers.

John Terraine states that French 'issued no written orders between 11.55 p.m. on August 21st and 8.25 p.m. on August 24th'.[24] It is certainly true that there are no written orders in General Staff records, but GHQ issued more than 30 orders (numbered OA62 to OA 95) between these times, many of them significant, and all logical on the information available to him.

3.6 5th Division Artillery, II Corps (Maps 4 & 8)

Immediately after his meetings on the morning of the 23rd, General Smith-Dorrien set about arranging his 'second position'. Every available unit was ordered to work on it. He probably thought his left flank as vulnerable as his right. He had stated as such in the secret briefing to his staff quoted above:

> At, as far as I recollect, about 9 a.m., I motored to the left of my outpost line at Pommeroeul, and leaving the car, crossed the bridge and saw an interesting scrap between the Cornwall's and German scouts. I then passed along east on the south side of the canal, when about 10 a.m., the first German shell I had seen fired burst in the road just in front of my car close to Jemappes.[25]

---

23 Edmonds, *Military Operations France and Belgium 1914*, Vol. I, p.92.
24 Terraine, *Mons: Retreat to Victory*, p.82.
25 Smith-Dorrien, *Memories of Forty-Eight Years' Service*, p.384.

Again, he uses anecdotes to deflect attention from what he is doing. He was consulting with General Ferguson; and it suggests that he, like General Haig, feared a battle of manoeuvre, and a severe threat to his left flank. On this left flank, the 5th Division's reserve brigade, the 15th Infantry Brigade was:

> [A]sked to reconnoitre and fix a line a line of defence if driven back from the canal. Did so with CRE [Commander Royal Engineers] V Div. Sent out working parties, two companies from each battalion, helped by civilian labour. Started about 12.30.[26]

The 'second position' was being chosen in partnership with the engineers, as was conventional where works were required. Decisions were made quickly, often before the guns had arrived. The line ran well south of the canal, starting at Wasmes, south-west of Mons and then largely following the undulating line of a railway, passing just north of Dour, to Elouges in the west. (Bois de Boussu, mentioned in General Smith-Dorrien's secret memo as being on the defence line was not the village of Boussu, but a wood one mile north of Dour.)

This 5th Division line was over 5 miles long and manned only by the 4000 men of the four battalions of the reserve 15th Infantry Brigade, supported by whatever artillery that could be mustered. The 5th Division refer to this line as the 'second position' from early in the day.[27]

Brigadier General Headlam, CRA 5th division, still had few resources to work with.[28] The 15th Brigade RFA had been at Dour overnight, and Lieutenant McLeod with the 80th Battery of this brigade, was ordered to prepare positions in the late morning of the 23rd:

> There was a field in the middle of the village close to Dour church and we left all the vehicles there, dismounted the gunners and marched through the village and turned into a turnip field with a railway running at the bottom. Here we started preparing a battery position along the only possible cover, behind a hedge bordering the railway. It was on a forward slope and somewhat to our surprise it was facing north-west. At the top of the slope was a factory we could use as an observation post. We cut gaps in the hedge and dug the gun pits so that the top of the hedge would be level with the tops of the gun shields. …We could see the infantry digging in along the hedge 500 yards in front of us, and soon others came even further back and started digging in just in front of us along the hedge on the other side of the railway track.[29]

---

26 TNA WO 95/1566: 15th Infantry Brigade, 23 August 1914.
27 TNA WO 95/1510: 5th Division, 23 August 1914.
28 TNA WO 95/1521: 5th Division Artillery, 23 August 1914.
29 RAM MD/115: McLeod, Journal, 23 August 1914.

The line at this point faced north-west. This took into account the possibility of a German encirclement manoeuvre round the left flank of II Corps. But the guns were aimed north to cover a line from Thulin eastwards.[30] On this flank, the railway was not particularly helpful for defence. Lieutenant McLeod did not relish being on a forward slope, and the infantry did not like the idea of being 500 yards forward with not much cover behind them. But they did their best to dig themselves in, and the rain that morning probably made this task easier than it might have been.

The 27th Brigade had billeted in Dour, and one battery, the 120th, already mentioned, and of which more anon, had gone up with forward elements of the 13th Infantry Brigade to St Ghislain; but most of the 5th Division artillery had been at Bavai overnight, and was now making its slow way to Dour, considerably held up by traffic congestion.

General Headlam decided on his main dispositions as the 'second position' was marked out. In the first instance, he split his artillery into three groups.[31] He kept his main force, under his own command, south and west of Dour, covering to the north, adjustable to the north-west. This initially consisted of only the 15th Brigade RFA, but his heavy battery (the 108th), and the 8th (Howitzer) Brigade, reached Dour during the afternoon. When the latter arrived, he sent their 37th Battery to reinforce his right group which he posted at Wasmes three miles back from St Ghislain.

This consisted of the 27th Brigade RFA, which was seconded to the 13th Infantry Brigade. His left group, consisting of the 28th Brigade RFA, was posted just north of Dour, similarly seconded to the 14th infantry brigade. These dispositions were fine as far as they went, but both infantry brigadiers were fully occupied with holding their canal positions, and unavailable to discuss the siting of guns on the 'second position'.

Just north of Dour, the line to which the 14th Infantry Brigade would fall back, this was not a problem. The wood just north of Dour (Bois de Boussu) was protected by a rail embankment, 'very suitable for observation'.[32] Siting the guns was relatively straight forward, and the infantry lines conformed.

But further east, towards Wasmes, the railway line undulated, and the battery captains of the 27th Brigade RFA had to site the guns 'depending entirely on their own judgement'.[33] (When the 13th Infantry Brigade did fall back in the dark that evening, they overshot the prepared lines in some places, and at least one gun-placement was dangerously far forward.)

The far left of II Corps was covered by the Cavalry Division, supported by two Horse Artillery brigades of light 13-pounder field guns, though these remained, in

---

30 TNA WO 95/1528: XV Brigade RFA, 23 August 1914.
31 TNA WO 95/1521: 5 Division Artillery, 23 August 1914.
32 TNA WO 95/1532: XXVIII Brigade RFA, 23 August 1914, p.47.
33 TNA WO 95/1529: XXVII Brigade RFA, 23 August 1914.

billets, back at Quievrain.³⁴ The main strength of the Cavalry had moved, behind the infantry, from the east flank to the west (not enjoying the cobbled roads) the previous evening. They were now patrolling over the canal facing the German cavalry screen in front of their approaching infantry. By the early afternoon, the Cavalry Division had taken up dismounted positions along the canal to the west, being relieved by the independent 19th Infantry Brigade as it arrived, without artillery, during the mid-afternoon. The 19th Brigade came immediately under the command of General Allenby.³⁵

3.7 3rd Division Artillery, II Corps (Maps 4, 6 & 7)

The same preparations were occurring to the east. The 3rd Division 'second position' again broadly followed the railway which tracked west, from the station at Harmignies, passing between Mons and Ciply, and then curved gently round to the northern edge of Frameries. (Even at this stage, it was clear that the left of the 3rd Division second position did not join up with the right of that of the 5th Division. There was a gap at Paturages, between Wasmes and Frameries. There were no reserves to be had. II Corps had to wait for I Corps reinforcements before this gap could be partially filled. That morning, General Smith-Dorrien could only be aware of the gap and hope for the best.)

The 7th Infantry Brigade, south of Mons was the reserve brigade of the 3rd Division. Their four battalions now had a line over four miles long to prepare. By noon, they had reconnoitred, and 'units began work preparing for defence. 1st Wiltshire Regt on the right, 3rd Worcestershire Regt in centre, 2nd Lancashire Regt on left. Owing to a misunderstanding, 3rd Worcestershire Regt began work on a position too far advanced towards Mons.' This caused problems the next day, as will be described. The 2nd Royal Irish Rifles, the fourth battalion of the brigade, were already lined out facing north-east on the railway to Harmignies station.³⁶ (The 2nd Royal Scots, of the 8th Infantry Brigade, were on the Mons to Harmignies road, also thinly spread, to their north-east.)

The three villages in which the three field artillery brigades of the division had billeted overnight, one south-west, one south and the other south-east of the town, were all south of the defence line. As has been said, Brigadier General Wing, CRA 3rd Division, had already identified positions 'selected with a view to delaying or preventing enemy's advance.'

---

34 TNA WO 95/1103: VII Brigade RHA, 23 August 1914.
35 TNA WP 95/1096: Cavalry Division, 23 August 1914.
36 TNA WO 95/1413: 7th Infantry Brigade, 22 August 1914.

The 42nd Brigade RFA, attached to the 7th Infantry Brigade, was at Nouvelles four miles south-east of Mons. They received orders to move forward and prepare their positions:

> 10 a.m. The OC brigade was ordered to reconnoitre positions for artillery on the high ground immediately north of Nouvelles …1.30 p.m. The three batteries moved from Nouvelles to entrench the positions selected….2 p.m. Lieutenant Colonel Geddes was ordered to reconnoitre and make arrangements to dig emplacements for the 23rd Brigade. Labour employed – men of brigade ammunition column and civilians.[37]

The 23rd brigade RFA were at Frameries to the west. They were supporting the 9th Infantry Brigade who were facing north in the salient. One battery was held back to dig in, but the other two batteries moved slightly forward to the south and south-west of Mons to positions from which they could cover the infantry if they had to fall back prematurely. They were south of the coal mine works and did not have line of sight over the canal. They could do nothing to support the front line. Only two rounds were fired by the brigade all day. They fell back in the evening to billets, just behind the emplacements that had been dug for them by the 42nd Brigade.[38]

The 40th brigade who were supporting the 8th Infantry Brigade facing east in the salient were also back, at Noirchain, south of Mons, though in the early hours of the morning their commanding officer re-visited Bois la Haut.[39] From this strategically important hill at the south-east edge of the town, they could cover the exposed right flank of II Corps, from which the Royal Irish Regiment had been withdrawn. But the 2nd Division were scheduled to take up these positions, and they made no move forward. The brigade remained on the back line.

Only one battery of the 30th (Howitzer) Brigade arrived at Ciply, south of Mons and that in mid-afternoon. They fired a few rounds but stopped hurriedly when they realised they were bombarding a British position by mistake.[40] The rest of the Howitzer brigade, and the Divisional Ammunition Column were still in transit, on trains somewhere in Northern France.

---

37 TNA WO 95/1401: XLII Brigade RFA, 23 August 1914.
38 TNA WO 95/1399: XXIII Brigade RFA, 23 August 1914.
39 TNA WO 95/1400: XL Brigade RFA, 23 August 1914.
40 Hutchison, *The Young Gunner*, p.9.

3.8 Summary of II Corps Artillery Dispositions

Thus, as the morning of 23 August dawned, the 5th Division, defending the canal, had only one battery forward, and that despite the misgivings of both infantry and artillery brigadiers, with four guns in action. The 3rd Division had no guns forward.

Field Service Regulation recommended that artillery should be close up to an outpost if it was to be firmly held.[41] They could fire on vulnerable enemy infantry as they advanced and could also neutralise enemy light artillery supporting that advance. But if the outpost position was not to be firmly held, guns forward would be vulnerable, and more useful in prepared positions, sited at relative leisure. II Corps had chosen the second option. But the preparation of the second line, and the arrival of the artillery to defend it, would take most of the day. The outpost positions had to be held for as long as possible. The one saving grace for the infantry was that they were almost invisible, dug in behind the canal. They had no cavalry to their front, though some units did post men over the canal where visibility forward was poor. There is a German source that suggests that their cavalry reconnoitred up to the line of the canal over the night of the 22nd, and reported the line as lightly held by the British, due to the lack of such outposts or a cavalry screen.[42]

3.9 The German Army and its Artillery (Map 4)

The German First Army, commanded by General Von Kluck, had even less information on British dispositions than the British had on his. On the 22nd, he responded to a rumour that the British Force was further west and turned one of his corps to face the threat. When his troops did, almost literally, stumble into the British positions at Mons, he ordered them in to attack as they arrived.

German Cavalry of both III and IX Corps reconnoitred the bridges soon after dawn and suffered some casualties. Further west, the German 9th Cavalry Division scouted. About 9 a.m., the cavalry and forward infantry units of IX Corps emerged from the woods about two miles from Mons. The latter marched into attack in columns down towards Nimy, accompanied by their field guns.[43] They were caught in a deadly crossfire from over the canal and fell back to the edge of the woods.

These woods were on higher ground, so the German light artillery, supporting their infantry, had a good view of the canal. Over the next few hours, the 17th and 18th Divisions of IX Corps arrived in their full strength and an increasingly fierce bombardment fell on the infantry defending Nimy, the point of the Mons salient,

---

41 *Field Service Regulations*, 1912, p.102.
42 Terence Zuber, British and German Cavalry, August 1914, <http://terencezuber.com/BritishandGermanCavalry.pdf> (undated) accessed March 2018.
43 TNA WO 95/1400: 8th Infantry Brigade, 23 August 1914.

Artist's impression of the German assault on Nimy bridge.

spreading east to Obourg gradually outflanking the British line. The vanguard of III Corps arrived on their right, and as their 5th and 6th divisions arrived, they spread out progressively further west along the line of the woods north of the canal. Their field guns also came into action on the edge of the woods. 'At 9 a.m. German guns were in position on the high ground north of the canal' and 'shells were bursting thickly along the whole line of the Middlesex and Royal Fusiliers,' says the Official History, though it was more probably 'from 9 a.m.' All accounts agree that the bombardments were both heavy and accurate.

At the same time, the German infantry attacks spread from this point both east, as the two divisions of IX Corps, renewed their attacks; and west as the two divisions of III Corps, came into action. The British infantry, in many places entrenched in positions partially dug by Belgian civilians, behind a canal 20 yards wide, used their expertise with the rifle with devastating effect on the advancing German infantry. In the first hours of the battle, only the German light field gun batteries, equipped with the 7.7 cm Feldkanone, were involved in the attacks, supporting their infantry, some of them advancing with the infantry as close as 500 yards from the canal.[44]

It is at this point that the single most important factor in the whole Mons campaign became apparent. The German field guns were almost useless. This is not strictly true. On the 22nd, the Cavalry Division submitted a cryptic report to I Corps which was forwarded to II Corps, received by them at 8.20 p.m. 'Cavalry engaged from 8 a.m. to 5 p.m. today. ...have charged both infantry and cavalry with success. German guns

44 Edmonds, *Military Operations France and Belgium 1914*, Vol. I, pp.76, 77, 94.

shoot well but their shells do not burst properly. Effect nil.'[45] This report was frankly unbelievable. And it was given no credence. But it was accurate.

The Middlesex Regiment of 8th Infantry Brigade, and the Royal Fusiliers of 9th Infantry Brigade, at the apex of the salient at Nimy, lost almost no casualties to artillery fire that morning. And nor did any other unit, bombarded exclusively by German field guns, suffer any significant losses, at any time in the battle. This is not to say that the German artillery as a whole was not a potent force. One in four of their forward batteries were equipped with the very effective 10.5 cm Feldhaubitze 98/09, although these guns were only used later in the day, and then mainly against 'field fortifications', i.e. barricades or machine gun posts, rather than the infantry line.

It is interesting to examine an accurate, but misinterpreted, account from an infantryman:

> "We were in the trenches waiting for them" an anonymous soldier told 'the Times', but we didn't expect anything like the smashing blow that struck us. All at once, the sky began to rain down bullets and shells. At first the shells went very wide, for their fire was bad, but after a time – I think it was a long time – they got our range and then they fairly mopped us up. I saw shells bursting to left and to right of me and I saw many a good comrade go out."[46]

This man was in the front line, and it did indeed rain air burst shrapnel overhead. Later in the battle, the anonymous soldier almost certainly came under the fire of the German howitzers targeting infantry strong points. They were indeed appalling weapons. But the earlier bombardment had not caused casualties. In the same account, 'a Royal Field Artillery officer noted in his diary: West Kent's, Middlesex and Northumberland's decimated by shell-fire,' which they were not, though it looked like it as the British positions were accurately targeted with air burst shrapnel. This perception was important and was to influence events. John Terraine, in his definitive book on the battle, fails to recognise the poor quality of the German Field ammunition, even surmising late in the battle that 'the shooting of the German artillery must have been very bad to allow any part of this splendid target to escape.'[47]

The task of the field guns in battle was to pin down and degrade enemy defensive positions in support of their own advancing infantry; to silence enemy counterfire; and to target organised units, wreck transport and, most importantly, kill horses to prevent a disciplined and successful withdrawal. The German field guns did none of these things. In 1913, a British Field Artillery expert guaranteed that one of his

---

45   TNA WO 95/629: II Corps Intelligence, 22 August 1914.
46   Terraine, *Mons: The Retreat to Victory*, p.92.
47   Ibid., p.117.

batteries could decimate an infantry formation, caught on an open road at 4000 yards, within two minutes.[48] There is no reason to doubt this assertion.

It was not of course immediately apparent to the British (or German) generals that this heavy initial bombardment was ineffective. The British feared the worst and quite reasonably. As already described, it was not even apparent to the British troops in the front line. The enemy fire was accurate. There were loud detonations both overhead and, on the ground, and a constant whistling of shrapnel through the air. It was terrifying. But the professional British infantry did not panic and kept up their accurate rifle fire despite all the distractions.

Most of the best eye-witness descriptions of this ineffective fire come later in the battle, so at the risk of disrupting the chronology to illustrate the point, it is worth quoting Lieutenant Schreiber, then a young Royal Field Artillery subaltern, later a distinguished Second World War general, who was watching the battle south east of Mons:

> I remember that morning seeing a salvo of airburst high explosive shells burst right over a wagon line in the valley in front of us. We expected to see a tangle of men and horses; all that happened was that the teams quietly trotted to a new halting place some three hundred yards to a flank – there was not a single casualty.[49]

3.10 The British Artillery in the Salient, 3rd Division (Map 9)

Brigadier General Wing, who commanded the 3rd Division artillery, was very conscious of the lack of support that his artillery was providing. Brigadier General Doran, commanding the 8th Infantry Brigade, occupying the north and east of the salient, was even more so. He had summoned the commanding officer of his usual supporting artillery, and together:

> [A]t dawn, O/C 40 FA Bde commenced reconnoitring positions for guns, resulting in finding good positions for guns about Bois la Haut for firing NE, E and SE, but in finding no satisfactory positions to fire north-west to assist the 4/Midd'x Regiment.[50]

There was increasing anxiety as the 2nd Division, who were supposed to be taking over this position failed to arrive. Their advanced party, ahead of their main body,

---

48 TNA WO 95/1521: 5th Division Artillery, lecture notes 1913, p.45.
49 Royal Artillery Museum, Larkhill, MD/425: Lt E Schreiber, XXV Brigade RFA journal, 23 August 1914.
50 TNA WO 95/1416: 8th Infantry Brigade, 23 August 1914.

did not reach 3rd Division headquarters till well after 9 a.m., too late for deployment deep into the salient.[51] At 10 a.m., realising this, General Wing released the 40th Brigade RFA, consisting of the 6th, 23rd and 49th Batteries to General Doran, and they reached the positions on Bois la Haut, two miles back from the canal by 11 a.m.[52] General Doran wanted guns further forward to support the Middlesex Regiment, who held the eastern end of the canal as far as the bridge to Obourg;[53] and a two-gun section of the 49th Battery was immediately sent to support them. This section was devastatingly effective when it found a good infantry target; but it was just two guns. One account of the Mons battle states that 'the defenders too had most effective support from the 107th Battery RFA entrenched behind them, the artillery observer in the firing line communicating the enemy's range with great accuracy.'[54] This is nonsense. No battery, least of all the 107th, was forward in the salient. It is jingoistic propaganda.

Mons was under attack by the 18th Division of IX Corps; and east to Obourg and beyond by the 17th Division of the same corps. The Middlesex were lined out along the canal as far as the Obourg bridge, but their right wing hung in the air, and the German infantry could, and did, outflank them. The 2nd Royal Irish, the 1st Gordon Highlanders and the 2nd Royal Scots were behind the Middlesex, facing east at the base of Bois la Haut set back on the Harmignies to Nimy road. (The latter were very stretched, their right wing just north of Harmignies, again still expecting relief from the 2nd Division.)

As the German infantry advanced, not only the right wing of the Middlesex Regiment, but their two supporting guns found themselves attacked from north and east, and later from the south-east. At that point, at about noon, they started to fall back from their eastern positions, probably a bit later than was entirely wise.[55] All but 30 of the company that guarded Obourg Bridge were lost, but they had savaged their assailants.[56]

Further destabilising the salient positions, at about the same time, the German infantry forced the canal at Nimy and Mons, held by the 4th Royal Fusiliers, of the 9th Infantry Brigade, who were on the railway to the left of the Middlesex positions. A few men of the 2nd Royal Irish Regiment had escorted a Royal Engineer detachment to Obourg Bridge, but the remainder, on the left of the Middlesex Regiment, fell back by stages with them from mid-morning, the Royal Fusiliers, on their left also falling back through Nimy. The far left of the Fusiliers, on the canal line at

51 TNA WO 95/630/1: II Corps Staff, 23 August 1914.
52 TNA WO 95/1400: XL Brigade RFA, 23 August 1914.
53 TNA WO 95/1416: 8th Infantry Brigade, 23 August 1914.
54 Ernest Hamilton, *The First Seven Divisions: Being a Detailed Account of the Fighting from Mons to Ypres* (London: Hurst & Blackett, 1916), p.5.
55 TNA WO 95/1416: 8th Infantry Brigade, 23 August 1914.
56 Charles Kingsford, *The Story of the Duke of Cambridge's Own (Middlesex Regiment)* (London, Country Life, 1916), p.166.

Mariette, failed to fall back 'owing to the telephone failing',[57] a euphemism for variance of orders:

> The forward companies of the Fifth (sic) Fusiliers meanwhile stuck to their position on the canal, in spite of the command to retire, in order to cover the engineers who were preparing the bridge at Mariette for destruction.[58]

The Fusiliers made their way through Mons north to south and exited the town with the Germans at their heels. Since early, they had defended the apex of the salient position, and come under heavy and sustained attack from many times their own number. Their concentrated rifle fire was devastatingly effective, particularly against the first German attacks in column formation. They had endured artillery bombardment for the whole morning and sustained repeated infantry attacks from the woods only 500 yards back from the canal. Due to their exposed positions defending Nimy Bridge, they had lost heavily to rifle and machine gun fire.[59] Remarkably their machine guns were knocked out, not by artillery, but by concentrated rifle fire, which riddled the water coolants and killed their crews. A regimental history describes the first stage of their withdrawal:

> They had about a mile to cover, the first 250 yards over open ground with the German guns firing shrapnel at 500 yards range and a heavy rifle fire. There were two railway embankments to cross; but the company suffered little beyond thrills, despite the heavy fire. The infantry were [sic] firing high, and even shrapnel burst too high to be effective.[60]

They had had a remarkable escape, losing only 150 men. They should have been annihilated. Once again, it was the ineffectiveness of the German field artillery that was decisive. Their exit from the southern edge of Mons was covered by four guns of the 109th Battery, which were sent forward by General Wing at 2 p.m. They offered only 'minor assistance to the infantry', much more effective being the rifles of the Lincolnshire Regiment, who were behind barricades, constructed that morning, on each of the three roads south out of the town. (A recent book cites this battery as performing effective work in the salient. It fired its only two shots of the day on this mission.[61]) The German infantry decided not to follow too closely and moved west inside the town. The guns fell back.

---

57 TNA WO 95/1425: 9th Infantry Brigade, 23 August 1914.
58 Edmonds, *Military Operations France and Belgium 1914*, Vol. I, p. 86.
59 TNA WO 95/1416: 8th Infantry Brigade, 23 August 1914.
60 H.C. O'Neill, *The Royal Fusiliers in the Great War* (London, Heinemann, 1922), pp.38-40.
61 TNA WO 95/1399: 109th Batt, XXIII Brigade RFA, 23 August 1914.

The 2nd Royal Irish also had a torrid time. By early afternoon, the Germans had bought up the howitzers of their 18th Division; and they proceeded, with good observation from high ground, to knock out the Irish machine guns and defences.[62] The battalion was closely engaged with the enemy, falling back under heavy rifle and artillery fire. No infantry accounts distinguish between field gun and howitzer attack, and this one is no exception. But in the third stage of their withdrawal, they were in the woods at the northern end of Bois la Haut.[63] A passing artillery subaltern described the scene.

Lieutenant Cyril Brownlow was with an ammunition party going up to the guns on Bois la Haut. He describes first the distinctive scream and black explosions of German heavy howitzer shells; then a bombardment by light howitzer shells; and finally records a dismissive reaction to earlier fire, presumably the 7.7 cm field gun, from the battery captain above. At about 2.30 p.m.:

> I was sent forward with four wagons of ammunition for the 23rd battery on Bois la Haut. We moved across a couple of meadows and up a road which skirts the left flank of the hill. …Suddenly I heard a whistling in the air which grew to the shriek of a soul in torment and ended in a terrific double crash and a hundred yards to my left there appeared two oily clouds of smoke. [15 cm heavy howitzer fire. No other account so clearly describes the characteristic howl and black smoke of this later much feared 5.9-inch gun.]
>
> To reach the battery it was necessary to go to the northern end of the hill and then to follow a rough track which doubled back to the crest in rear. Leaving the road, we swung at a trot through a gate on the right and up a sandy track. On the left, fifty yards away were trees and undergrowth where shells were bursting continuously. [and where the Royal Irish Regiment had entrenched.] The noise and concussion of the explosions was terrific; trunks, branches and leaves were cut down and splinters struck the ground about us with deadly smacks… [10.5 cm Feldhaubitze fire.] I found…the battery in a clearing among the woods. As the ammunition was wanted at once, I took my wagons direct to the gun position. The six guns, each with an ammunition wagon alongside, lay in line just below the crest…. While my wagons were being unloaded I spoke to the captain, who said "It's quiet now, but they have been shelling us periodically. Luckily they have not done much damage."[64]

---

62 Edmonds, *History of the Great War*, p.84.
63 Brig. Gen. S. Geoghegan, *The Campaigns and History of the Royal Irish Regiment*, Vol. II (Edinburgh, Blackwood & Sons, 1927), p.27.
64 Lieutenant Cyril Brownlow, 40th Brigade Ammunition Column, quoted in John Hutton, *The Gunners of 1914: Baptism of Fire* (Barnsley, Pen & Sword, 2014), p.50.

The casualties of the Royal Irish Regiment, under this howitzer fire, were heavy. It is premature to record this, but their full casualties in the battle were 20 killed, including 4 officers, 60 wounded and 226 missing (of whom only 87 re-joined).[65]

It is this damaging fire of the 10.5 cm Feldhaubitze that has to some extent masked the ineffective fire of the 77 feldkanone in the battle. The 8th Infantry Brigade diary also describes losses when a hastily erected barricade in Mons is destroyed by enemy guns.

The German infantry, advancing from the east, south of the canal, made two determined attacks towards Bois la Haut, the first at about 1 p.m. and the second at about 4 p.m. Both attacks were enfiladed by the rifles and machine guns of the Scottish regiments on the full length of the Nimy to Harmignies road and brought to a standstill with heavy losses. The 40th Brigade RFA on Bois la Haut contributed to this defence. The 6th Battery and 23rd Battery both fired at an enemy field battery coming into action, and both also had infantry targets, all at about 3000 yards, nearly two miles.[66] The Brigade diary is cryptic, but confirms that they were in covered positions, meaning that they were directed by observers.

The 49th Battery, on the northern spur of Bois la Haut, alone had two guns forward at risk, in close support of the Middlesex Regiment. They were extricated later with great difficulty under machine gun and rifle fire. Very few men from the right of the Middlesex line survived, and, according to a regimental history, only 258 men answered their first roll call after the battle, while 368 men were lost.[67]

Meanwhile the rest of the 8th Infantry Brigade, on the road in front of Bois la Haut, was heavily shelled throughout the afternoon, 'but without much effect'[68], (the Royal Irish presumably dissenting from this view,) this being attributed in the Official History to the British positions being hidden from the German guns. This is wrong. They used forward observers too. Their light artillery fire was just ineffective.

Between 3.15 and 4 p.m., the remnants of the Royal Irish and the Middlesex Regiments retired in good order to link up with the left of the Gordon Highlanders on the Nimy to Harmignies road in the lull between the German attacks from the east. On their right, the 2nd Royal Scots were thinly spread on the road down to Harmignies.

They also came under attack, and by mid-day, were under real pressure. Their colonel appealed for help, to the 2nd South Staffordshire Regiment, on the left of the recently arrived, 2nd Division, 6th Infantry Brigade line, and it was provided immediately. Brigadier General Davies, commanding the 6th Infantry, reported this development at 1.45 p.m.:

---

65 Geoghegan, *Campaigns of the Royal Irish Regiment*, p.29.
66 TNA WO 95/1400: XL Brigade RFA, 23 August 1914.
67 Kingsford, *Duke of Cambridge's Own (Middlesex Regiment)*, p.166.
68 Edmonds, *History of the Great War*, p.83.

Royal Scots immediately north of Harmignies are attacked and have appealed for support from South Staffords. AAA S Staffords have sent their reserve company to help them. AAA I am moving half battalion of my reserve battalion towards Harmignies as precautionary measure, as hill occupied by Royal Scots overlooks and enfilades my position. AAA No other infantry of 2nd Division have yet arrived.[69]

A battalion of the 4th (Guards) Brigade was supposed to be up at Harmignies, linking with the two taking over the eastern salient at Mons, relieving battalions of the 3rd Division. They were not in position. It was causing problems to the front lines of both corps.

3.11 The 4th (Guards) Brigade (Maps 6, 7, 8 & 9)

The 4th Guards had had very clear orders, as already described, at 2 a.m. that morning. They were to advance and take up positions, two battalions in the eastern salient, covered by their own artillery on Bois la Haut, linking with a third battalion which was to occupy the ground north of Harmignies. These orders were known to the 3rd Division, and to the 6th Infantry Brigade at Harmignies. The war diary of the 4th (Guards) Brigade, uniquely, is missing. (Entries up to 18 August 1914 are intact, implying that it was not lost during the retreat.) This makes interpretation of its movements difficult.

The 6th Infantry Brigade was the first brigade of the 2nd Division to advance that morning, heading for the line between the 1st Division, who were already in position, and Harmignies. They arrived about midday. The 4th (Guards) Brigade had left their billets east of Bavai at 3 a.m. and marched just behind them.

Of their four battalions, the 2nd Grenadier Guards and the 3rd Coldstream Guards marched to Quevy, the former stopping there as brigade reserve, the latter marching on, heading for Harmignies, to link up with the left flank of the 6th Infantry. The 1st Irish Guards and the 2nd Coldstream Guards, together with the 16th and 17th Batteries of the 41st Brigade RFA, marched direct to Mons, with a view to arriving by 6 a.m., under orders issued by GHQ the previous day. They arrived between 10 and 11 a.m.:

> On approaching Mons, orders were received to entrench a line just east of Mons. The battery was ordered to take up a position on the high ground near Bas-la-Haut [sic] to cover the infantry when entrenching. On arrival on the ground to reconnoitre the position of the battery, I found that the third division were already entrenching and that they had guns at Bas-la-Haut. On returning to

69   TNA WO 95/1283: 2nd Division, 23 August 1914, p.50.

2nd Grenadier Guards, 4th (Guards) Brigade on the march, August 1914.

report to the advanced Guards commander, it was found that orders had been cancelled and the battery marched with 4th Gds Bde for Quevy-le-Petit.[70]

Their orders to support II Corps had been rescinded. Meanwhile, the 3rd Coldstream Guards had been 'ordered to take up a line on a ridge north of Harmignies … The battalion left the main column and passing through … Quevy [and] … arrived at Harveng which was found to be occupied by British troops. We then received orders to go no further until ordered to do so.'[71]

Their orders had been rescinded too. In the early morning, I Corps diary says, erroneously, that the 4th (Guards) were in position at Bois la Haut.[72] But at noon, it records a gloomy situation report, stating that Charleroi and Péronnes were in flames; and that four German corps were approaching Mons from the north. The '6th Brigade is holding from Harmignies village' south, and 'the remainder of the 2nd Division is about Quevy'. There is no mention of the salient contingent. The 5th Infantry Brigade had already been 'ordered into billets about …Genly'.[73] Haig, in his account, says that, 'at 10.45 a.m.', all the 2nd Division, with the exception of the 6th Brigade, were 'in reserve', the 4th (Guards) Brigade 'at Quevy'; and that the junction between the 2nd and 3rd Divisions was at Harmignies.[74] It will be remembered that General Smith-Dorrien had informed General Haig of his intention to withdraw to a line between Harmignies and Ciply in the event of heavy attack.[75] So, it seems that Haig decided, in mid-morning, to cancel the deployment of any I Corps units north of Harmignies. He informed neither II Corps, nor his own 6th Infantry Brigade, of this decision.

70 TNA WO 95/1326: XLI Brigade RFA, 23 August 1914.
71 TNA WO 95/1342: 3rd Coldstream Guards, 23 August 1914.
72 TNA WO 95/630/1: II Corps Staff, 23 August 1914.
73 TNA WO 95/1283: 2nd Division, 23 August 1914, diary and p.47.
74 TNA WO 95/588/4: I Corps staff, 23 August 1914.
75 TNA WO 95/630: II Corps Staff, 23 August 1914, p.75.

The three battalions of the 4th (Guards) Brigade and accompanying artillery, marched back to Quevy-le-Petit to find their headquarters, reaching there about 4 p.m.[76] (Quevy and Quevy-le-Petit are less than a mile apart, separated by a stream.) GHQ orders pertaining to the 4th (Guards) Brigade had been countermanded, and they were being sent into billets to the south of the 2nd Division line, adjacent to the southern main road to Bavai, and well placed for withdrawal.

3.12 General Haig's Account of I Corps Dispositions (Map 6)

General Haig denies attending the conference of the generals at 6 a.m. that morning. He says that this occurred at 10.30 a.m., and that at this conference, it was decided that 'the right of the 2nd Corps was to extend up to and include Point 93, one mile north of Harmignies.'[77] This can be explained as an attempt by General Haig to legitimise his apparently unilateral decision to withhold troops from the salient and Hill 93, at this precise time. He goes on to say that the 5th Cavalry Brigade was 'not under my orders', though his own staff,[78] GHQ orders and cavalry records,[79] indicate that it was. It is at this stage that one is forced to the conclusion that General Haig's account in I Corps records is unreliable as a factual account, from the moment that he cancelled his 2nd Division's advance at 7 p.m. on the 22nd. It is a personal account, typed as a final draft, and labelled 'final copy',[80] clearly intended as his definitive account of the campaign. He is not glossing over 'facts'. He is inventing new ones and denying others. The narrative is duplicated in personal 'diaries' in his private papers.[81] These have additional letters and supporting anecdotes, some of which have already been quoted, and many of which fit uneasily with the narrative. If these had been the papers of an insignificant general, who sank into obscurity, one might regard it as evidence of that general's unfitness for high command. But this is General Haig. The issue has to be addressed. But to return to his official account, the 'morning and early afternoon passed quietly', he says.[82] II Corps, and indeed the left flank of the 6th Infantry Brigade, would have disputed this assessment.

---

76 TNA WO 95/1342: 1st Irish Guards, 23 August 1914.
77 TNA WO 95/588/4: I Corps staff, 23 August 1914.
78 TNA WO 95/630/1: II Corps Staff, 23 August 1914.
79 TNA WO 95/1138: 5th Cavalry Brigade, 23 August 1914.
80 TNA WO 95/588/4: I Corps Staff, 1914, p.37.
81 NLS, Acc. 3155/96 and 3155/98: Douglas Haig Papers, August 1914.
82 TNA WO 95/588/4: I Corps staff, 23 August 1914.

Times of arrival of British artillery units in Northern France, August 1914

The march from the divisional concentration areas towards Mons started at 4 am on 21 August

Date	Time	Unit	Division	Railhead	Marched to:	Distance	To destination given at:
20th		1st Division Artillery collected, except 39th Bde and Divisional Ammunition Column (DAC).					
		2nd Division Artillery collected, except 44th Bde (How), 35th Batt (Heavy) and DAC.					
	01:30	27th Bde	5th		Marched with division for entire advance		
	18:15	40th Bde	3rd		Marched with division for entire advance;		
		40th Bde AC			Mis-guided and marched 20 miles – 'done in'.		

All subsequent arrivals were significantly to the rear of their divisions as they advanced.

Date	Time	Unit	Division	Railhead	Marched to:	Distance	To destination given at:
21st	19:20	15th Bde	5th	Le Cateau	Bavai	20m	04:00 22nd
	pm	44th Bde (How)	2nd	3 different	Laval (in rear)	10m	pm 22nd
	pm	35th (Heavy)	2nd		Laval (in rear)	10m	pm 22nd
	19:30	23rd Bde	3rd	Landrecies	S of Mons	25m	14:00 22nd
	23:00	42nd Bde	3rd	Hautmont	S of Mons	16m	16:30 22nd
	overnight	39th Bde	1st	3 different	SE of Givry	10–23m	After dark 22nd
	overnight	DAC	1st	Etreux	SE of Givry	23m	After dark 22nd
22nd	01:00	48th (Heavy)	3rd	Hautmont	S of Mons	16m	during 22nd

All subsequent arrivals were unavailable for the action at Mons during the morning.

Date	Time	Unit	Division	Railhead	Marched to:	Distance	To destination given at:
21st	23:00	28th Bde	5th	Le Cateau	Bavai	20m	16:30 22nd
22nd	05:00	8th Bde (How)	5th	Landrecies	Bavai	14m	pm 22nd
	08:00	61st Bt/8th Bde	5th	Le Cateau	Bavai	20m	late 22nd
	15:00	DAC (half)	2nd	Landrecies	billeted	N of Maubeuge	pm 23rd

Date	Time	Unit	Division	Railhead	Marched to:	Distance	To destination given at:
23rd	00:00	DAC	3rd	Valenciennes	S of Mons	20m	14:00 approx
	02:00	130th batt/30 bde	3rd	Valenciennes	Ciply via Bavai	27m	15:00
	morning	DAC	5th	Valenciennes	2m S of Dour	15m	Early evening
	13:30	DAC (half)	2nd	Aulnoye	N. of Maubeuge	12m	21:00
	10:00	30th Bde (How)	3rd	Valenciennes	Ciply via Bavai	27m	04:00 24th

Roads north from Bavai to Dour and Mons were very congested.
Two 3rd Division howitzer batteries never made it to Mons on the 23rd.

The plan of the 20th was that the 3rd Division should be 5 miles north east of Mons on the 23rd.

All dates and times in this table are taken from the war diaries of the various units.

Mons Artillery

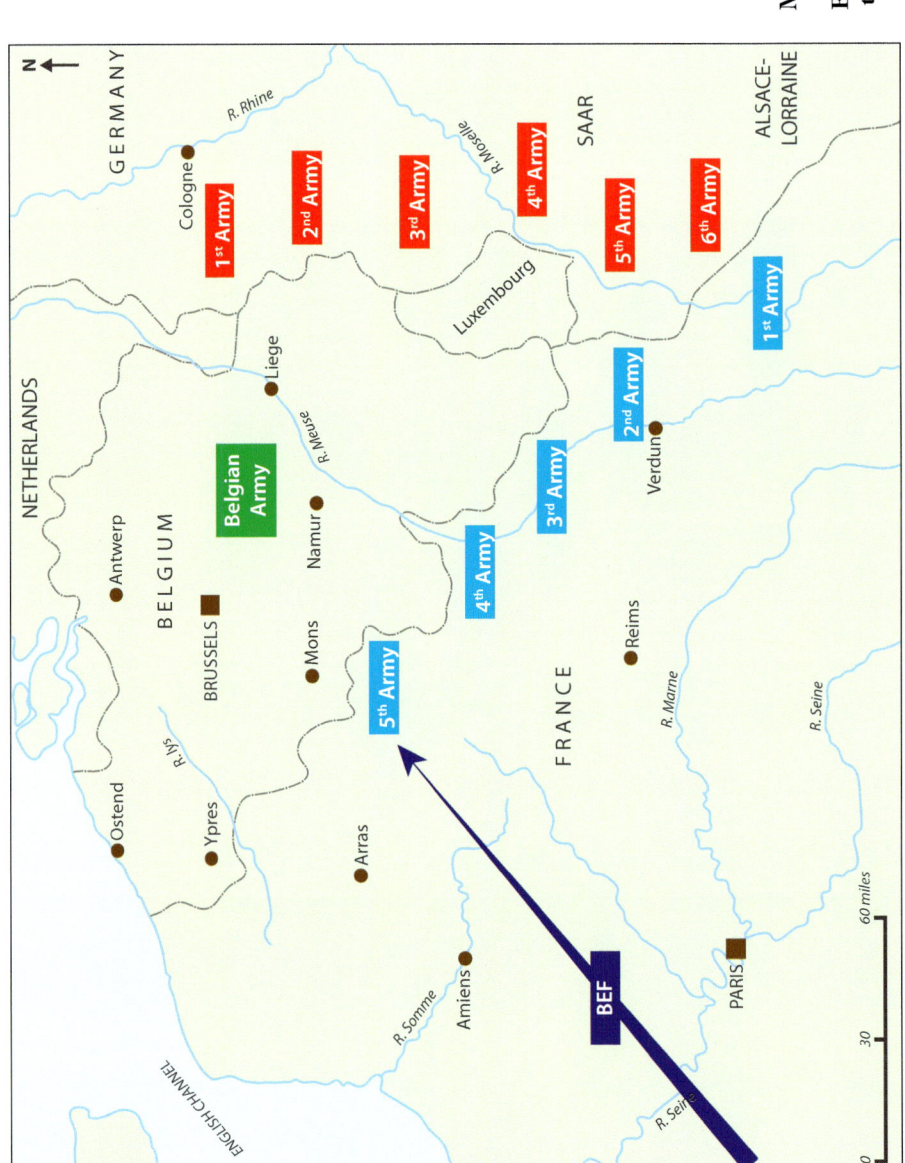

Map 1. The advance of the British Expeditionary Force to Northern France from 17 August.

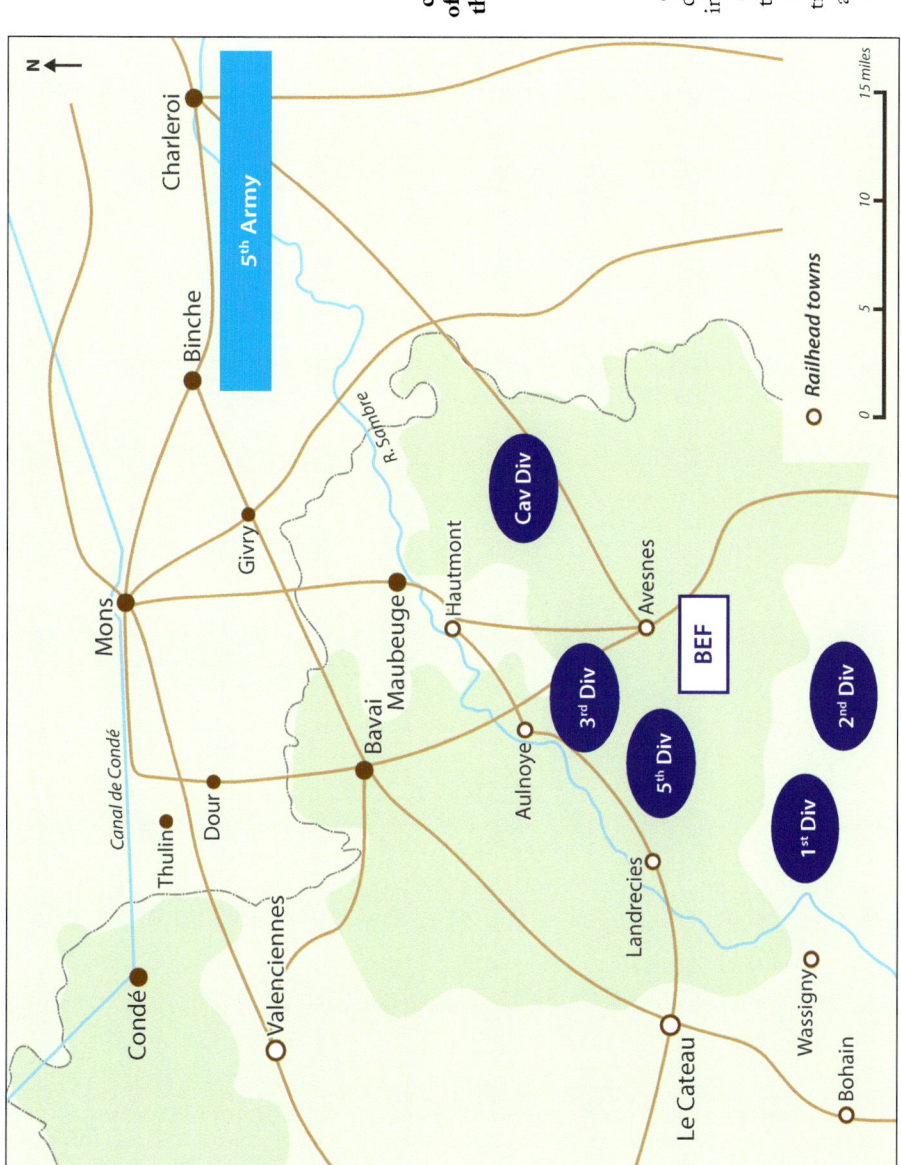

Map 2. The concentration areas of the five divisions of the BEF in Northern France, showing railheads.

From the 17 to 20 August, the five divisions of the initial BEF force concentrated. Each division was billeted in an allocated cluster of villages. Most of the army, and all the artillery, arrived by train, usually, but not always, at a railhead town close to their final destination.

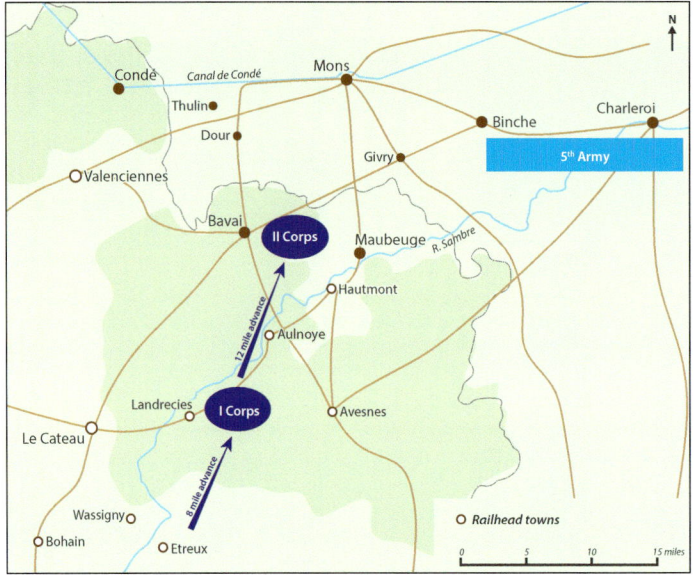

Map 3a. I and II Corps start their advance into Belgium on 21 August.
The advance began in the early hours of 21 August. Neither corps had completed their concentration. The cavalry scouted forward as far as Binche and Mons, between the French and British forces.

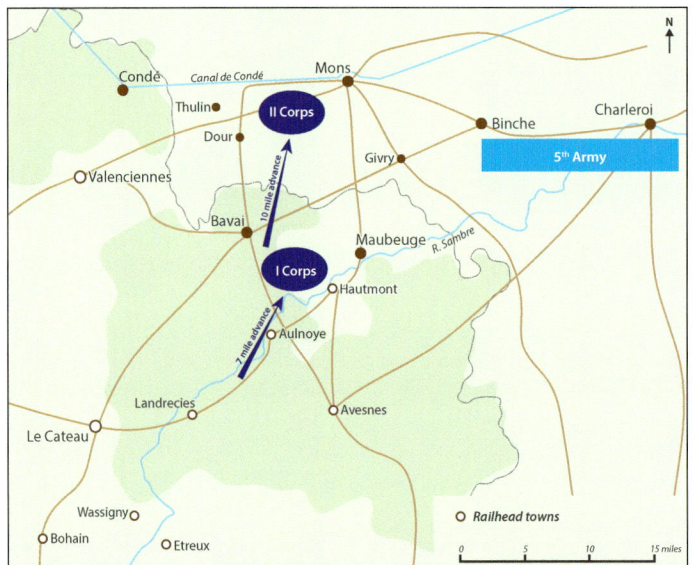

Map 3b. I and II Corps continue the advance into Belgium on 22 August.
The advance continued in the early hours. Units still arriving at railhead towns were following behind, trying to catch up.

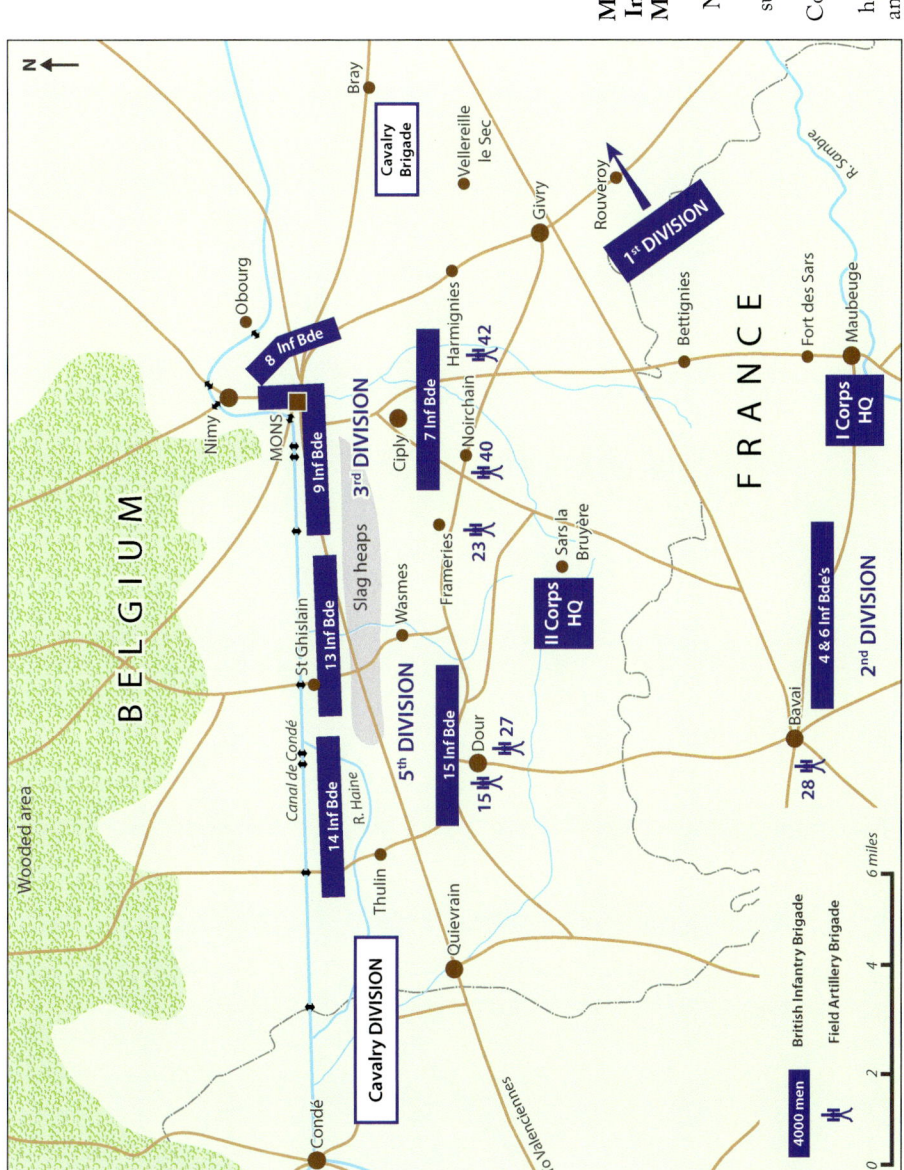

Map 4. Artillery and Infantry positions at Mons on the evening of 22 August.
No artillery brigade was deployed to support the infantry outposts on the Condé Canal. Neither division had their howitzer brigades or ammunition columns.

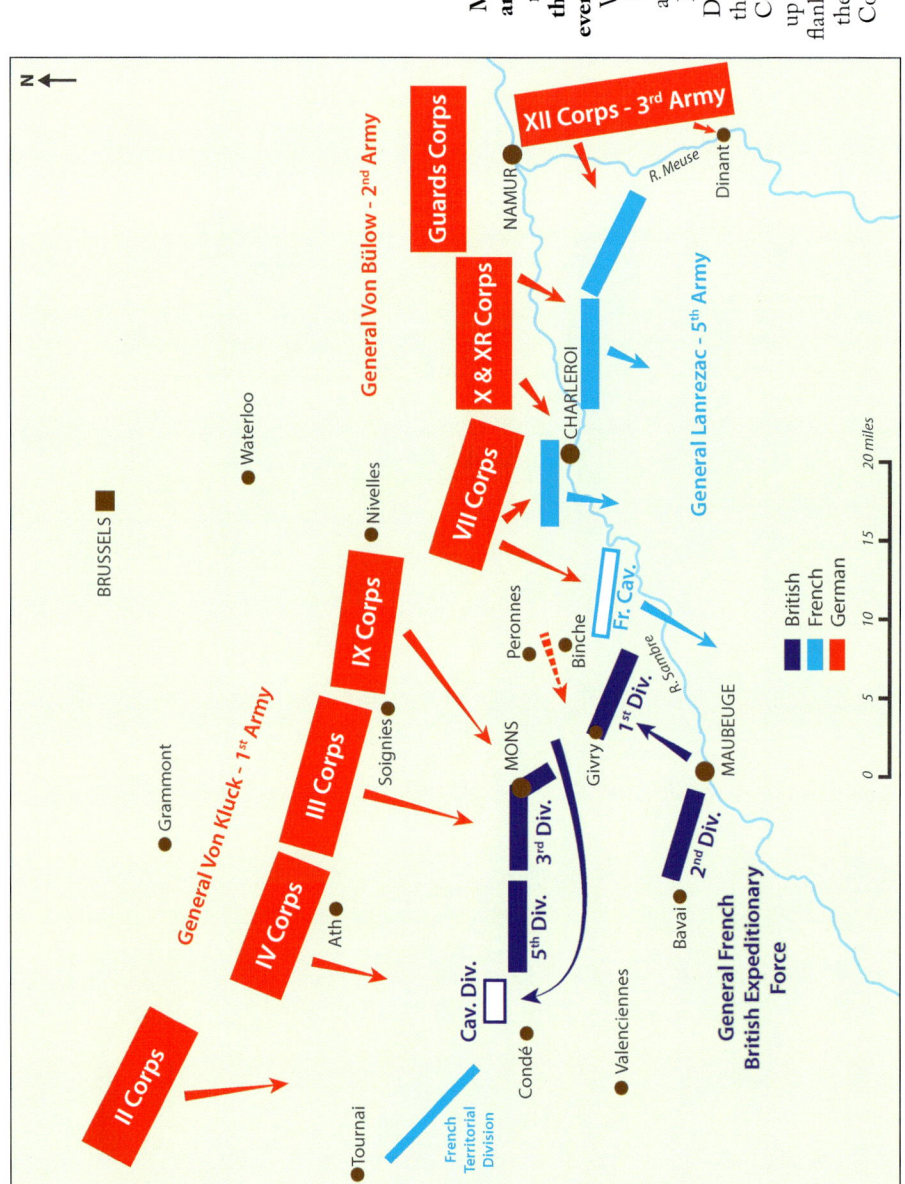

Map 5. German and British Army movements on the afternoon and evening of 22 August. With significant German forces approaching, the British Cavalry Division moved to the left flank, and I Corps was ordered up to cover the right flank of II Corps. Only the 1st Division of I Corps responded to this order.

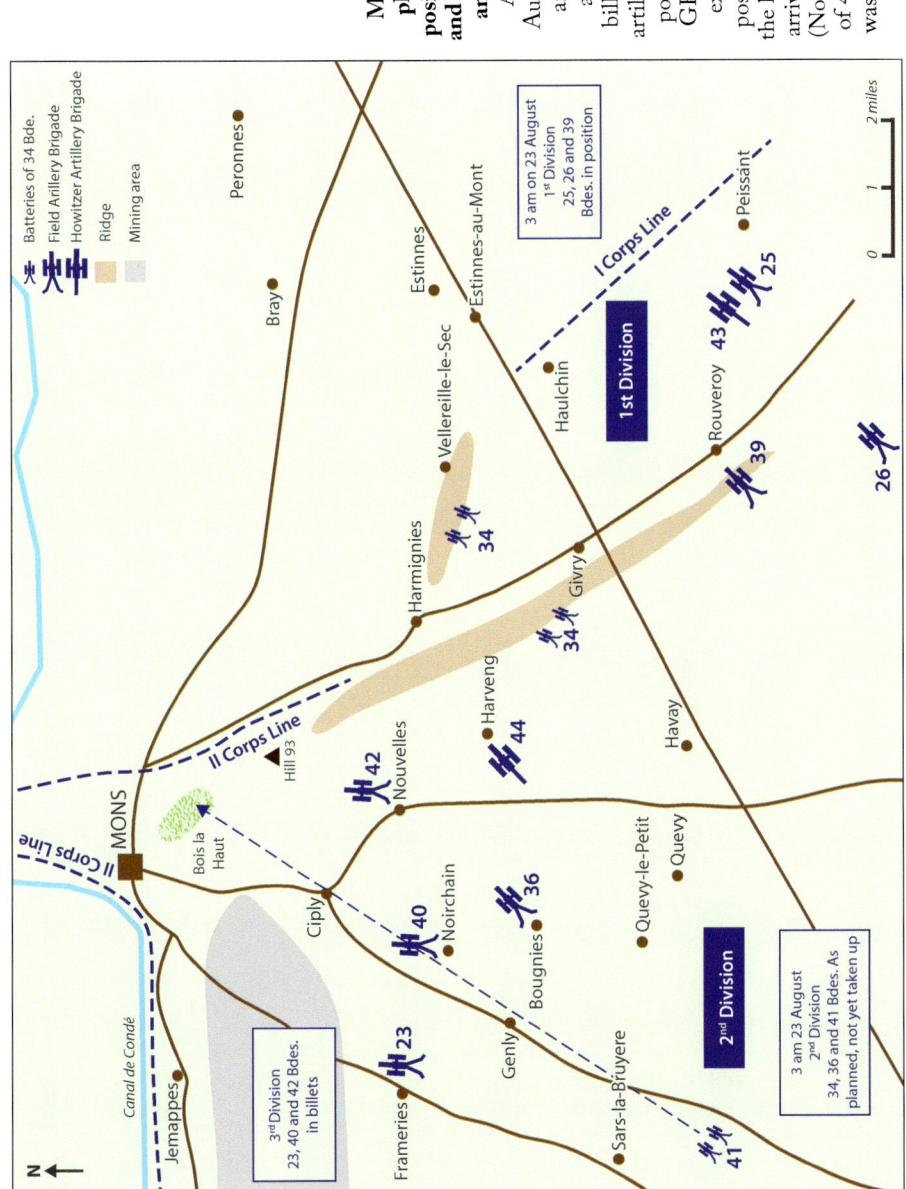

Map 6. Actual or planned artillery positions for 1st, 2nd and 3rd Divisions at 3 am on 23 August.

At 3 a.m. on 23 August, 1st Division and 3rd Division artillery were in billets. 2nd Division artillery had identified positions as shown. GHQ and II Corps expected them in position by 6 a.m. at the latest. They did not arrive till after 11 a.m. (Note that one battery of 41st Brigade RFA was seconded to 34th Brigade RFA).

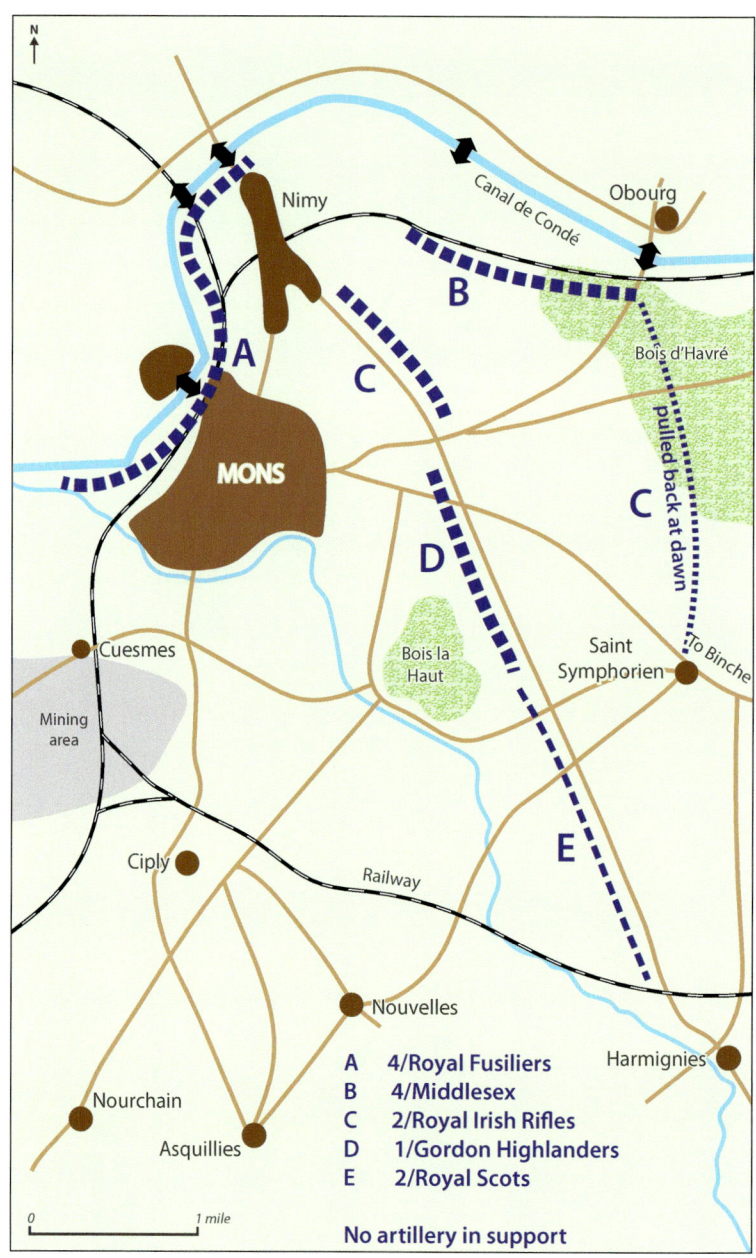

Map 7. 3rd Division Infantry in the Mons salient in early hours of 23 August.
3rd Division infantry dispositions in the salient at Mons, midnight of 22 August: Only from Bois-le-Haut, allocated to guns of the 2nd Division, could the field artillery support the infantry from behind the front line. The divisional howitzers, which might have supported the infantry, were still in transit.

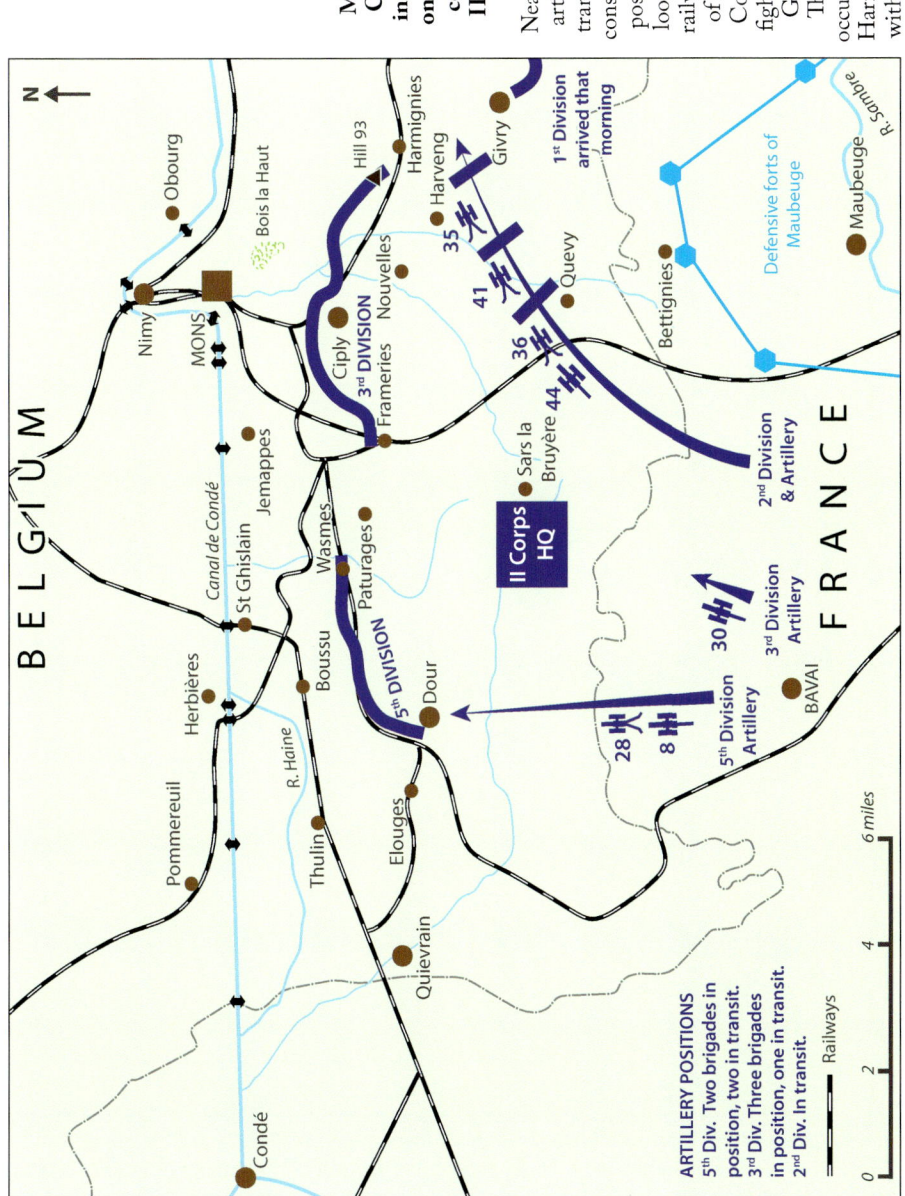

Map 8. I and II Corps Artillery in transit at noon on 23 August, and construction of II Corps 'second position'.

Nearly half of BEF's artillery was still in transit. II Corps was constructing a 'second position' line, which loosely followed the railway. The outposts of II Corps on the Condé Canal were fighting to delay the German advance. The 2nd Division occupied the line from Harmignies to join up with the 1st Division.

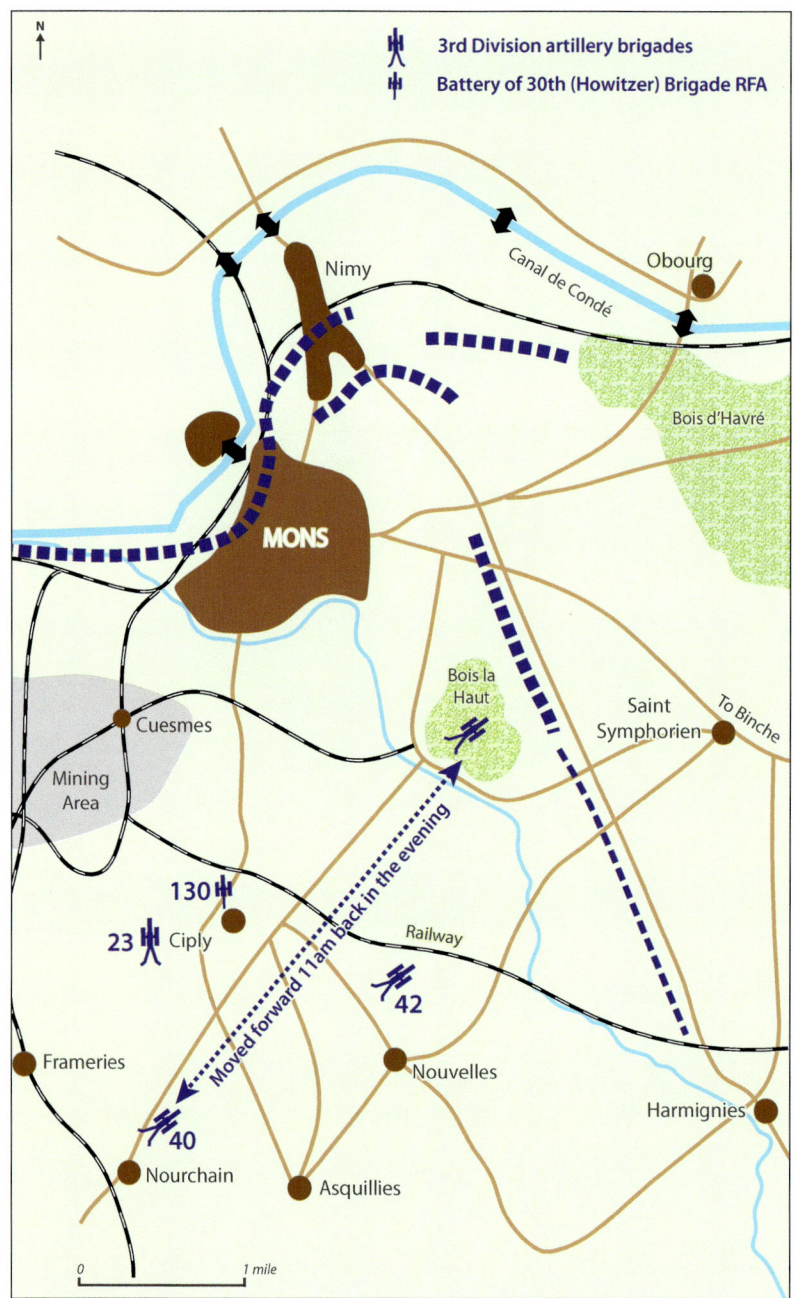

Map 9. 3rd Division Artillery in the Mons salient at midday on 23 August.
23rd and 42nd Brigades RFA hardly fired a shot; 40th Brigade RFA took up positions on Bois-le-Haut because 41st Brigade, of 2nd Division, failed to arrive in time.

Map 10. II Corps retirement to 'second positions' from the Mons salient and Conde Canal on 23 August; the gap at Paturages.

By early evening, German attacks on Mons had driven the 3rd Division outpost line back. The 5th Division outpost line was giving ground, but still holding. The divisional howitzers and heavy battery had arrived and were digging in, in three 'groups', to strengthen their second line'. A potential gap was opening between the two divisions. The railway line in front of Paturages was undefended.

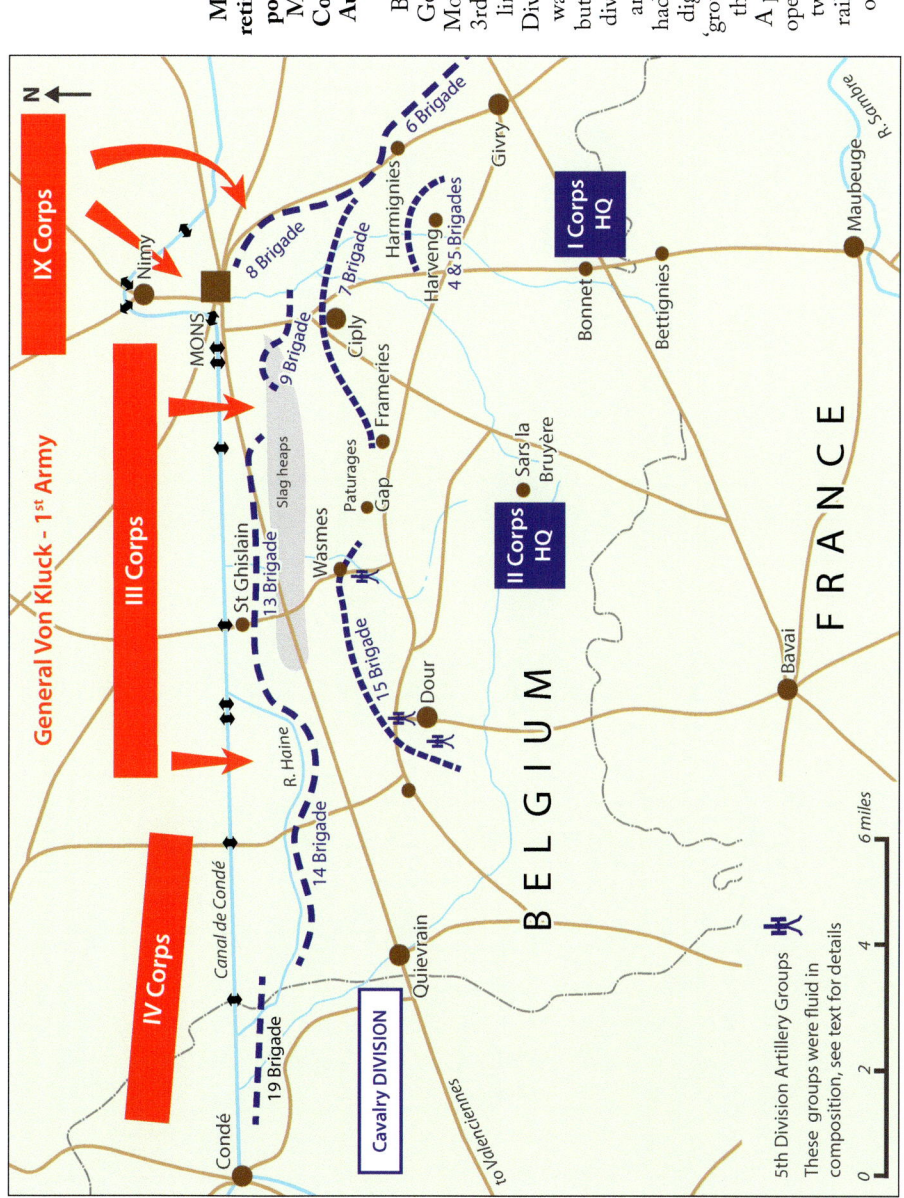

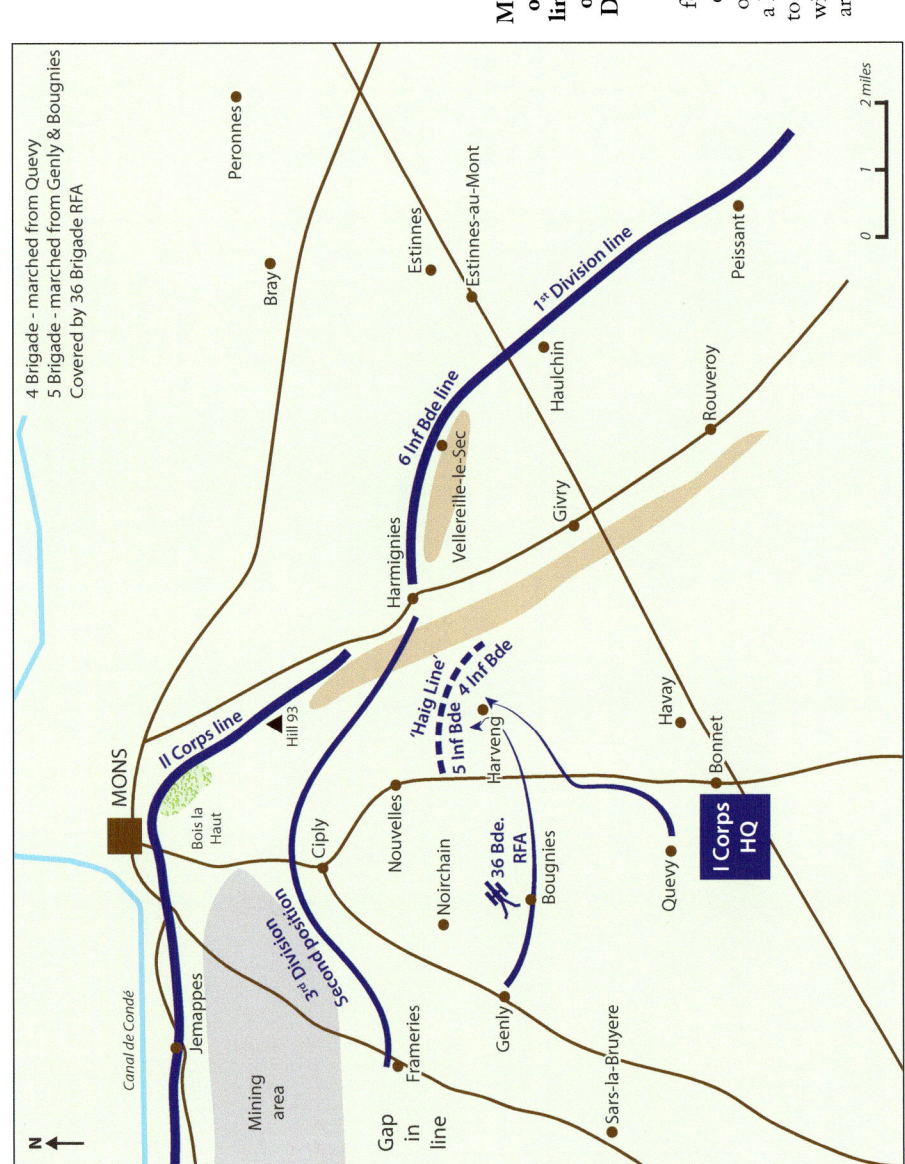

Map 11. Construction of the 'Haig' defence line at Harveng, south of Mons, by the 2nd Division, from 5 p.m. on 23 August.

General Haig, foreseeing the defeat of the 3rd Division, orders the digging of a line around Harveng to cover a 2nd Division withdrawal, covered by artillery. He instructed the 1st Division to prepare to retreat.

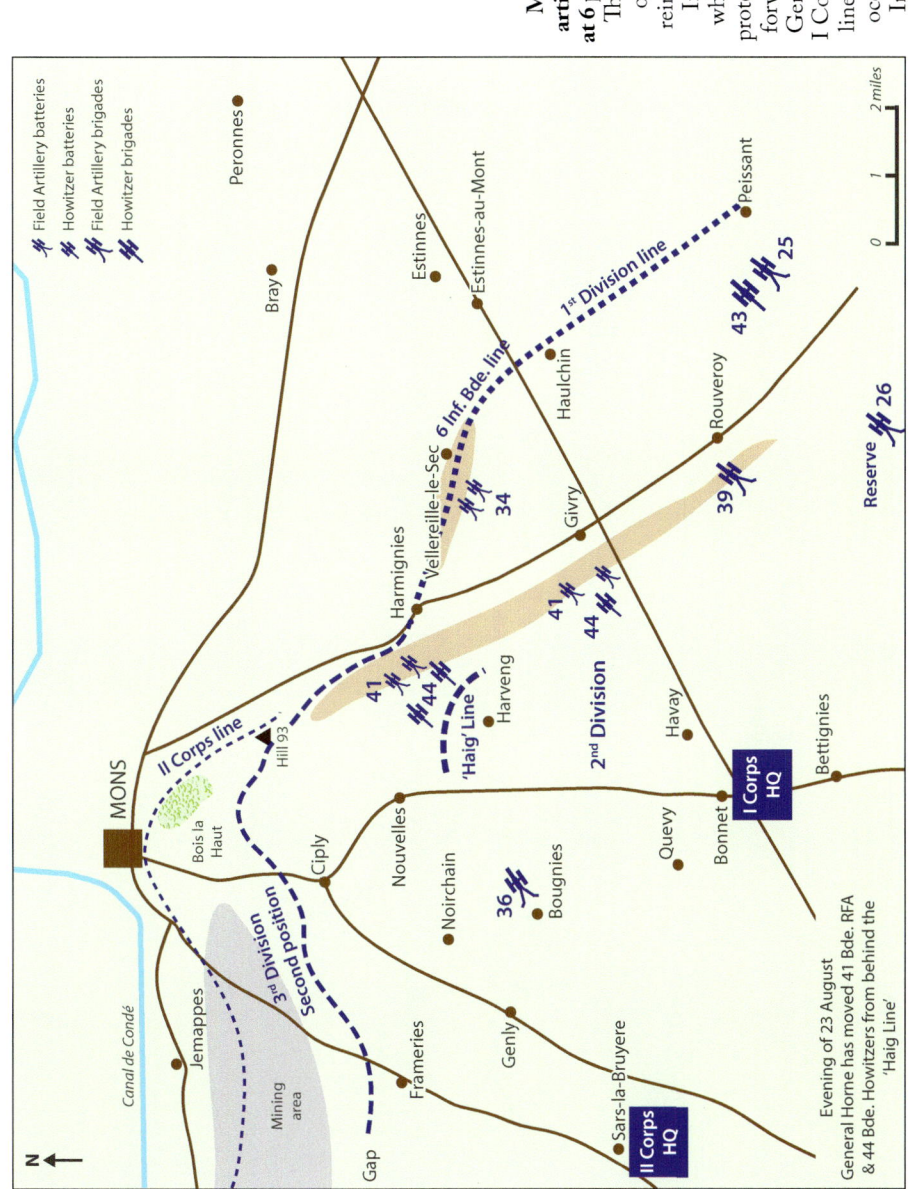

Map 12. I Corps artillery dispositions at 6 p.m. on 23 August. The weak line north of Harmignies is reinforced by the 4th Infantry Brigade, who are deployed to protect the guns moved forward by Brigadier-General Horne, CRA I Corps. This section of line should have been occupied by the 4th Infantry at 6 a.m.

xiii

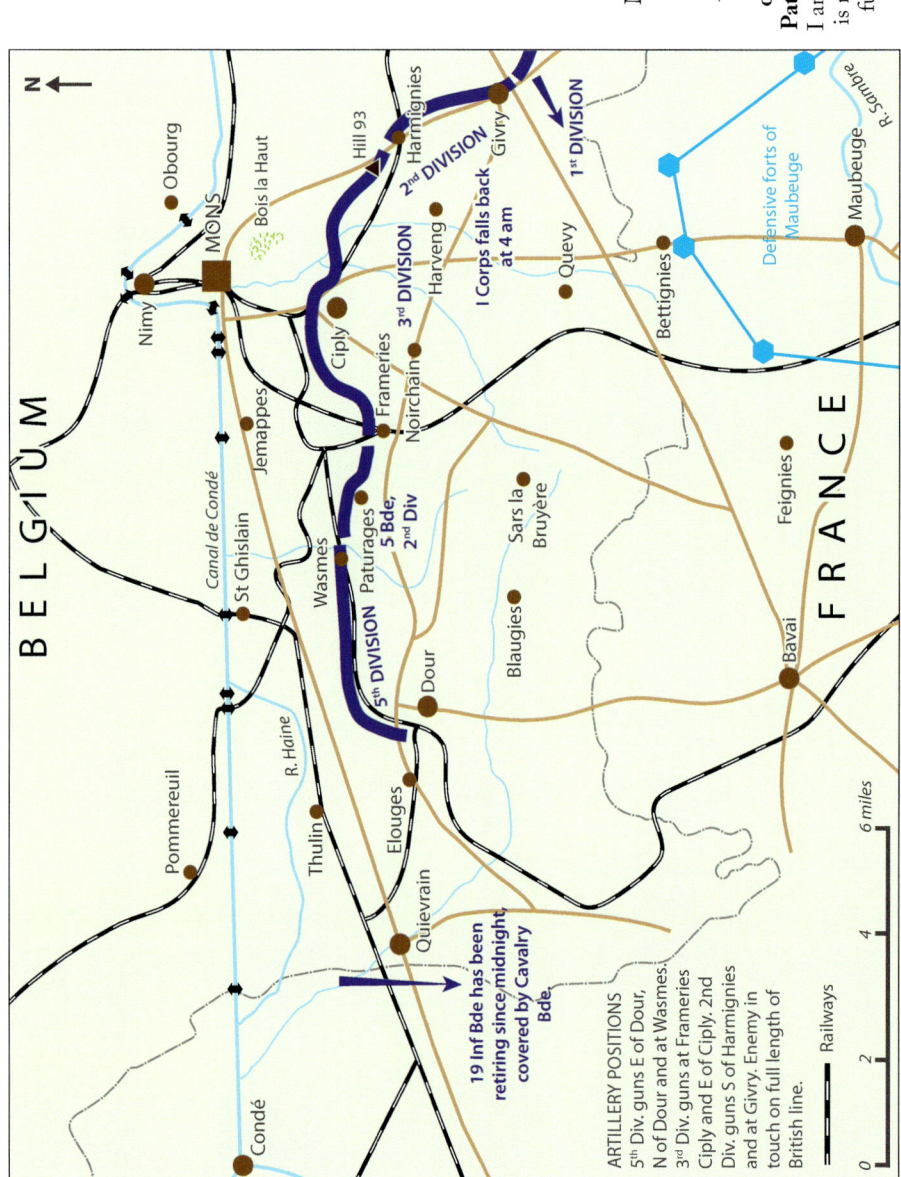

Map 13. Second position' lines at 3 a.m. on 24 August. I Corps reinforcements occupy the gap at Paturages at 2.30 a.m. I and II Corps artillery is now supporting the full length of a line south of Mons.

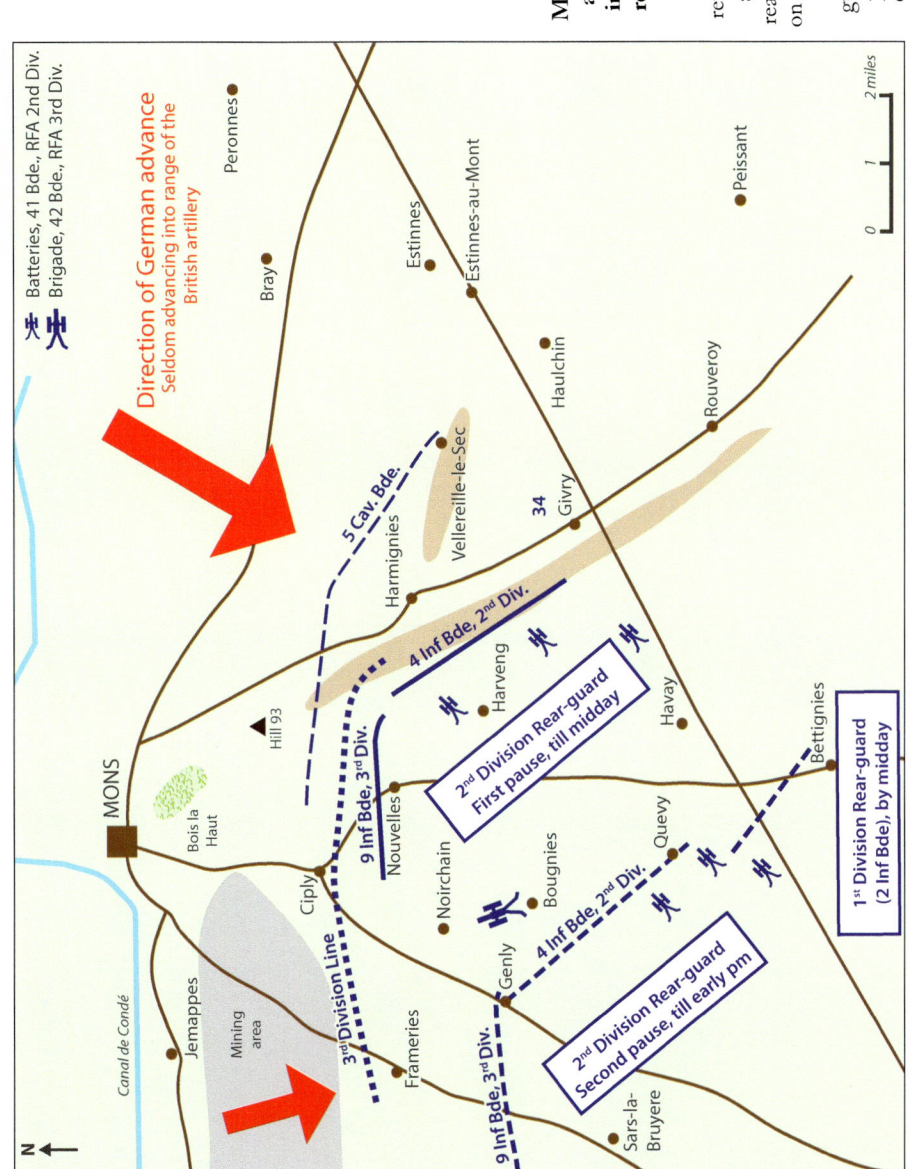

Map 14. Rear-guard artillery positions in first hours of the retreat, morning of 24 August.

The coordinated retirement of the 2nd and 3rd divisional rear-guards after dawn on 24 August. Artillery cover of the rear-guard is maintained, preventing enemy offensive pressure.

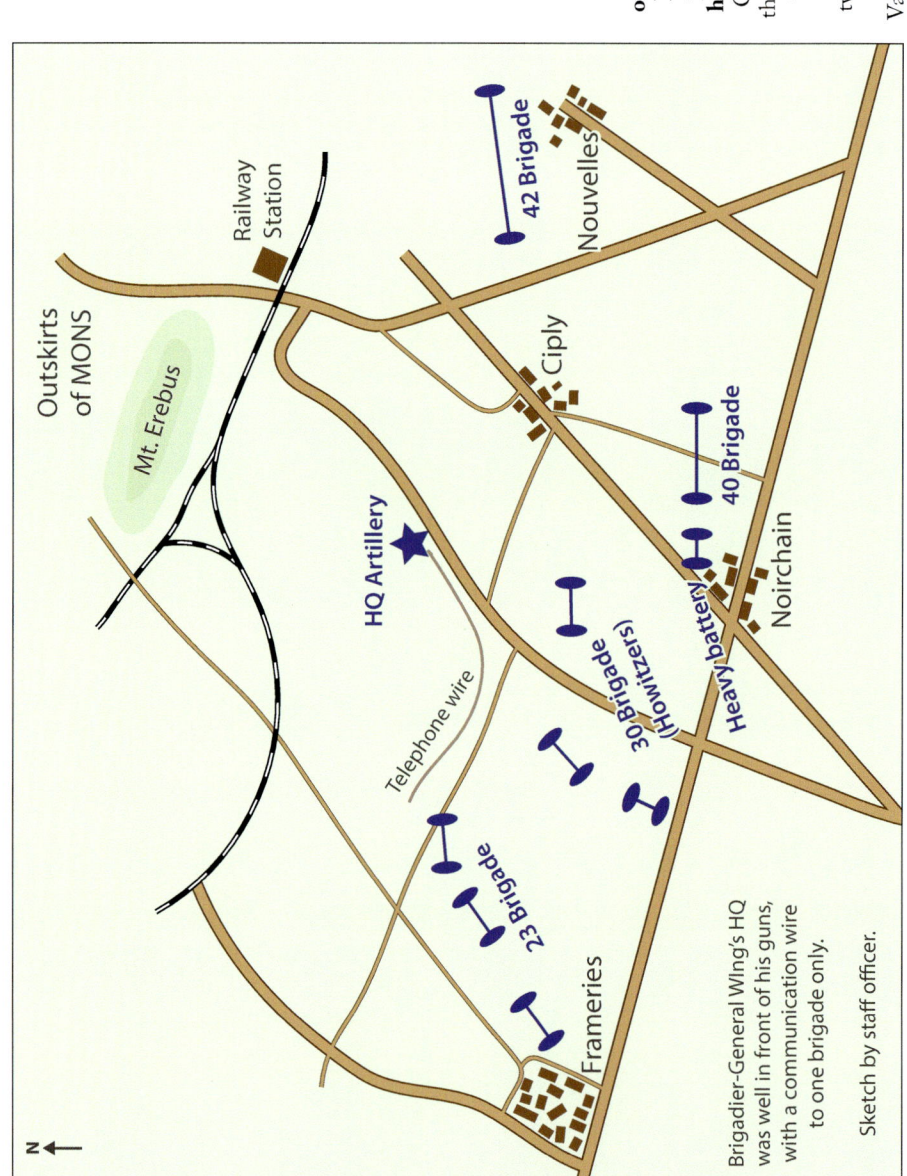

Map 15. Staff officer sketch of 3rd Division artillery positions in early hours of 24 August. Only the eastern of the howitzer batteries was in position as shown. The other two were still on the march from their Valenciennes railhead.

3.13 British Artillery along the Canal, 5th Division (Maps 4, 8 & 10)

Whilst the decisive battle in holding the German advance that morning was fought at the eastern end of the canal line, that is not to say that there was not heavy fighting along the whole length of the canal. The focal points of attack by the German III Corps, their 5th Division, close to Mons, and their 6th, further west, were the bridges. The 9th Infantry Brigade, of the 3rd Division, defended three, the first two at Jamappes, two miles west of Mons, and the third at Mariette, another one and a half miles on. All were attacked in turn, the further west, the later the hour of attack. German methods were the same in every case. First massed infantry moved forward, incurring heavy losses to accurate rifle fire, and then more circumspect infantry advances, supported by machine guns and artillery, made progress. The Germans were advancing through water-logged low ground, the rain of the early morning very likely making conditions difficult for a brisk advance.

The tenacity with which the German light artillery supported their infantry is illustrated at Mariette where two field guns were brought up within half a mile of the canal. A high explosive shell from one of these guns burst inside a house close to the bridge during their bombardment, unsurprisingly causing casualties.[83] There are very few accounts that attribute a death so definitely to a German field gun.

Hauptmann Heubner of the German 20th Infantry Regiment (5th Division, III Corps) participated in the assault on Jamappes. He described 'numerous wounded' and 'heavy losses' to his regiment.[84] The German attack was courageously pressed, not only over the canal, but beyond.

One and a half miles further west, the 120th Battery, of 27th Brigade RFA, was supporting the 13th Infantry Brigade of the 5th Division at St Ghislain, five miles from Mons. Two sections of the battery were on the tow-path of the canal, supporting a rear-guard action of a single company of the West Kent Regiment who were initially north of the canal, first coming under attack by III Corps at about 11 a.m. The infantry brigadier was not unnaturally concerned. The 'enemy soon brought up a large number (18) of field guns to within about 1200 yards of the canal opposite St Ghislain and soon silenced our one battery. The lack of any artillery assistance on our side was very seriously felt.'[85] Silenced, they were not. They were in semi-covered positions, dug in. They should have been annihilated. But they fell back, with minimal casualties, to resume their fire from covered positions. The following accounts describe the futility of the German light artillery fire:

6 a.m. to 11 a.m. Entrenched 4 guns on canal bank.

---

83   Edmonds, *Military Operations France and Belgium 1914*, Vol. I, p.78.
84   Hauptmann Heubner, *Unter Emmich vor Lüttich, Unter Kluck vor Paris*, pp. 69, 74, quoted in Edmonds, *Military Operations France and Belgium*, Vol. I, p.78.
85   TNA WO 95/1548: 13th Infantry Brigade, 23 August 1914.

11 a.m. Enemy attacked battery with field guns and rifles.

Noon. OC battery decided to withdraw guns due to increasing severity. Guns were run back, limbered up and taken to Town Hall. One man killed and two wounded during retirement.

3 p.m. Two guns brought into action under cover 200 yards east of former position – guns could only just clear the crest, platforms very bad. Engaged hostile battery in open with effect. German artillery and infantry both fired on false crest, where Major Holland was observing. At 3.30 p.m. he was killed by a rifle bullet.

6.30 p.m. Guns taken in reverse by rifle fire. It was decided to retire the guns which were in reserve with the wagon line. One of the guns which was in action was removed. One gun had to be left where it was, and another which had been brought up close to the position had to be left as they were surrounded by enemy infantry.[86]

Albert George, an artillery NCO, was with the guns:

About 12.15 p.m. … the Germans were approaching so rapidly that we were firing at a low range of 600 yards and every shell killed dozens as they were advancing in close order. The German gunners found our battery and things got very hot. The shells were dropping all around, but not doing serious damage, only ploughing up the ground. At 1.15 we retired into the town. About 3 p.m., … shells were bursting over our heads. At 6 p.m. the attack became hotter … Our casualties for the day were very small – 2 killed 1 wounded.[87]

Neither the air bursting shrapnel, nor the ground bursting high explosive shells, had any significant lethal effect. It is probably significant that it had rained in the early morning after dawn. High explosive rounds burying themselves in moist earth would indeed 'plough up the ground'. Second Lieutenant Robert Thornhagh-Foljambe was also with the battery:

At 3 p.m. the infantry were [sic] practically back to the line of the guns and were holding on until we got them away. We walked away under a heavy but inaccurate fire…all the German shrapnel burst far too high and I don't think there was a single casualty.[88]

---

86 TNA WO 95/1529: 120th Battery, XXVII Brigade RFA, 23 August 1914.
87 IWM 18429: Col. Albert Cyril Laurence George, private papers. 23 August 1914.
88 RAM MD2960: Robert Francis Foljambe MC, 120th Battery RFA, diary, 23 August 1914.

Not only were the British artillery casualties insignificant, the infantry got off very lightly too. 'The enemy pushed forward three batteries to within twelve hundred yards of the canal about St. Ghislain, and smothered the 13th Brigade, 5th Division, with shells, but did remarkably little damage,' says the official history. This is one of a number of episodes in the battle in which the futility of the German light artillery fire is frankly unbelievable. One can only surmise when the German artillery men started to realise this. In the early stages of the battle they supported their infantry with great panache and at considerable cost. They do seem to have become more circumspect as the battle progressed.

German infantry managed to force the bridge in the early afternoon and there were British infantry losses, but few in comparison to the German assailants. The two guns of the 120th Battery were the only guns lost in the battle that day. The Brandenberg Grenadiers are described as losing five out of six company commanders and half their men in the attacks on St Ghislain, the account specifically mentioning losses to the British artillery. Artillery fire from this battery was both described in a British account, and confirmed by a German account, as devastating.[89]

Further west, the two bridges at Les Herbières were defended by the East Surrey Regiment of the 14th Infantry Brigade. 'The enemy plied the East Surrey defences with shrapnel for half an hour, causing no casualties,' and the following infantry attack by 2000 men (again of the German III Corps) in open order was stopped with huge loss by accurate rifle fire. 'It was not till about 6 p.m. when guns were brought up within close range and destroyed the barricade over Les Herbières road bridge,' says the official history.[90] 'The last man had only just left the house… at the bridgehead, when an enemy's shell completely destroyed it.'[91]

This was not a field gun shell, even at close range. This was a shell from a German howitzer, probably the heavier 15cm (5.9 inch) schwere Feldhaubitze 13 field howitzer, being deployed against their 'field fortification' defences. It was a devastating weapon, and their casualties reflect this. 'If they hit anything direct, not very much remains,' says Colin Hutchison a few weeks later on the Aisne.[92] The East Surrey regiment lost 139 men that evening, most of them reported missing, though some would have re-joined later. The other three battalions of the 14th Infantry Brigade lost only 27 men between them.[93]

As with Brigadier General Wing CRA 3rd Division, Brigadier General Headlam of the 5th Division artillery was conscious of the lack of support his guns were providing for the front-line infantry. He sent the 119th Battery, a sister to the 120th already in action at St Ghislain, to the Bois d'Haine two miles further west to cover the bridge

---

89 Walter Bloem, *Vormarsch* quoted in Edmonds, *Military Operations France and Belgium*, Vol. I, p. 80.
90 Edmonds, p.86.
91 TNA WO 95/1563: 1st East Surrey Regiment, 23 August 1914
92 Hutchison, *The Young Gunner*, p.27.
93 TNA WO 95/1560: 14th Infantry Brigade, 23 August 1914.

to Pommeroeul over which British patrols north of the canal would need to retreat and to cover a partial withdrawal of the 14th Infantry Brigade.[94]

Unlike the 13th Infantry Brigade, the 14th did not stay on the canal line once the Germans started to get close. A mile behind them was a significant obstacle, the water courses of the River Haine, and they had no wish to get trapped between the two waterways. The 119th Battery covered their retreat. About 6 p.m., it fired on enemy infantry of the German IV Corps (7th and 8th Divisions) approaching the canal. At a range of about 4000 yards:

> [A] column of the enemy were [sic] seen moving through Ville Pommeroeul. A section was then brought into action with immediate result, and the section was then employed searching for German guns which had opened on our trenches from several directions. Shortly afterwards however the infantry fell back from the canal to the River Haine and the battery was then withdrawn.[95]

Yet again they did not remain on the front line. The infantry was still in outpost positions, poised to fall back further. General Headlam briefly sent two other batteries half forward further west, but they quickly returned as dusk fell, without coming into action. He also ordered his 60 pounders to fire at long range over the canal, and they claimed a hit on an ammunition wagon; though the adjutant who wrote up the report was inclined to think this wishful thinking. His wording is careful.[96]

Yet again, this activity should not be allowed to disguise the main tactical dispositions of the 5th Division artillery. In line with General Smith-Dorrien's strategy, General Headlam had a second position to defend, which broadly followed the railway line from Mons to Dour. This crossed the low-lying country, much of it on an embankment, suitable for both protection and observation.[97] His 27th Brigade RFA was at Wasmes, on the right, waiting for the 13th Infantry Brigade to fall back, and his 28th Brigade RFA was at Dour, on the left, similarly waiting for the 14th Infantry Brigade. The rest of his command was south of Dour, in reserve.

It was a bit more complicated than this. From the right, he had deployed the 119th Battery of the 27th Brigade to the west, so he moved the 37th Battery of the 8th (Howitzer) Brigade to replace it; and the 119th fell back to his reserve group at Dour:

His reserve group, south of Dour, was covering the ground to the north, but also poised to react to any German enveloping manoeuvre from the north-west. The 15th Brigade RFA, his heavy battery (the 108th), two batteries of 8th Brigade (howitzers), and now the 119th Battery, were in this group under his direct command.[98]

---

94 TNA WO 95/1521: 5th Division Artillery, 23 August 1914.
95 Ibid., 23 August 1914.
96 Ibid., 23 August 1914.
97 TNA WO 95/1532: 123 Battery, XXVIII Brigade RFA, 23 August 1914.
98 TNA WO 95/1521: 5th Division Artillery, 23 August 1914.

The far left of II Corps was covered by the Cavalry Division, supported by two brigades of light 13-pounder field guns. But the cavalry guns were kept in reserve, at Quievrain. William Collins was a medical orderly with the 7th Brigade RHA, of which one battery advanced briefly that afternoon:

> That afternoon we moved forward and later on, approaching a wood, I heard my first shell burst some 50 yards ahead. It was shrapnel, a high burst, a cloud of white smoke and then a sound like a hundred shrill whistles as the pellets spread around. No one was wounded but the shrill of the shrapnel bullets lives with me still …[99]

One can allow for some exaggeration from a medical orderly as to how close this shell burst, but they were certainly ineffectively targeted by German light artillery. At nightfall, this small advance force fell back again to Quievrain, without coming in to action.[100]

Throughout the afternoon, the cavalry on the canal were relieved by the 19th Infantry Brigade, which had marched in from Valenciennes, just in time to face the advanced patrols of the 8th Division of IV Corps, (the 7th Division on their left) who were on the right of the German line. They exchanged fire with enemy forward patrols.

3.14 I Corps Artillery (Maps 6, 8 & 12)

The siting of the guns of I Corps had been decided in the early hours of the morning by Brigadier General Horne, CRA I Corps, and his two divisional brigadiers. Most of these positions were taken up, behind a low ridge, and the guns fired over the heads of the infantry at the very few targets of opportunity they were offered, discouraging any enemy advance from east or north, not that any was planned or intended.

The 1st Division, on the south-eastern flank of the British forces, had been in position since the evening before. At 8 a.m., the line of the 3rd Infantry Brigade was extended north to securely hold the high ground at Vellereille-le-sec, until relieved by the 6th Infantry Brigade of the 2nd Division later that morning, when they dropped back again.[101]

Of the 1st Division artillery, the 26th Brigade RFA was three miles south of Rouveroy with the 1st (Guards) Brigade as a divisional reserve. The 25th Brigade RFA and 43rd (Howitzer) Brigade were a mile or two east of Rouveroy in positions behind the 3rd Infantry, looking north-east. One battery of the 25th fired 20 rounds towards

---

99 RAM MD657: Sergeant William Collins RAMC, Note, 23 August 1914.
100 TNA WO 95/1103: VII Brigade RHA, 23 August 1914.
101 TNA WO 95/1227: 1st Division, 23 August 1914.

the flashes of an enemy battery at 4,700 yards, without much perceived result, in the early evening. They then moved north at Brigadier General Findlay's instigation, to try to target a battery that was troubling the 2nd division lines, but at a range of 6000 yards, they could not accurately locate its position and fell back at nightfall without firing. The 39th Brigade RFA entrenched at Rouveroy, with the 2nd Infantry Brigade. They did not fire a shot.[102]

Collectively, the guns of the 1st Division made almost no contribution to the battle, although the German cavalry was aware of their presence and gave them a wide berth.

The 2nd Division artillery had billeted the evening before south and east of Bavai, but were roused just before 1 a.m. to continue their advance to the road between Mons and the 1st Division at Rouveroy. They moved somewhat quicker than the infantry, and most arrived at Quevy during the late morning. The 6th Infantry Brigade made up the lead infantry of the 2nd Division. They arrived at Givry at 11 a.m., and moved up to the line from there, relieving the 1st Division at Vellereille-le-Sec, and gaining touch with the 3rd Division at Harmignies from about noon, as previously described.[103]

On the march, the 4th (Guards) Brigade were three miles behind, with the 5th Infantry Brigade five miles behind them. Brigadier General Percival had seconded his three field artillery brigades to the three Infantry Brigades and sent his howitzer brigade and heavy guns to reserve positions at Harveng, a mile west of Harmignies, just south west of the point where the 3rd and 2nd Divisions would join up.[104] Of his field artillery, the 36th Brigade RFA, with the 5th Infantry Brigade formed the divisional reserve, and billeted, with the infantry, well back at Bougnies, and Genly.[105] Once billeted, it would take two hours to ready themselves for a further march.

The 34th Brigade RFA, and the 9th Battery of the 41st Brigade RFA, went forward with the 6th Infantry Brigade. The 9th Battery, and the 22nd Battery of the 34th, remained at Givry, while the 50th and 70th Batteries, of the 34th, went forward to Vellereille-le-Sec.

The 16th and 17th Batteries of the 41st Brigade had been allocated to the two battalions of the 4th (Guards) Brigade, who had been ordered to take over the eastern flank of the salient at Mons. Specifically, they were to take up positions on Bois la Haut.[106]

Thus, the initial dispositions of the 2nd Division artillery gave very good support to the section of line around Givry and Vellereille-le-Sec, the latter with a good view north, which covered the ground east of Harmignies. But there were at this stage no guns in action further north, at Harmignies.

---

102 TNA WO 95/1239: 1st Division Artillery, & unit diaries, 23 August 1914.
103 TNA WO 95/1352: 6th Infantry Brigade, 23 August 1914.
104 TNA WO 95/1313: 2nd Division Artillery, 23 August 1914.
105 TNA WO 95/1343: 5th Infantry Brigade, 23 August 1914.
106 TNA WO 95/1326: XLI Brigade RFA, 9th Battery, 23 August 1914.

3.15 First Request for Assistance by II Corps (Maps 8, 9 & 11)

The lack of enthusiasm that the lead German infantry showed on the southern exits from Mons, in failing to follow up their breaching of the canal and capture of the town centre, was entirely understandable, given the fact they had been fighting for many hours and suffered heavy casualties. They knew that it would be some time before their artillery could get across the canal to support an attack on the 3rd Division second line, manned by the 7th Infantry Brigade just south of Mons. But, further east, the fighting was very heavy, and there was still doubt as to whether the forward British infantry battalions could extricate themselves. The units at Bois la Haut were almost completely surrounded, with more infantry of the German 17th Division (IX Corps) attacking from the east. The 3rd Division line faced additional threats. There were weaknesses in the defence line on either flank, most significantly in the gap at Paturages on their left, but also on their right, south-east of Bois la Haut to Harmignies.

The problem at Bois la Haut itself, had to be, and was toughed-out through the afternoon and into the evening, as will be described. But the 3rd Division was still attempting to screen its right flank down to Harmignies, supported only by the one company of the 2nd South Staffordshire Regiment (of the 6th Infantry Brigade) who had moved north of Harmignies on local initiative. They had no reserves and were receiving none of the expected help from the 2nd Division's 4th (Guards). Even the 6th Infantry Brigade was asking where they were.

Both General Smith-Dorrien and General Hamilton of the 3rd Division were worried. II Corps times the first request for information and help at 2.38 p.m., when they asked if I Corps 'could assist to fill gap between positions if contingency arises'. This calm and reasonable entry in the II Corps record probably does not reflect General Hamilton's demeanour as he made this appeal in person. He was in the throes of organising a dangerous and difficult withdrawal from the salient, fearing heavy casualties to his forward battalions. He desperately wanted the reassurance of any 2nd Division support. Three battalions had been promised. None had materialised. The noise of battle was considerable, and doubtless increasing: 'At 2 p.m., it became apparent the enemy were advancing', report 2nd Division staff, and warned the 5th Infantry Brigade in billets to prepare for movement.[107] They passed General Hamilton's appeal on to I Corps headquarters.

Hamilton's staff were at least partially reassured, by their reply at about 3 p.m., stating that '2 Inf Brigades are in position of readiness at crossroads 4 miles south of Mons.'[108] But the 5th Infantry Brigade, of the 2nd Division, were in billets at Genly and Bougnies, and would take at least two hours from 2 p.m. to be ready to move. The 4th (Guards) Brigade was out of position, just then on the march to Quevy. Neither

107 TNA WO 95/1283: 2nd Division, 23 August 1914.
108 TNA WO 95/630/1: II Corps Staff, 23 August 1914.

brigade could reasonably be described as either in position, or in readiness. II Corps waited in vain for any further information.

By this time, the news coming to I Corps from Mons was anything but reassuring. Frightened civilians and British wounded clogged the roads, fuelling rumours. It has already been mentioned that an artillery officer believed that the 'West Kent's, Middlesex and Northumberland's [had been] decimated by shell-fire.'[109] It was reasonable to ask if the 3rd Division could possibly hold out.

I Corps staff interpreted Hamilton's appeal, along with other reports, as a warning to expect an imminent breakthrough, and not as a measured request for support. They issued a series of orders. The first, at 3.50 p.m., was to the 1st Division. It started by saying that 'two brigades, 2nd Division, have been called upon to support 3rd Division, retiring from Mons,' and went on to advise that 'impedimenta not required for action [was] to be ready to move at a moment's notice'.[110] Panic is perhaps too strong a word, but calm there was not. The worst was clearly feared. 'We heard verbally from General Lomax, commanding the 1st Division, that we might have to retire,' says his forward infantry brigade at 6 p.m.[111] It seems that Haig was preparing to execute the retirement plan agreed with General Murray that morning.

The second, at 4 p.m., was to the 4th (Guards) Brigade. The Brigade was to concentrate at Harveng.[112] It is not clear if I Corps staff was aware that the two battalions who had marched to Mons were back at Quevy. Whatever they thought, all four battalions of the 4th (Guards) Brigade, along with the two batteries of the 41st Brigade RFA, now marched from Quevy, where most had just arrived, back to Harveng. Morale at this stage was not high. All but one battalion had just come from there. They were marching in circles. Most of the Battalion diaries simply leave a gap in the narrative. That of the 3rd Coldstream Guards reveals the disarray. They arrived at Harveng 'in consequence of alarming reports. On arrival there, the utmost confusion seemed to prevail, the flat plateau above Harveng was crowded with artillery, the village and street were equally crowded, and no-one seemed to know whither to go or what to do.'[113]

The third order issued by I Corps staff was to the 5th Infantry Brigade, now in readiness. 'At about 4.30', I Corps staff ordered them to march to a crossroads of country lanes, just north of Harveng, from their reserve billets at Genly and Bougnies.[114]

The 4th (Guards) Brigade were just arriving at Harveng. At least, 8,000 men were now converging on the tiny hamlet, which already hosted both artillery reserves and infantry headquarters. The 'divisional commander explained the situation', when the 5th Infantry Brigade arrived, although their diary does not enlarge on what that explanation was.

---

109 Terraine, *Mons: The Retreat to Victory*, p.117.
110 TNA WO 95/1227: 1st Division, 23 August 1914.
111 TNA WO 95/1274: 3rd Infantry Brigade, 23 August 1914.
112 TNA WO 95/588/1: I Corps staff, 23 August 1914.
113 TNA WO 95/1342: 3rd Coldstream Guards, 23 August 1914.
114 TNA WO 95/1343: 5th Infantry Brigade, 23 August 1914.

The 35th Heavy Battery of the 2nd Division also arrived at Harveng about 5 p.m., and 'halted. Alarm of attack on column. Road lined with dismounted men with rifles. No enemy seen. …a fierce action was going on. Nearly all the men of the second division were involved.'[115] False rumours were sweeping along the crowded roads. The noise of battle was continuous. Nobody knew what was happening.

Both the 4th and 5th Infantry Brigades were seriously fatigued by hours of marching; many of them had set off that morning without breakfast. There is an hour's gap in the narrative of every unit; and it is 6.15 p.m. before the 2nd Division diary record that all four battalions of the 5th Infantry Brigade, and two battalions of the 4th (Guards) had been instructed to dig a defence line north and north-east, respectively, of Harveng.[116] For clarity, this new line will be referred to as the Haig line.

The 36th Brigade RFA, attached to the 5th Infantry, took up positions at Bougnies at 7 p.m., to the west, facing east. '48th and 71st Batteries brought into action with the object of covering withdrawal of our troops in the neighbourhood of Harveng.'[117]

It is the artillery dispositions that clarify what is happening. It was feared that the 3rd Division was being overwhelmed; and a rear-guard line in anticipation of a rapid retreat was being prepared for the 2nd Division, with the 5th Infantry Brigade north of Harveng, and two battalions of the 4th (Guards) north-east, covered by these guns. The 5th Brigade and half the 4th Brigade were preparing defensive positions only a mile south of the 3rd Division 'second positions' already laid out, and only a mile south and east of the 3rd Division and 6th Brigade positions which met at Harmignies.

Haig's account in I Corps describes his reaction to the 2 p.m. appeal by Hamilton:

> A message was now received from the GOC 3rd Division stating that he was being heavily attacked, that his advanced troops had been driven back from the canal north and north-east of Mons, and that he needed assistance. As the situation on my right was not yet clear, for the enemy were still shelling the 6th Brigade hard, I judged it unwise to detach any force to attack in the Mons direction, but I ordered two battalions of the 4th Brigade to take over the defence of Point 93, and to relieve the troops of the 3rd Division who were holding that point. The two remaining battalions of the 4th Guards Brigade entrenched a position covering Harveng from the northeast.[118]

The bombardment of the 6th Infantry Brigade positions did not start till 4.30 p.m.[119] There is no supporting evidence that he ordered two battalions to Hill 93 immediately. They were not ordered to advance from Harveng till 6.15 p.m. He does not

---

115 TNA WO 95/481/2: 35th (Heavy) Battery, 2 Division, 23 August 1914.
116 TNA WO 95/1283: 2nd Division, 23 August 1914.
117 TNA WO 95/1325: XXXVI Brigade RFA, 23 August 1914.
118 TNA WO 95/588/4: I Corps staff, 23 August 1914.
119 TNA WO 95/1352: 6th Infantry Brigade, 23 August 1914.

mention the 5th Infantry Brigade entrenching the Haig line, north of Harveng, and the confusion this caused, as they prepared for a fighting withdrawal.

3.16 2nd Division Artillery Dispositions (Maps 11 & 12)

Brigadier General Horne, CRA I Corps, went to Harveng to help Major General Monro, commanding the 2nd Division, with his artillery dispositions on the Haig line. It is more than likely that Haig had issued him with verbal instructions, bypassing his staff, as he had when he tried to cancel the advance of the 1st Division the previous day. It did not take General Horne long to realise that his guns were in the wrong place. It will be remembered that he had planned the siting of the 2nd Division guns with Brigadier General Percival at 3 a.m. that morning. Uniquely, General Horne took the 16th and 17th Batteries of the 41st Brigade RFA, who had gone to Mons and back, under his personal command during the late afternoon, and sent them into action, north of Harveng, facing north-east to cover the real front line.[120] The 2nd Division Artillery diary makes no mention of this.

At about the same time, the 47th (Howitzer) Battery was detached south to Givry, and the other two batteries of this 44th (Howitzer) Brigade came in to action east of Harveng, again to support the northern flank of the 6th Infantry Brigade.[121] All these artillery dispositions ignored the needs of the Haig line. The fearful near panic of two hours earlier was being steadied. Instead of preparing for a breakthrough, steps were now being taken to prevent it. Only the division's heavy battery, the 35th, prepared positions west of Harveng, to support the reserve 36th Brigade RFA at Bougnies.[122]

At 6 p.m., the 2nd Division reports heavy shelling to the north and east, specifically on the 'Mons to Harmignies road … where are troops of the 3rd Division,'[123] not, it can be noted, 'where are our troops'. Fifteen minutes later, the two remaining battalions of the 4th (Guards) Brigade, who had been waiting over an hour in the confusion at Harveng,[124] were at last ordered forward to support the right flank of the 3rd Division, where they would be covered by the artillery movements already described.[125] This order emanates from Monro; and it seems likely that Horne, was involved in the discussion. General Haig may have given verbal instructions to General Horne, which were not recorded. Indeed, it is not impossible that these two battalions were now under corps control, along with their guns. The 2nd Division summary of the battle, in I Corps records, is at odds with its own war diary. It says that the concentration at Harveng occurred at 2 p.m., which was the time the two battalions of the

---

120 TNA WO 95/1326: XLI Brigade RFA, 23 August 1914.
121 TNA WO 95/1313: 2nd Division Artillery, 23 August 1914.
122 TNA WO 95/481/2: 35th (Heavy) Battery, 2 Division, 23 August 1914.
123 TNA WO 95/1283: 2nd Division, 23 August 1914.
124 TNA WO 95/1342: 1st Irish Guards, 23 August 1914.
125 TNA WO 95/1283: 2nd Division, 23 August 1914.

4th Guards were marching through the hamlet on their way to Quevy. It also says that the 4th Guards were at Harveng at 4.30 p.m. but took two hours to advance the one and a half miles to north of Harmignies.[126] Its account disguises the confusion which reigned, and the energy that went in to creating the Haig lines.

The 3rd Division second position, between Ciply and Harmignies, was sparsely manned by the 2nd Royal Irish Rifles of the 7th Infantry Brigade, covering a front of over a mile. (In front of them, and to their left, was the right flank of the 2nd Royal Scots on the northern end of the Mons to Harmignies road.) Both were under heavy artillery and rifle fire as the Germans occupied the east of the salient to their north. Near dusk, the 1st Irish Guards of the 4th Brigade who had been marching, almost continuously since 3 a.m., arrived, footsore and weary, having at last been:

> [O]rdered to go and support the 3rd division on a chalk ridge stretching from just north of Harmignies station. …Colonel Bird, commanding the Irish Rifles, was in command of this section, and No 2 company was sent to reinforce the Irish Rifles on the left, and No 1 company on the right. This was the first time the Battalion was under fire and during the evening five men were wounded.[127]

The Irish Guards was delighted to be in action at last and supporting another Irish regiment. It details its casualties in so doing with pride. The Grenadier Guards, on their right front, came up to support the Royal Scots and South Staffords. Only now, at about 7 p.m., was Hill 93 occupied by the 4th (Guards).

3.17 The Salient in late afternoon (Maps 9, 10 & 12)

The 4th Middlesex Regiment and 2nd Royal Irish Regiment, being the last to disengage in the salient, lost heavily in the final throes of a disciplined and at times selfless withdrawal, but astonishingly all the 40th Brigade guns got safely back. They had to leave Bois la Haut down the track at its northern end and circle west and then south. The brigade diary is somewhat cryptic:

> [At] 6 p.m., enemy attacking road Mons – Givry. Guns formed in a circle, Gordon Highlanders in intervals, no attacks by enemy. 7.30 p.m., guns withdrawn by hand and hooked in at bottom of hill. Return to Nouvelles.[128]
>
> [A recent book is more informative, though not referenced.] As the 23rd Battery left its positions on the hill, it encountered German infantry moving along the road to Hyon. The front horses and drivers were all shot down.

---

126 TNA WO 95/588/3: I Corps staff, 2nd Division, 23 August 1914.
127 TNA WO 95/134: 1st Irish Guards, 23 August 1914.
128 TNA WO 95/1400: XL Brigade RFA, 23 August 1914.

The gunners had no choice but to become infantry themselves, alongside the Gordon Highlanders tasked with escorting the guns. Engaging the enemy with their rifles, they drove the enemy back into the village. After further skirmishing, the guns would be safely got away after dark from within 200 yards of the enemy.

The 6th Battery also had a narrow escape. For most of the early evening they expected to be attacked by enemy infantry. The guns were placed in a semi-circle and defended by parties of the Royal Irish, Gordon Highlanders and the gunners themselves, facing to the north, west and south. The attack never came. Just before midnight, the guns were manhandled to the foot of the Bois la Haut, the teams hooked in and the battery made good its escape.[129]

Almost all of the German units sounded a ceasefire at night-fall, hunkering down where they were and ignoring night-time noises.[130] The British gunners, like the infantry who escorted them, lost casualties to rifle and machine gun fire in this last phase, but since the brigade diary was lost in the Retreat, full details of casualties are not available. Two artillery officers were wounded, and the artillery medical officer stayed behind at his dressing station in the hospital on Bois la Haut with them and other casualties.[131] Brigadier General Doran, commanding the 8th Brigade, had pulled off a largely successful withdrawal from the salient. Nevertheless, it should not be forgotten that this frantic activity involved only one brigade of the 3rd Division artillery. Most did not fire a shot all day and were preparing positions to defend General Smith-Dorrien's 'second position', which had been, and still was, being created by working parties of the 7th Infantry Brigade and their artillery.

3.18 I Corps Artillery in Action (Map 12)

In the late afternoon, the 6th Infantry Brigade positions from Vellereille-le-Sec to Harmignies came under fire from six batteries of the German 17th Division. Some VII Corps units (it was they who had captured Péronnes), covered by one infantry and one cavalry regiment, may also have been involved.[132] 'The enemy's cavalry and advanced troops opened a heavy artillery fire at 4.30 p.m.'[133] It was accurate, but totally innocuous: 'The 6th Infantry Brigade, on the right of the 2nd Division line,

---

129 Hutton, *The Gunners of 1914*, p.51.
130 Reichsarchiv, *Die Schlacht bei Mons* quoted in Edmonds, *Military Operations France and Belgium 1914*, Vol. I, p. 94.
131 TNA WO 95/1395: RAMC, 3rd Division, 23 August 1914.
132 Reichsarchiv, *Die Schlacht bei Mons* quoted Edmonds, *Military Operations France and Belgium*, 1914, p. 94.
133 TNA WO 95/1352: 6th Infantry Brigade, 23 August 1914.

was shelled heavily all afternoon, but suffered no casualties.'¹³⁴ But it was perceptions and reports that were important.

The 9th Battery, the one battery of the 41st Brigade RFA which did not march to Mons and back, had been told off to support the 6th Infantry. It was sited adjacent to 2nd Division Headquarters at Givry:

> Marched to Givry arriving about 2 p.m. A defensive position to be occupied. Battery took up position of observation on reverse slope of heights about one mile north east of Givry, and just south of railway line, with 4 guns. 5 p.m. Enemy opened fire on us from concealed position to north-east. Fire very heavy and battery had heavy casualties, losing 2 officers and 12 men killed and wounded. Fired at enemy cavalry just north of Mons to Binchy road. Fire apparently effective.
>
> Our shields gave no protection against enemy's high explosive shell fired with time fuses, the fragments of which strike vertically downwards and penetrate shields.¹³⁵

German howitzer fire was extremely unpleasant: 'One battery … was badly knocked about' according to Haig's account.¹³⁶ I Corps staff drew their own conclusions on the effectiveness of the German artillery. Heavy casualties as a result of accurate German light artillery fire had been assumed by the British generals all day. It is easy to understand how 'alarming' reports were magnified in the telling, becoming a threat to objective action.

Lieutenant J.L. Dent, 2nd South Staffordshire Battalion, at Harmignies, described in his diary a scene of 'many dead men, and struggling and riderless horses' following an artillery bombardment of British cavalry. He also describes buildings 'collapsing in clouds of smoke' at 'the railway station and village, held by the Royal Berkshire Regiment on our right'. He did not see these sights because they never happened, but he was assuming, not unreasonably, that accurate enemy artillery fire was effective. After the battle he says that 'the Royal Berkshires, who we imagined must have suffered so severely, had very few casualties.'¹³⁷ They had none. The 5th Cavalry Brigade spent most of the day '1 1/2 kilos [sic] SW of Givry in readiness for action. No action took place … I Corps Infantry, the 6th Bde especially, were very hard pressed', their diary reports, confirming the prevailing perception that evening.¹³⁸

Lieutenant Le Breton was with the 50th Battery at Vellereille-le-Sec. He describes being targeted by a field battery using both high explosive and shrapnel:

---

134 TNA WO 95/588/4: I Corps staff, 23 August 1914.
135 TNA WO 95/1326: XLI Brigade RFA, 9 Battery, 23 August 1914.
136 TNA WO 95/588/4: I Corps staff, 23 August 1914.
137 J.A. Jones, *A History of the South Staffordshire Regiment (1705-1923)* (Wolverhampton: Whitehead Brothers, 1923), p.249.
138 TNA WO 95/1138: 5th Cavalry Brigade, 23 August 1914.

> At 5.30 p.m. they turned their fire on us. About 5% of their shells landed in the battery. I was twice hit by clods of earth. Fryers of my section had a shell burst right under him as he was running up with ammunition. He was wounded in seven places, but not badly. In fact, he managed to run on to the gun pit. Bombardier Brothers was hit at No 6 gun. None of the horses were hit, though frequently shell burst right over the places where they had been shortly before.[139]

This inability of the German field artillery shrapnel to kill horses was absolutely critical. If enough horses were killed, batteries were crippled. The 70th Battery was next to the 50th at Vellereile-le-Sec:

> [Both] were subjected to a very heavy shell fire during the afternoon, 70th having two hostile howitzers turned on it; both batteries however maintained their fire. Lieutenants Robertson and Durand, 70th Battery wounded, 3 NCOs and men killed, 27 NCOs and men wounded.[140]

Yet again, a howitzer attack was the one to fear. Many officers, including staff officers from the 1st Division,[141] watched these two batteries in action from the road south of Givry. It was not reassuring. Lieutenant Schreiber of 115th Battery, 25th Brigade, 1st Division, was amongst them:

> We could see batteries of 2 Division in action behind a crest about 2 miles to the north… Our batteries appeared to be having a very bad time. Time after time, salvoes of shrapnel and air burst high explosive appeared to obliterate our guns… We waited anxiously to see the effect when the smoke cleared. Great was our relief to see the flashes of our guns as they continued their fire apparently unharmed…. The noise of the explosion was perhaps the worst part of them as they burst with a most terrifying crash.[142]

The 2nd Division artillery was deployed in counter battery work. As previously mentioned, the 47th (Howitzer) Battery of the 44th Brigade was sent to support the two field batteries at Givry:

> At Harveng till 6 p.m., and then received orders to join 6th Brigade at Givry. Entrenched a position north of Givry on left of 34th Brigade RFA. Finished

---

139 IWM 15384: Private Papers of Lt Francis Henry Le Breton. 23 August 1914.
140 TNA WO 95/1324: 50th Battery, XXXIV Brigade RFA 23 August 1914.
141 TNA WO 95/1274: 3rd Infantry Brigade, 23 August 1914.
142 RAM MD/425: Schreiber, 23 August 1914.

entrenching at 2 a.m. Beautiful observing station 3.30 a.m. and engaged German batteries 3,500 yards to the north.[143]

There is certainly a contrast between field guns coming in to action, and this howitzer battery. 'Beautiful' positions maybe, but they took over six hours to start their counter battery work. Field battery arrangements were much more perfunctory.

Both the 2nd Grenadier Guards, of 4th (Guards) Brigade and the 6th Infantry regiments, at Harmignies, also came under heavy and accurate artillery fire. Neither suffered any casualties, but it was very uncomfortable. They wanted counter battery fire to take the pressure off. Help was provided by the 16th and 17th Batteries of the 41st Brigade RFA, which General Horne had posted behind them earlier. They targeted one enemy battery, and then the 17th Battery sent forward a section of guns in close support, in an unsuccessful attempt to get a better view. The reverse slope was too steep to lay the guns, and they decided against taking up a position on the crest of the ridge due to the weight of fire sweeping across it. They fell back again at nightfall.[144]

German infantry never attacked the I Corps line south of Harmignies, and the German field artillery fire caused no casualties at all. But at this stage of the battle, it was perceptions (and rumours) that mattered. Nobody knew how ineffective the German field artillery fire was.

3.19 Second Request for Assistance by II Corps (Maps 10 & 11)

In the absence of any assistance materialising following General Hamilton's request for help, General Smith-Dorrien personally renewed the request for help for his 3rd Division.[145] His lack of reserves was becoming critical.

There had always been a gap in the 'second position' line between the 5th Division at Wasmes, and the 3rd Division at Frameries. This gap was opening as the 9th Infantry Brigade of the 3rd Division fell back south of Mons, while the 13th Brigade of the 5th Division remained up at the canal. The Royal Scots Fusiliers, falling back from Mons, was still being harried on the northern edge of Frameries that evening, losing two officers and 30 men to an infantry attack. By early evening, all the 9th Infantry Brigade were back on the 3rd Division second position.[146] But some German infantry units were uncomfortably close in front of them.

The 1st Dorsetshire Regiment, 15th Infantry Brigade, facing north at Wasmes, was at the eastern end of the 5th Division second position. It watched the 9th Infantry fall

---

143 TNA WO 95/1327: 47th Battery, XLIV Brigade RFA, 23 August 1914.
144 TNA WO 95/1326: XLI Brigade RFA, 23 August 1914.
145 TNA WO 95/630/1: II Corps Staff, 23 August 1914.
146 TNA WO 95/1425: 9th Infantry Brigade, 23 August 1914.

back at 4.30 p.m., and reported at 5.30, that a German battalion was following up at 1000 yards.¹⁴⁷ It was very likely this report which caused General Smith-Dorrien to rush to I Corps Headquarters, but first composing a message:

> To G.H.Q., G 271, August 23rd. Third Division report at 6.47 p.m. the Germans are in front of his main position and are not attacking at present. They are, however, working round 3rd Division on left flank. If it should appear that there is a danger of my centre being pierced I can see no course but to order a general retirement on Bavai position. Have I your permission to adopt this course if it appears necessary? From II Corps, 7.15 p.m.¹⁴⁸

The 3rd Division was back on their second position. General Murray, Field Marshal French's Chief of Staff, that morning, had insisted that General Smith Dorrien obtain GHQ approval for any general withdrawal. This dispatch was a warning that the time for withdrawal was near.

Prior to this in the timeline is a letter found in Haig's personal papers. It was allegedly written from his headquarters at Bonnet, at 5.35 p.m.:

> Dear Smith-Dorrien, I felt sorry that I could not comply with your request to fill the gap between the left of your 3rd and right of your 5th Divisions. … The best I could do was to relieve your detachments on Hill 93, near Harmignies by two Battalions of Guards thus setting free two of Hamilton's Battalions. The rest of the 4th Brigade is near Hartweg [sic]. Haking's [5th Infantry] Brigade in readiness near X roads NE of Bougnies. Let me know your views for tomorrow… If all goes well on my right, I should like to support Hamilton in driving enemy back into Mons. …Unless you and I meet, coordination between our two corps will be difficult.¹⁴⁹

Haig had just issued orders to facilitate the withdrawal of both his divisions and had stopped his troops going to Hill 93. There is no evidence that he was aware at this time that the gap at Paturages was a problem. The misspelling of Harveng, repeated in his retrospective diaries, but nowhere else, is inexplicable. General Smith Dorrien had no intention of going on to the offensive. The first two letters in this series are of questionable provenance. This, the third in the series, has so many factual anomalies as to render it almost unbelievable as a contemporary missive. His account in I Corps records is factual:

---

147 TNA WO 95/1572/2: 1st Dorsetshire Regiment, 23 August 1914.
148 Smith-Dorrien, *Memories of Forty-Eight Years' Service*, p.385.
149 NLS, Acc.3155/98: Douglas Haig papers, 23 August 1914, p.88-89.

About 6.30 p.m., the GOC 2nd Corps came to my Headquarters at Bonnet and stated that a gap had been laid open about Frameries between the 3rd and 5th Divisions and asked for the assistance of a couple of battalions. Three battalions of the 5th Brigade were immediately placed at his disposal. It was now nearly dark and on the arrival of this detachment no enemy was to be found.[150]

In fact, Haig delayed issuing the order. There was no 'immediate' about it. Now the 6th Infantry Brigade was being bombarded. It was feared that they were sustaining heavy casualties. At 5.20 p.m., I Corps had ordered the 1st Division to send two battalions, with supporting artillery, to Givry to support the right wing of the 2nd Division in expectation of attack.[151] Note the specific nature of this order. It is not 'brief and very general instructions'. An infantry attack was expected. 'Enemy advanced from direction of Binche, but retired at dusk', report General Haig's staff.[152]

II Corps reported at 7.20 p.m. that General Haig had agreed the request, probably the time General Smith-Dorrien returned to his headquarters at Sars-la-Bruyère. But it was not till 8 p.m., when it was nearly dark, that the 2nd Division received the necessary order. At about the same time, GHQ's response (OA90) to II Corps' enquiry about possible retirement (G271) arrived, instructing II Corps to 'hold ground, unless ordered to retire, and to ask for assistance from I Corps if necessary'.[153]

The 2nd Division was ordered to send three battalions to 'the occupation of ground which had been abandoned [sic]'.[154] This last was neither true, nor reassuring. 'Alarming' reports had been circulating in I Corps all day, and they were keyed up for a fighting withdrawal. Who knew what state the 3rd Division was in?

General Monro of 2nd Division was put on the horns of a dilemma. On the one hand, his orders to hold the Haig line north of Harveng had not been cancelled. On the other hand, he was being ordered to send the troops manning this line to the north-west. The only solution he could come up with was to withdraw the two 4th (Guards) Brigade battalions he had just ordered up north of Harmignies back to the Haig line.

Brigadier General Scott-Kerr, commanding, was keen on this solution, reporting that the road north of Harmignies, was 'a regular shell trap and untenable'. (The 8th Infantry Brigade who had held it all day would have been grimly amused by this assessment.) So, Monro ordered the two batteries of the 41st Brigade RFA, the howitzer battery, the Irish Guards and the Grenadier Guards to fall back. The field guns, now under Corps command, refused to comply. General Horne had given them a task, and Monro could not use them, until they were released from that task. The

---

150 TNA WO 95/588/4: I Corps staff, 23 August 1914.
151 TNA WO 95/1227: 1st Division, 23 August 1914.
152 TNA WO 95/588/1: I Corps staff, 23 August 1914.
153 TNA WO 95/630/1: II Corps Staff, 23 August 1914.
154 TNA WO 95/1283: 2nd Division, 23 August 1914.

howitzer battery did fall back, but the infantry in front of the field guns had to endure yet another order and counter order and stay put to protect the guns. General Scott-Kerr was told to hold his ground north of Harmignies. One of the two battalions of the 4th (Guards), digging in east of Harveng, was ordered to the line north of Harveng.[155] A dangerous (for the late evening) withdrawal was prevented by the artillery dispositions of General Horne.

So, it was not till 10 p.m. that three battalions of the 5th Infantry Brigade, on the Haig Line at Harveng, were released from their task of digging in, and received their instructions, the remaining battalion remaining in the Haig line:

> About 10 p.m., a message came from I Corps headquarters ordering 3 battalions of the 5th Brigade to march to turn the Germans out of Paturages village, where it was reported they had penetrated between the 3rd and 5th Divisions. After considerable trouble the Oxfords, Worcester's and HLI were collected …and about 11.30 p.m. the march commenced. Bns moved in fours with bayonets fixed. On reaching Hqrs of 3rd Division in Noirchain, the situation did not seem so serious as was thought at first, but the brigade continued its march to Framerie … It was apparently uncertain if the Germans were or were not in Paturages, but if they were, they were not showing themselves. About 1 a.m., the Brigade continued to advance and succeeded in occupying the N edge of Paturages by 2.30 a.m.[156]

By the time the 5th Infantry battalions received their orders, they were exhausted. They had been roused at 1 a.m., south of Bavai, marched many miles, spent most of the afternoon in alarm and confusion, and been digging trenches for the last four hours. Another march, at worst to face a rampant enemy, at best to dig more trenches, was not a welcome prospect.

They were far too late, but as often happens in war, much was made of a potential problem. General Hamilton believed I Corps' assertion that the 5th Infantry Brigade was moving to Paturages at 7.30 p.m., and, greatly reassured, recorded it as fact.[157] General Smith-Dorrien had also been under enormous stress that afternoon when the battle was in the balance. It seems likely that he was equally reassured at the time, but II Corps knew at 10.57 p.m., that the gap was still unfilled.[158]

In the heat of the moment, he, and General Hamilton earlier, had probably exaggerated the threats to their positions, confirming General Haig and General Monro's fear that the general breakthrough they had expected all day was imminent. In expectation of this breakthrough General Haig had refused to commit troops north of Harmignies all afternoon, despite his orders from GHQ; and he had concentrated

---

155 TNA WO 95/1283: 2nd Division, 23 August 1914.
156 TNA WO 95/1343: 5th Infantry Brigade, 23 August 1914.
157 TNA WO95/1375: 3rd Division, 23 August 1914.
158 TNA WO 95/630/1: II Corps staff, 23 August 1914.

his forces to protect Harveng, which was never actually under threat. But the extent to which the advancing German battalions had been exhausted by their exertions was underestimated by both General Smith-Dorrien and General Hamilton. As previously described, all the German forces ceased fire and billeted where they were at dusk. The 1st Bedfordshire Regiment, covering the right rear flank of the Dorsetshire Regiment at Wasmes, scouted forward after dark, and located the enemy, previously spotted by the Dorset's, now halted about two miles from Frameries. They reported this 'by breaking into railway telegraph room and using instruments' to communicate with their divisional headquarters.[159] The German infantry moving towards Paturages had withdrawn and hunkered down for the night. The gap in the defence line was filled without drama at 2.30 a.m., and this was important for the next morning. All previous accounts of the Battle of Mons imply that this gap at Paturages was filled in the early evening of the 23rd.[160] It was not. This episode has often been cited as evidence of cooperation between the two corps. It was anything but.

3.20 II Corps Retirement to Second Positions (Maps 10 & 13)

By mid-afternoon, General Smith-Dorrien was trying to orchestrate an orderly withdrawal of his troops from the canal to his second position. It was not easy. The corps signals company had arrived at his headquarters at Sars-la-Bruyère on the 22nd at '10 a.m. ... and laid lines to 3rd and 5th division. 23 August – laid fresh lines to 3rd as first unsatisfactory, heavy fighting and many lines cut.'[161]

The retirement of the 3rd Division had started in the late morning, and although the retirement of the left flank of the 9th Infantry Brigade, covering the bridge at Mariette, was delayed as they covered a demolition engineer, almost all had retired to the second position, running along the railway from Frameries to Harmignies, by early evening.[162] Only the right flanks of both the 7th and 8th Infantry Brigades, did not fall back to this line at dusk, continuing to hold the strategically important Hill 93, north of Harmignies, along with the two battalions of the 4th (Guards).

In the centre of the British line, only the 13th Infantry Brigade, 5th Division, was still up at the canal; they had to adjust their right flank when the 9th Infantry retired, and their left flank when the 14th Infantry fell back behind the River Haine in the late afternoon, (as previously described). At 7.30 p.m., it too received orders to fall back 'to second position', beginning the retirement at 9 p.m.[163] Due to German encroachment over the canal on both flanks, the initial stages of their withdrawal were difficult and

---

159 TNA WO 95/1570/1: 1st Bedfordshire Regiment, 23 August 1914.
160 Edmonds, *Military Operations France and Belgium 1914*, Vol. I, p.90.
161 TNA WO 95/646: II Corps Signals Company, 23 August 1914.
162 TNA WO 95/1425: 9th Infantry Brigade, 23 August 1914.
163 TNA WO 95/1510: 5th Division, 23 August 1914.

slow. They were not safely back on their defence line until about dawn, the next day. Further west, the 14th Infantry Brigade, on the River Haine, also received orders to withdraw to their second positions, starting at 9.45 p.m. They were able to comply much more quickly.[164]

To the far west, the 19th Infantry Brigade, under General Allenby, stayed put until midnight, holding their line with little difficulty. They were attacked, and lost six men killed, twenty-one wounded and eight missing by the time they had withdrawn.[165] Thus, the withdrawal of II Corps to their second position was largely complete by midnight. Most units, with the exception of the 13th Infantry, were getting what rest they could after an exhausting twenty-four hours. General Fergusson of the 5th Division kept half his reserve 15th Infantry Brigade on the left flank, and the other half covered his weak right flank between Wasmes and Paturages. He asked the Bedfordshire Regiment to link with the 5th Infantry Brigade battalions of the 2nd Division at Paturages. (It was they who notified II Corps that this contingent had still not arrived at 10.57 p.m.) The Dorset Regiment was between them and the 13th Infantry Brigade. There was every intention of holding this line the next morning. The Infantry Brigades of the 3rd Division received a divisional order at about 1 a.m.: '[R]eceived instruction that position was to be held to the last (ms 3rd Div G155 attached)'.[166]

A 5th Division battery also recorded orders to hold to the last.[167] General Smith-Dorrien was following the battle plan agreed that morning with General Murray. No further retirement was planned unless authorised by GHQ.

3.21 I Corps on the evening of 23 August (Map 13)

The 1st Division had seen no action but was still expecting the order to retire at any minute at 6 p.m. The 3rd Infantry Brigade, with their brigade headquarters at Rouveroy, manned the front lines. Their diary is a delight to read, and gently records their indecisive handling:

> Heavy artillery firing to be heard most of the afternoon towards Mons, and a good deal to our east…
>
> 7 p.m. Received orders from 1st Division (verbal) to get Queens ready for a possible local counter-attack, but as Gloucs [sic] had not apparently fired a shot yet, there seemed no possible target. …Went out with the general and General Lomax to watch the German shrapnel bursting over our 2nd Division batteries.

---

164 TNA WO 95/1560: 14th Infantry Brigade, 23 August 1914.
165 TNA WO 95/1364: 19th Infantry Brigade, 23-24 August 1914.
166 TNA WO 95/1413: 7th Infantry Brigade, 24 August 1914.
167 TNA WO 95/1529: 120th Battery, XXVII Brigade RFA, 24 August 1914.

> 10pm. Called to conference at Divisional HQ. (We had previously heard verbally, 6 p.m., that we might have to retire.) Decided there to fight tomorrow, if attacked in our present position, which… is better than changed orders and a move in the dark.[168]

The 2nd Division had a somewhat nervy evening: 'At 1.30 a.m.… reports were received that an attack was being made. No local attack developed.'[169]

Also at 1.30 a.m., the two 4th (Guards) battalions were again ordered to retire from the hill north of Harmignies and this time they did so.[170] The 16th and 17th Batteries of the 41st Brigade had already fallen back after dark to billet. Both the Royal Irish Rifles and the 2nd Royal Scots of II Corps were retiring to the 3rd Division second position at Nouvelles, north of Harveng.[171] There is no record of who issued the retirement order to the 4th (Guards) battalions, and there is no doubt it was a mistake. Probably when the guns fell back and no longer needed to be protected, the officer commanding the two battalions followed suit, obeying the last order he had received from division only a few hours before. The 2nd Division diary reports that the 'g.o.c.' – General Haig, why he, unless division thought these two battalions were still, like the guns, under corps control? – ordered reoccupation of the hill, following the retirement. The two battalions, if they received this order, took no notice. Presumably enough was enough. It was their sixth counter order of the day. II Corps and the 8th Infantry Brigade thought they were still in place at dawn.

Why this mistake occurred is not clarified by notes in General Haig's private papers, stating that Brigadier General Scott-Kerr, commanding the 4th (Guards), sought advice, at 11 p.m., from General Haig.[172] Curiously, he was by-passing General Monro, his immediate superior, implying that the two battalions were under corps control at the time. A letter, allegedly written to Monro, follows:

> The GOC 4th Gds Bde has come to see me regarding how Point 93 north of Harmignies is to be held tomorrow. At present there are parts of 5 Batt on that hill. The troops belonging to the 3rd Division should be sent to rejoin their Bde.
>
> As regards the others, will you please dispose them as you consider best. As GOC 2nd Division, you are in command of the troops holding from General Lomax's left near Estinnes Station, through Vellereille le Sec and Point 93 (N of Harmignies) to the rising ground north east of Bougnies village. Your objective is to hold that line …[173]

---

168 TNA WO 95/1274: 3rd Infantry Brigade, 23 August 1914.
169 TNA WO 95/1352: 6th Infantry Brigade, 23-24 August 1914.
170 TNA WO 95/1342: 1st Irish Guards and TNA WO 95/1342, 2 Grenadier Guards, 24 August 1914.
171 TNA WO 95/1413: 7th Infantry Brigade, 24 August 1914.
172 NLS Acc.3155/98: Douglas Haig Papers, 23 August 1914, p. 94.
173 Ibid., 23 August 1914, pp. 90-91.

Haig was, for no obvious reason, informing Monro where his own troops were posted. If genuine, the letter places blame for the mistake on Monro. The 4th (Guards) Brigade war diary, which might have shed some light on events is missing. It is likely that this episode, now a mere footnote, was significant at the time.

3.22 GHQ Reaction to the events of 23 August (Map 13)

II Corps received two orders from GHQ during the evening. The first, already referred to, at 8.05 p.m., ordered the Corps to 'hold ground unless ordered to retire and to call on I Corps for assistance if necessary', (OA90). This was followed up at 8.40 p.m. with 'positions now held to be strengthened with a view to meeting enemy attacks on it tonight or tomorrow', (OA95).[174] They had no impact on II Corps dispositions, and they continued to fall back to their second positions, which they did indeed strengthen as effectively as they could. GHQ recorded their interpretation of the day's events as follows:

> Enemy attacked Mons and line of canal W of it early in morning. Troops ordered to hold their positions. By the evening, 3rd Div had been driven out of Mons with loss, and hill of Bas Haut; 5th Div had fallen back on Boussu. Germans penetrated between 3rd and 5th Divs and 3 battalions were sent by I Corps to support in the gap.[175]

This was a profoundly negative take on the battle, and it was not even accurate. The Germans had not penetrated the line, and nor were I Corps battalions supporting the gap at the time of writing. The 5th Division was in the process of falling back through the village of Boussu. The truth was that two British divisions, with almost no artillery support, had fought six German divisions to a standstill in a rear-guard action, and were now back in prepared positions, ready to resist further German advance, with their artillery in close support, and just as importantly, completely intact. They even had their Divisional Ammunition Columns.

This GHQ report completely misinterpreted the battle which General Smith-Dorrien had fought, and it is clear that BEF Chief-of-Staff Murray had been unable to put a positive gloss on events, despite his presumed awareness that all had essentially gone to plan. It is hard to think of another battle in history where a Commander-in-Chief appears less informed of the strategy his army was employing.

174 TNA WO 95/630/1: II Corps Staff, 23 August 1914.
175 TNA WO 95/1/2: General Staff, 23 August 1914.

4

Second Day of Battle – 24 August 1914

4.1 GHQ Orders a Withdrawal

By the evening of the 23rd, Field Marshal French, at his headquarters in Le Cateau, was fully aware of the precipitate retreat of the French 5th Army which had left his right flank almost completely exposed. He had also, at last, accepted that II Corps was being heavily attacked by three German corps, though not till evening was it noted in the GHQ record that '3 or 4 German Corps were in front and flank of the army.'[1] In fact, it was five. IV, III and IX Corps were engaged; II Cavalry Corps was approaching behind IV Corps; and VII Corps, following up on the French retreat, was south-east of IX Corps.[2]

He called a meeting at Le Cateau, demanding personal attendance of the Corps Chiefs-of-Staff. This meeting is said to have taken place at 1 a.m., though it may have been earlier.[3] I Corps say the call to attend came at 7.30 p.m., II Corps say 'overnight'. French ordered 'a general retirement to be carried out by the two corps commanders in conjunction.'[4] Brigadier General Gough, Chief-of-Staff, I Corps enlarges in his message to General Haig, timed at 1.30 a.m. 'C in C orders that 2nd Corps retires under cover of First Corps. … Corps commanders to arrange cooperation in retirement.'[5] The extent of the withdrawal was back to a line on Bavai.

Haig received the message by telegram at 2 a.m., and made no attempt to liaise with II Corps. He leapt into his car and embarked on a whirlwind tour of his commanders from north to south, to activate his retirement:

---

1 TNA WO 95/1/2: General Staff, 23 August 1914.
2 Reichsarchiv, *Die Schlacht bei Mons* quoted in Edmonds, *Military Operations France and Belgium 1914*, Vol. I, p.94.
3 Edmonds, *Military Operations France and Belgium 1914*, Vol. I, p.97.
4 TNA WO 95/630/1: II Corps Staff, 23 August 1914.
5 TNA WO 95/588/1: I Corps staff, 24 August 1914, p. 20.

The GOC 1st Corps then motored to the Headquarters of the 2nd Division and saw General Munro [Monro]; thence to Givry where he met Generals Davies and Bulfin; thence to the Chateau at Rouveroy, the Headquarters of the 1st Division. Orders were thus given personally in the space of 45 minutes, and the movement was started on certain lines in a way impossible by means of written orders in the time.[6]

Conspicuous by its absence is any consultation with his staff, liaison with II Corps, or contact with the 5th Cavalry Brigade he was commanding. His initial orders to the 2nd Division exposed rather than covered the right flank of II Corps. Haig's I Corps staff diary for the day records the receipt of the order to retire in an untimed entry, and then nothing at all. There is no evidence that General Haig's staff made any contribution to the organisation of the withdrawal.[7] (Some of I Corps staff records were lost at Landrecies on 25 August. This may explain some of the poor record of events.)[8]

Coordination appears to have been left entirely to Brigadier General Horne, who was already commanding the artillery at Harveng. Before 4 a.m., he took control of the 5th Cavalry Brigade, and subsequently assumed command of the 4th (Guards) Brigade to make up an all-arms rear-guard force to cover the withdrawal of both corps.[9] Nowhere is it recorded that this was planned. His command evolved out of necessity.

It was 4 a.m. before General Smith-Dorrien was informed of the decision to withdraw. His telephone line was down, and his Chief of Staff had to drive the 25 miles from Le Cateau to Sars-la-Bruyère to deliver the message.

4.2 GHQ Orders to the left flank (Map 13)

It is not in doubt that GHQ issued an operation order to General Allenby concerning a withdrawal, but there are no details in the records. According to the Official History, the Cavalry Division was ordered to conform with the retreat of a French territorial division at Condé.[10] The 19th (Independent) Infantry Brigade received orders, presumably from GHQ, at midnight to fall back from its position on the far-left flank towards Elouges;[11] and was then immediately put back under the command of General Allenby.

---

6   TNA WO 95/588/4: I Corps Staff, 23 August 1914.
7   TNA WO 95/588/1: I Corps staff, 24 August 1914.
8   Brigadier-General John Charteris, *Field Marshal Earl Haig*, (London, Cassell and Company LTD, 1929) p.94.
9   TNA WO 95/1283: 2nd Division, 24 August 1914.
10 Edmonds, *Military Operations France and Belgium 1914*, Vol. I, p.103.
11 TNA WO 95/1364: 19th Infantry Brigade, 23 August 1914.

The Cavalry Division received a message, at 8.20 p.m. (on the 23rd) from the 5th Division, that the left flank held by the 14th Brigade was intending to fall back to Dour in the next hour; and a message from GHQ 'during the evening' advising them to be ready to move forward at dawn the next morning.[12] The 2nd Cavalry Brigade covered the retirement of the 19th Infantry, noting that they were very tired, as well they might be, after their exertions of the day before. The Cavalry Division diary describes events:

> The Second Brigade became engaged just north of Elouges, the enemy opening with his guns at about 6 a.m. … Communication with the 5th Division on our right was found difficult.
>
> Owing to the operation orders issued the night before and the allotment of roads which were at an angle to the line occupied by our forces, it was necessary in case of a retirement to clear the road Audregnies – Roisin for the 5th Division. The 19th Infantry Brigade were therefore sent off to Rombies to join the 4th Cavalry Brigade. …At about 6.45…the GOC, under the belief that the 5th Division had also commenced its retirement, determined to move on Rombies and there concentrate the Division.[13]

Instead of stopping at Elouges and forming up on the left of the 5th Division, the 19th Brigade marched on to Quievrain, and from there to Rombies, further southwest. The Cavalry Division diary, quoted above, makes it clear that this was a mistake, caused by General Allenby thinking that the 5th Division were falling back from their second position immediately. What a change it is to see an honest mistake honestly admitted!

The mistake implies that General Allenby had not been briefed either by General Ferguson of the 5th Division, or by General Smith-Dorrien of II Corps, on the plan to establish a firm second position, running east from Dour. It was not till 9.10 a.m. that General Ferguson made this clear in a request for continuing cover of his positions.[14] Allenby had earlier lost touch with the 5th Division and withdrawn his infantry too far and too fast. It was his responsibility, but, in his defence, GHQ may have advised him that the 5th Division was to retire immediately.

4.3 German Intentions on 24 August

General Von Kluck had been ordered to outflank the French Fifth Army, which he had done. He had not expected a significant British force to delay this envelopment. But he still had IV Corps, with II Cavalry Corps not far behind them, outflanking

---

12   TNA WO 95/1096: 1st Cavalry Division, 23 August 1914.
13   Ibid., 24 August 1914.
14   Ibid., 24 August 1914, p.54.

the west of the British lines. He could use them to swing round the British left flank and bundle them towards Maubeuge.

The IV Corps, at the western end of the line, was still on the march at midday on the 23rd and did not reach the canal till the late afternoon or cross the canal in any force till midnight. Although they had been marching hard, they were relatively fresh. Thus, while the fighting by the German III and IX Corps against the 3rd Division was quietening after nightfall, the German IV Corps was preparing to advance.[15]

Both Smith-Dorrien and Haig had feared this envelopment manoeuvre from the west. There had been no evidence of it on the first day of battle, but with the German IV Corps now crossing the canal west of the 5th Division's line, it was becoming a

General Alexander von Kluck.

significant threat to the British positions. General Ferguson and General Smith-Dorrien had to hope that the 5th Division could retire quickly enough to avoid being entrapped, but they relied on the 19th Infantry Brigade, now withdrawn, to slow the German advance.

An envelopment manoeuvre was most effective if the force to be enveloped was held in place by frontal attack, not with any expectation of great success, but to tie the troops attacked down to be caught by the envelopment. In addition, horses, and indeed men, were vulnerable to artillery fire on the move, and a heavy bombardment might be expected to cause significant difficulties to any attempted retreat. In line with this strategy, von Kluck ordered heavy bombardments on the British line, while his infantry moved forward, picking their way carefully through the abandoned British positions.

The German divisions of III and IX Corps had suffered heavy losses and were exhausted by a long day's fighting. As night fell, with many units badly mauled, they had billeted where they were. There was a significant lull in the fighting. However, from dawn, these units started to reorganise as reserves moved forward. The IX Corps was the more damaged, and it was not till relatively late that infantry attacks out of

15 Edmonds, *Military Operations France and Belgium 1914*, Vol. I, p.94.

Mons were arranged. Few infantry were south-east of Mons, but a heavy artillery barrage was opened there at dawn. Only cavalry detachments were present in significant numbers further south-east, on the I Corps front.

Meanwhile, west of Mons, III Corps sent forward reserves over the canal, behind a heavy artillery barrage, which fell initially on abandoned territory. But the infantry eventually made contact with the British second positions. They were immediately sent into attack. The German artillery moved forward to support these attacks. As with the day before, the infantry attacks rolled from east to west.

4.4 Withdrawal of I Corps (Maps 12, 13 & 14)

I Corps started to retreat at 4 a.m. having had very little rest. They had also had very few casualties; the Official History estimates forty on the 23rd.[16] This is an underestimate, though not by much. The first division reported four. In the 2nd Division, the 9th, 50th and 70th batteries alone lost 46 on the 23rd, and the 1st Irish Guards five. The attached cavalry brigade lost at least two. The 2nd Worcestershire Regiment had five the next morning at Paturages. The true figure is about sixty. Given the concern shown by the artillery brigadiers and their infantry counterparts of the 4th and 6th Brigades at the heavy and relentless shelling of their lines, the figure is unbelievably small.

The road south to Maubeuge was closed to I Corps, since it was full of French troops falling back. The main direction of their withdrawal was therefore just south of west, towards Bavai. It was some time, of course, before the forward units could move, since the transport had to go first. It was not till 6.10 a.m. that the 3rd Infantry Brigade of the 1st Division issued precise orders to its forward battalions on the order of retreat. 'The artillery will cover the retirement.' This they did. It was all very professional. The battalions were the 1st South Wales Borderers, the 2nd Welch, the 1st Gloucestershire and the 1st Queens (Royal West Surrey):

> 7 a.m. Order to SWB, Welsh and Gloucs to commence to retire sent out. Moved Bde HQ to the edge of the village where we could get a good view of the proceedings. At 8.30 a.m., the Gloucs moved through the Queens. They had got away without any trouble … The Glosters [sic] rightly came back through Croix les Rouveroy, and not as suggested in Bde orders past Givry, as the open slope in that direction might have been shelled. 8.45 a.m. An Uhlan patrol rode into the Queens and then galloped across their front at 400 yards. The Queens shot well and only one got away. The Welsh and Gloucs also shot a few cavalry patrols and the SWB exchanged shots with some more. A mass of German cavalry seen halted at 3000 to 4000 yards off towards Binche. After some delay, the 115th

16 Ibid., p.91.

Battery, and one Batt 43rd [howitzer] Brigade opened fire on them and they moved off SE towards the woods.[17]

Prior to this last excitement, the 115th Battery (25th Brigade RFA) also had an encounter with a German cavalry patrol, as recounted by Lieutenant Schreiber:

> The day was very hot. Everything appeared to be very quiet on our front and we were all lying down near the guns. Suddenly there was an outburst of musketry on our right. I jumped up and saw a patrol of about six German cavalry galloping across our front about 100 yards away. Sergt. Greest, the Number 1 of my right-hand gun, shouted, 'I am on them, Sir'. One round and the patrol seemed to melt. A second round and when the smoke had cleared one dismounted man was seen to run over the crest in front. The men of the battery were highly elated at the first shot they had fired in war. The Major went out and destroyed the wounded horses.[18]

The 3rd Infantry Brigade now fell further back through the 2nd Infantry Brigade, who made up the rear-guard of the 1st Division. The latter were shelled, as were 6th Infantry Brigade, of the 2nd Division, further north as they fell back.

Lieutenant Le Breton, with the 50th Battery, still at Vellereile-le-Sec, recorded the ineffectiveness of the German bombardment: 'The same battery the next morning from 4.30 a.m. started plunking shell over our heads again. They must have fired off 500 rounds at us in 1 1/2 hours. We had no casualty.'[19]

The hostile artillery fire proved no hindrance to the withdrawal of I Corps. During the morning, the 2nd Brigade retired to Bettignies, and dug in, covered by the 39th Brigade RFA. Their 54th Battery had earlier fired 'about 50 rounds at infantry – result not observed' while at Rouveroy, but the brigade did not fire again that day.[20] This 1st Division rear-guard force linked up with that of the 2nd Division rear-guard soon after midday.

As previously related, the I Corps rear-guard further north consisted of the 4th (Guards) Brigade, the 41st Brigade RFA, the 5th Cavalry Brigade and J Battery RHA, under the command of Brigadier General Horne, CRA I Corps. He also took command of the 36th Brigade RFA, (still at Bougnies, covering the Haig line).

The 6th Infantry Brigade of 2nd Division withdrew through this rear-guard following the Givry to Bavai Road. The early abandonment of Hill 93, already described, and of Harmignies soon after that, made the 3rd Division adjust rapidly, when they became aware of it, at 5.30 a.m. (The 2nd Division withdrawal did not

17   TNA WO 95/1274: 3rd Infantry Brigade, 24 August 1914.
18   RAM MD/425: Schreiber, 24 August 1914.
19   IWM 15384: Lt Le Breton. 24 August 1914.
20   TNA WO 95/1249: XXXIX Brigade RFA, 24 August 1914.

include the 5th Infantry Brigade – less one battalion which had remained at Harveng – situated at Paturages on the II Corps defence line.)

As rear-guard, the two batteries of the 41st Brigade were in position a mile west of Harmignies, (having remained harnessed up all night), and they came into action at 4 a.m. to cover the first line of the retirement.[21] The 36th Brigade were ordered to just north of Quevy to hold the second line of withdrawal on the day. They came into action, but did not fire, falling back with some elements of the 5th Infantry Brigade who had stayed to support them, when the 41st Brigade fell back to them after midday.[22] The good sense of these dispositions is obvious from a look at the map. There were three main routes south to Bavai, down which the 2nd and 3rd Divisions would have to retreat. The first position covered the eastern of these roads, the second the western two.

From just west of Harmignies, the 2nd Division batteries were in a position to bombard any enemy that might threaten from the east, and by 6 a.m., General Horne had liaised with the 3rd Division to ensure continuity of artillery cover at the junction between the two Corps.[23] This is arguably the first instance of effective liaison between the two corps in the battle.

General Horne held the forward infantry just behind the Harmignies to Givry road, until just short of midday, waiting for the road south of Mons through Ciply towards Quevy to become clear of retreating 3rd Division troops. His forward guns and infantry line then retired west to a line about two miles behind this, between Genly and Quevy, covering the Ciply to Bavai road. His cavalry patrolled to the north and east.

The 5th Cavalry Brigade covered an arc from Vellereille-le-Sec round through Harmignies to Ciply. Their 'positions were heavily shelled, partly by our own artillery,'[24] this last being an occupational hazard of all forward troops in the battles of that era. Quite possibly, it was the 1st Division, already mentioned, but J Battery RHA covering the cavalry patrolling to the north, could also have been the culprit:

> The battery came into action east of Bougnies near the Mons Maubeuge road in dispersed sections, under cover, the Cavalry holding the line in front. The battery came under heavy shell fire. After covering the retirement of the Infantry and Cavalry, the battery was withdrawn.[25]

Horne could not but be aware of the positions of the 3rd Division infantry as the dense columns retired down these roads, but he needed a cool head, as he positioned his left

---

21　TNA WO 95/1326: XLI Brigade RFA, 24 August 1914.
22　TNA WO 95/1325: XXXVI Brigade RFA, 24 August 1914.
23　TNA WO 95/630/1: II Corps Staff, 24 August 1914.
24　TNA WO 95/1138: 5th Cavalry Brigade, 24 August 1914.
25　TNA WO 95/1135: J Battery RHA, 24 August 1914.

flank so that the right flank of their rear-guard could link up with his left. He then coordinated his withdrawal with that of the 3rd Division. Their rear-guard, provided by the 9th Infantry Brigade, had to open to allow some of the 7th and most of the 8th Brigades to fall back through them. Once those on the right had withdrawn, and the road was clear, the combined rear-guard fell back west to repeat the process with the left of the 3rd Division front line which was also in full retreat.

Of the batteries of the 41st brigade RFA, which covered the retreat, the 17th fired 77 rounds from west of Harmignies at an enemy infantry column, forcing it to take refuge in a roadside ditch. This battery remained in position until midday, when it retired to just north of Quevy, (relieving the 36th Brigade and allowing them to retire), to cover the road at Givry behind the still retreating 4th (Guards) Brigade. In this second position, German howitzers tried to bombard them, but they were just out of range and the shells fell short.[26] The effective fire of this battery in defence, is what the German generals would have been hoping for from their own advancing artillery. It can only be guessed as to how the British retreat would have fared in the face of lethal fire from the German light artillery.

The 16th Battery came into action on a similar line of withdrawal but had no targets. The damaged 9th Battery retreated on the more southerly road, which was covered by the 1st Division rear-guard and later by J Battery after it had left Bougnies 'and moved to Havay, where the battery came into action and fired on the enemy near Givry after 2 p.m. (Fired up the road at some dark objects thought to be German guns, found to be abandoned infantry cookers. Also engaged by a field battery.)'[27] Another mistake engagingly admitted by a cavalry unit; there was a good culture in General Allenby's command, but they had prematurely revealed their positions.

It all sounds brilliantly orchestrated and it was. But it was not as difficult as it sounds. It was almost a field exercise. All the roads were full of retiring troops, and it was a matter of the I Corps rear-guard staying east of those roads until the last of the retreating troops had moved south. Colin Hutchison, a 3rd Division artillery subaltern, describes the scene. 'We arrived at last at the main road, only to see a never-ending column, all sorts of units mixed up, marching two columns deep.'[28]

It was a well-coordinated and successful withdrawal. Once again, the I Corps staff summary is very misleading. It implies that the rear-guard was never under any threat, and II Corps is not even mentioned. General Horne was apparently able to report it complete at 11.10 a.m., when he was in the middle of the most dangerous part of the coordinated withdrawal. It severely deprecates his achievement.[29] As night fell, the 41st Brigade RFA, and indeed the whole rear-guard force retired west of Feignies to bivouac.

26   TNA WO 95/1326: XLI Brigade RFA, 24 August 1914.
27   TNA WO 95/1135: J Battery RHA, 24 August 1914.
28   Hutchison, *The Young Gunner*, p.11.
29   TNA WO 95/588/4: I Corps staff, 24 August 1914.

4.5 II Corps Prepares for Withdrawal
(Maps 13 & 14)

Major General Hubert Hamilton.

Withdrawal was an altogether harder task for II Corps. As already described, General Smith-Dorrien did not receive his orders to withdraw till 4 a.m. He immediately ordered the roads south to be cleared of parked wagons, but it was not till 6 a.m. that his staff issued orders to the divisions, based on the plans which it will be remembered had been worked up that morning. His II Corps was not prepared for an immediate withdrawal. They were in the process of consolidating his second position with every intention of holding it. Only minutes after receiving the orders to retire, he received the news of the withdrawal of the 2nd Division of I Corps, which started at 4.45 a.m., leaving his right flank vulnerable. General Hamilton of the 3rd Division, and Brigadier General Doran of the 8th Infantry Brigade adjusted positions to cover the gaps left by the early abandonment of Hill 93 at 1.30 a.m., and then by the unexpected retirement of the 2nd Division at Harmignies from 7 a.m.[30] (There may later have been some robust questioning of I Corps as to what occurred on this flank. Early liaison there was not.) The 8th Infantry started their retirement at 8 a.m., falling back to south of Genly, digging in there at 10.30 a.m.

At 7 a.m., General Smith-Dorrien's main concern was for his right flank, but he sent a message, at 7.15 a.m. to General Fergusson of the 5th Division telling him that the 3rd Division would soon have to fall back as far as his headquarters at Sars-la-Bruyère, and instructing them to conform to 3rd Division movements, meaning they should fall back simultaneously when the order was given. This was a council of perfection, and for various reasons proved impossible to obey.

It was no easy matter to move 35,000 men and all their accoutrements down the four or five roads that were available to them, and the transport had to go first. They started to move as they received their orders, but there was no way his front-line infantry could begin to fall back for many hours. The roads were completely full. They had to hold the enemy for the time being. At dawn on the 24th, the corps defence line was fully manned with the guns of both the 3rd and 5th Divisions well dug in, in prepared positions.

However, by dawn the guns of the German IV Corps had established positions and started bombarding the left of the British line. By 5.15 a.m., the guns were firing

---

30 TNA WO 95/1416: 8th Infantry Brigade, 24 August 1914.

along the whole length of the German line, signalling the probability of further infantry attacks. But along the canal as far east as Jamappes, the German artillery was heavily bombarding positions which had already been abandoned: 'The German guns opened a bombardment before dawn, and continued it steadily for four hours, though to little purpose.'[31]

All of the villages of the mining strip south of the canal came in for attention. German infantry cautiously moved forward through this difficult terrain, meeting no resistance. The British infantry line, behind which their guns were entrenched, was back on the railway line from Mons to Dour. It was some time before the German infantry was far enough forward to be in attack positions.

The 28th Brigade RFA formed the left group of the forward 5th Division artillery and had entrenched itself just south of Dour the afternoon before. It had a quiet time till well after dawn. But the closer to Mons, the more prepared were the German infantry for further attacks. Fresh infantry had crossed the bridges of Jamappes and St Ghislain in some strength and were lining up in readiness. Happily, for the 3rd Division, the German forces occupying the outskirts of Mons and the ground further east, were not in a position to renew their attacks in the early hours of the morning. An attack here was not so important in furtherance of German plans, though it is also true that IX Corps had suffered such that it needed time before it could be marshalled for a further advance.

4.6 First German Infantry Advance (Maps 13, 14 & 15)

The first German infantry attack, soon after dawn, fell on the forward battalions on the left flank of the 3rd Division. The line at Frameries was held by the 1st Lincolnshire Regiment, of the 9th Infantry Brigade with the 2nd South Lancashire Regiment, of the 7th Infantry Brigade on their right, at Ciply, just south of Mons. (The 8th Brigade had been in the front line in the salient, but had fallen back through the second positions, manned by the 7th Brigade, south of Mons.)

At Frameries, the 1st Lincolnshire Regiment, entrenched in an orchard, had to endure 'very heavy artillery fire causing many casualties' defending the northern edge of the village.[32] This is only the third time during the battle that a battalion recorded the effectiveness of German artillery fire. Again, it was howitzers. A German account records the bombardment:

> A continuous stream of gun and howitzer shells thundered out, hurtling over our heads and bursting in smoke and dust on the edge of the village. No human being could possibly live there. At 7 a.m., six companies of the regiment advanced to

---

31 Edmonds, *Military Operations France and Belgium 1914*, Vol. I, p.101.
32 TNA WO 95/1425: 9 Infantry Brigade, 24 August 1914.

the attack. If we thought that the English had been shelled enough to be storm-ripe we were greatly mistaken. They met us with well-aimed fire.[33]

The same source states that the attack was pressed by a whole division across an open field. It was not only accurate rifle fire from entrenched positions which kept the Germans at bay. The Lincolns had considerable help from the 109th Battery of the 23rd Brigade RFA, which was covering this sector. Most of the brigade guns were aimed in the wrong direction, expecting attacks from Mons and the east. Even the guns of the 109th Battery were not initially well placed to counter this attack from due north.

The battery had gone forward to Frameries before dawn (3.45 a.m.) and taken up their forward position on the eastern edge of the orchard occupied by the Lincolnshire Regiment, but facing west. 'Enemy invisible', and they did not fire. They endured the heavy German field artillery fire for nearly four hours, having two horses killed and six wounded. At 7.30 a.m., two guns of the centre section turned and moved to face north, as it became clear from which direction the infantry attack was developing. From a covered position, they fired, with observation from a nearby house, 'with effect' and 'continuously against the German supports and a battery'. Despite being heavily shelled for the next two hours, they sustained no casualties except a subaltern reconnoitring forward, who was wounded, and another 3 horses killed.[34] They were lucky not to be targeted by the enemy howitzers. But the German bombardment had set a factory on fire on the edge of the village, and the resultant smoke obscured visibility.

The 107th, to their right, also took up covered positions at 3.30 a.m., behind the 2nd South Lancashire Regiment at Ciply, but facing east. The enemy artillery fire, and the subsequent infantry attack, came mainly from the north-west, as outlined in the somewhat breathless account in the battery diary:

> Attack came from spoil banks north of Frameries. Battery was swung round to the left and observation station moved forward. Fired a lot at advancing German infantry north of the spoil banks. Ordered to retire. Limbered up under heavy musketry fire. 2nd Lieutenant Gray wounded, and 5 NCOs and men – 11 horses killed. Left on the position: one wagon and limber overturned with broken pole, and one wagon body with broken eye. Retired to position north of Noirchain and fired a few shells at infantry advancing on to our late position.[35]

The brigade diary is a little more measured. The 107th moved left behind the lines of the 2nd South Lancashire Regiment, at about 4.30 a.m. with 'German infantry and

---

33 Major-General C.R. Simpson (ed.), *The History of The Lincolnshire Regiment, 1914-1918* (London, The Medici Society, Ltd, 1931) p.13.
34 TNA WO 95/1399: XXIII Brigade RFA, 24 August 1914.
35 Ibid., 107th Batt, 24 August 1914.

guns then massing against them'.³⁶ This regiment and its supporting artillery held an attack by two German battalions. But, at 8.45 a.m., the Lincolnshire Regiment, having lost 105 casualties, killed or wounded, with 29 missing, fell back from their orchard. Many of their wounded were left on the battlefield, as they retired hurriedly, but in relatively good order.³⁷

This retirement enabled the Germans to occupy the northern outskirts of Frameries, where they were able to site a machine gun, firing east, to enfilade the South Lancashire Regiment, who had not retired simultaneously with the Lincolns' and 'lost heavily' as a consequence, on their left (western) flank. It was not till 9.30 that their trenches were completely evacuated; and it was 9.45, before the 107th Battery behind them was ordered to retire.

The 108th was on the right of their brigade position, facing the outskirts east of Mons, and covering the 3rd Worcestershire Regiment, again of the 7th Infantry Brigade. No attack developed from there in the early morning.

It will be recalled that the 3rd Worcestershire Regiment 'owing to a misunderstanding' had dug lines closer to Mons than intended, forming a small salient. So, when an infantry attack, supported by artillery, developed from Mons just as they started to retire, it was a problem. They responded with accurate rifle fire at 500 yards. By that time, the main body of the 108th Battery had withdrawn. But one section was still covering them. It 'fired on advancing infantry for about half an hour'. The battery lost one man wounded by rifle-fire, and two horses killed, presumably at this stage of their battle.³⁸ The Worcester's, by now the most forward of the British infantry, had open ground to their rear, swept by enemy artillery. Their final 'company had to withdraw by single sections or half platoons to dodge the shell-bursts', losing 50 casualties.³⁹ This again sounds like howitzer fire.

The withdrawal of most of the artillery was coordinated with the complete evacuation of both forward infantry brigades from their entrenched lines. The 8th Infantry Brigade, 3rd Division, aligned towards Harmignies, had already retired without incident, their attached 40th Brigade RFA withdrawing at 11 a.m., having had 'no target'. All the British batteries had been placed behind the infantry, in covered positions, well dug in, with their horses protected. By the time a forward battery was ready to move, another battery, or section of a battery, was covering that move from further back. It was all very professional. A German infantryman observed in his diary that day: 'English beaten at Frameries. We had very heavy losses.'⁴⁰

36 Ibid., 24 August 1914.
37 TNA WO 95/1429: 1st Lincolnshire Regiment, 24 August 1914.
38 TNA WO 95/1399: XXIII Brigade RFA, 24 August 1914.
39 The Worcestershire Regiment <http://www.worcestershireregiment.com/bat_2_1914.php> (Accessed October 2017).
40 TNA WO 95/629: II Corps Intelligence, 24 August 1914, p.72.

4.7 Rear-guard of 3rd Division (Map 14)

The 9th Infantry Brigade had been nominated to provide the rear-guard to the 3rd Division, and this is why batteries of the 23rd Brigade RFA were covering the retreat of half the 7th Infantry Brigade. Flexibility was key. The 42nd Brigade RFA, which was initially covering the 7th Infantry, came under the command of Brigadier General McCracken, of the 9th Infantry, and was ordered back to a position just north of Bougnies, from where, at 10.30 a.m., they fired over his forces at a German column of infantry and guns, who were trying to follow up on the British retirement. The 42nd only remained in this position until the guns of the 23rd Brigade RFA could get back to perform this role, subsequently re-joining their 7th Infantry Brigade, and making their way south with them. The 3rd Division infantry was disengaging successfully, thanks to the smooth and rapid movements of the guns which covered them. On the retirement of the infantry, the 5th Cavalry Brigade moved in front of them at Ciply to delay the enemy advance, themselves covered by J Battery, also at Bougnies.

Bougnies was behind the left flank of the 2nd Division rear-guard. The 4th (Guards) Brigade of the 2nd Division had taken up a position on a front of three miles facing north-east, just behind Harmignies. By 10.30 a.m., the 9th Brigade of the 3rd Division had dropped back to link up, facing about, with its right flank on the Guards left. The 7th and 8th Brigades fell back through the 9th Brigade to a mile south east of Sars-la-Bruyère, where some elements halted and faced about. The three 2nd Division battalions of the 5th Infantry Brigade, who had been at Paturages since 2.30 a.m., received orders to retire simultaneously with the 3rd Division and did so. Only their forward battalion was under fire that morning, sustaining five casualties. They arrived back to just in front of Sars-la Bruyère by about 11 a.m., as did the 8th Brigade after them on the same roads.

Brigadier General Horne, II Corps artillery commander, commanded the right of the line on which the 3rd Division organised their retreat. It was the only truly cooperative manoeuvre between I and II Corps of the whole campaign. None of the unit diaries provide much detail, precisely because it was so smooth; sporadic, but effective artillery fire, and the cavalry, preventing any precipitate German advance over the dead ground between the two forces.

Three battalions lost significant casualties during the retirement. The 3rd Worcestershire, 7th Brigade, and the 1st Lincolnshire, 9th Brigade, to enemy howitzers and the South Lancashire, 7th Brigade, to machine gun enfilade. The latter lost 35 killed, 75 wounded and 348 missing (though it is likely that many of these found their way back to their unit). Given the weight of the attacks and the number of German batteries targeting the withdrawal, the British had got off very lightly.

Of the remainder of 3rd Division artillery, the Divisional Ammunition Column had long gone, starting at 8 a.m. For no obvious reason, the 30th (howitzer) brigade did not withdraw with the rest, of which more anon.

4.8 Second German Infantry Advance (Map 13)

The second major push by German infantry that morning fell on the right of the 5th Division. Both infantry and artillery had crossed the canal in force at St Ghislain, while their artillery heavily bombarded the deserted mine works in front of them, as previously described. These troops made their way through the coal-mining strip to emerge south and a few hundred yards east of the bridge at St Ghislain. From there they attempted to advance on Wasmes against the 13th Infantry Brigade, which was supported by Brigadier General Headlam's right artillery group.

The 13th Infantry Brigade had not fallen back till midnight to the line dug by the Bedford and Dorset Regiments of the reserve 15th Infantry, who had themselves already moved towards Paturages as a reserve on the right flank. And in the dark, some Battalions fell back beyond the partially prepared lines, closer to the railway; 'obviously too far south', as the 15th Brigade war diary observed.

The 27th Brigade RFA battery captains had tried to forecast the 'second position' line the infantry would take up, 'depending entirely on their own judgement' to select positions the previous day. They did not always get it right. One gun of the 121st battery, which covered the centre of the 'right artillery group', found itself actually in front of the infantry line:

> The gun which had been placed in the pit engaged hostile infantry and machine guns on the neighbouring pit heaps commencing at 3.30 a.m. on the 24th inst., the range being about 750 yards. At about 6 a.m., a German battery opened fire on the infantry trenches and gun pit at a range of about 1000 yards, and a German machine gun opened fire at a range of about 200 yards. The infantry occupying the trenches were relieved at about 7 a.m., but owing to the intensity of the fire, the relieving troops were unable to reach the trenches on either side of the gun pit and in consequence the gun and its detachment were now entirely isolated. As the enemy were still pressing, the breech block of the gun was taken out and sent to the rear, and Lieutenant Chapman and his detachment set to work to manhandle the gun back. This was done under a concentrated artillery and machine gun fire, the gun being finally limbered up behind a house which had already been frequently hit by shells. The limber of the gun was brought up entirely on the initiative of Driver Birkett. From this cottage where the gun was limbered up, to the nearest cover there was a space of 200 yards across which the gun was successfully taken, though the area was being shelled and swept by machine gun fire.[41]

Once again, the ineffectiveness of German artillery fire in preventing the British retreat is remarkable. A German battery engaged one British gun at 1000 yards and failed to prevent its withdrawal. 'About 10' casualties were sustained by the two-gun

---

41 TNA WO 95/1529: XXVII Brigade RFA, 24 August 1914.

section. Once under cover of buildings, this section met up with the Lieutenant McLeod of the 80th Battery, of which more anon. Young Lieutenant Chapman was still in a state of euphoria:

> I found halted there a section of guns under Lieut. Chapman of the 27th Brigade. He told me that he had been in action that morning in the front-line trenches and had taken on the Germans at 70 [sic, probably 700] yards range as they topped a small bank in front of his guns. He had wrought tremendous execution in their dense masses, legs, arms and heads flying in all directions. They had finally turned machine guns onto him and he had got out with a few casualties.[42]

The remainder of the 27th Brigade guns in this right group were also having 'a hot time … under heavy fire.'[43] The remaining four guns of the 120th Battery, who had been up at the canal, had fallen back with the infantry to cover the left of the 13th Infantry line:

> [The battery was] rather behind the infantry trenches … The country was flat, and no covered positions were available without leaving dead ground in front of the infantry . About noon, scattered German infantry appeared from the north, and our guns were heavily shelled by field guns and howitzers, without however suffering many casualties. The fire of our guns kept back the enemy infantry, and the enemy's guns kept under cover of the pit heaps.[44]

Certainly, the 2nd King's Own, Yorkshire Light Infantry (KOYLI), on this left flank of the 13th infantry Brigade positions, appreciated their help. 'The divisional artillery … were of the utmost assistance during the day.' Or as the brigade diary put it, 'the guns … prevented the enemy from getting within effective range of the positions.'[45] The left flank of the 5th Division had by this time already retired, and General Headlam had ordered the 80th Battery of his reserve 15th Brigade from their positions west of Dour to come under the orders of the 27th Brigade defending this sector; hence the reference to the 'divisional artillery'. Lieutenant McLeod of this battery takes up the story:

> [We had rendezvoused at] Dour church, and while there a messenger arrived with orders for us to come under the orders of the 27th Brigade RFA. Evidently reinforcements were needed further east. [We moved] …about 2 miles [initially to] about 300 yards south of the railway embankment at Wasmes …which was the front line [and then a mile south to come into action.] The KOYLI's were

---

42 RAM MD/1150: McLeod journal, 24 August 1914.
43 TNA WO 95/1529: XXVII Brigade RFA, 24 August 1914.
44 TNA WO 95/1529: 120th Battery, XXVII Brigade RFA, 24 August 1914.
45 TNA WO 95/1548: 13th Infantry Brigade, 24 August 1914.

holding a slag heap about 2000 yards to the north of us. Nearer was another slag heap …on which was one of our machine guns. They were obviously in the front line and hotly engaged, so we opened fire beyond them at a range of about 2,400 yards. One of our howitzer batteries was also assisting the KOYLI by dropping shells beyond the slag heap. Soon after this the KOYLIs began retiring by small detachments. … They said … that we had done great execution among the Germans, and if it had not been for us they would not have got away.[46]

The 37th Howitzer Battery was also in this right group 'entrenched in gun pits', south of the village of Wasmes. They were behind the other guns, with their observer on the top floor of a house. Not only German howitzer fire was effective. They 'engaged enemy's infantry with great success. The Dorset's sent a message to say that the fire was effective, and the enemy could make no way against it.' They were targeted by enemy batteries – 'casualties were mainly in the firing line, 7 horses and 3 men wounded.'[47] It is interesting to note that they kept horses up in the firing line, not a practice ever recorded later in the war. The horses and limbers were usually at least a few yards back under cover. The German infantry sustained heavy losses, attacking at least three times against the 1st Dorsetshire Regiment despite this defensive artillery fire.

The Germans were employing howitzers against the 1st Bedfordshire Regiment on the railway. A forward company was 'holding houses and bridges along railway line' and 'they were eventually driven back slowly as houses were knocked down by shells'.[48] The hard fighting of both these battalions, as rear-guard to the division, and being targeted by howitzers, was reflected in their casualties, the Bedford's losing 68 killed, wounded or missing, the Dorset's 134.

The retirement of the 5th Division was not an easy exercise. The 3rd Division and the reserve brigade of the 2nd Division had retired on the road south from Frameries by a few minutes after 9.30, and the Germans had advanced to occupy Frameries, just south-west of Mons, thus blocking 5th Division access to this road. They had to withdraw almost due west, to pick up the next road south, and this was towards Dour, which was already being occupied from the west. Worse still, just as the left flank of the 3rd Division forward battalion had been enfiladed by the capture of Frameries, so the right flank of the forward battalion of the 5th Division's 13th Infantry Brigade, the 2nd Duke of Wellingtons, West Riding Regiment, was exposed. By 10 a.m., the Germans had machine guns in place at Frameries, and they too suffered significant losses before they were able to pull back their flank to join up with the Bedfordshire Regiment to their southeast.[49] It and the Dorsetshire Regiment, 15th Infantry Brigade reserve, were back, and to the east of the right flank of the 13th Infantry, the Dorsets

---

46 RAM MD/1150: McLeod journal, 24 August 1914.
47 TNA WO95/1527: VIII Brigade RFA, 24 August 1914.
48 TNA WO 95/1570/1: 1st Bedfordshire Regiment, 24 August 1914.
49 TNA WO 95/1548: 13th Infantry Brigade, 24 August 1914.

having already moved further back to cover Paturages, following the withdrawal of the 5th Infantry Brigade I Corps contingent. But the right of the Bedford's was now 'somewhat en l'air' as the Infantry Brigade diary rather delightfully puts it and would also be laid open by any further enemy advance.

The withdrawal of these units started at about noon, and it did not go smoothly. The right of the 13th Infantry, with the Bedford and Dorset Regiments as rear-guard facing east, started to fall back west in order to pick up the main roads south. But then, a command pathway problem involving the Yorkshire Light Infantry, on the left of their line, caused a long delay. The 27th Brigade RFA were covering them as previously described:

> About 2.30 p.m. … orders to retire first reached the officer commanding 27 Brigade from the Brigade Major 14th Infantry, but having been detailed to the 13th Infantry, he refused to …[50] retire his guns, the OC Manchester Regt refused to retire until the guns had gone, as did the OC Yorkshire Light Inf of the 13th Brigade on the right of the guns. About 3 p.m., the OC Yorkshire Light Inf received a written order to retire, and this order also contained orders for the RFA to retire.[51]

This is from the artillery records. The 14th Infantry diary says that the colonel of the 2nd Manchester's failed to receive his orders.[52] But it is clear that he did, and that he refused to obey his order to retire until the artillery did. Perhaps, on this occasion, the artillery colonel should not have followed the strict rule of delegated command, but he was allowed to be correct, and control was maintained – just:

> The 120th Battery retired first and then the leading section of the 121st Battery in the infantry trench, and then the rear section. The men of the Manchester's assisted to run the guns back from the trenches, and the whole battalion waited until the guns were back until they retired themselves. The Yorkshire's also waited for the guns. The limbering of the guns and subsequent withdrawal was carried out under heavy shellfire, but only four casualties occurred in the 121st Battery, two men being killed and two wounded by one shell.[53]

These two infantry battalions were the last to disengage facing north, but necessarily, the Bedfordshire and Dorsetshire Regiments of the 15th Infantry, making up the eastern rear-guard, had to hold, and were only 'withdrawn at the very last moment'.

Albert George of 120th Battery described the withdrawal of his battery from their position in front of the railway. 'The retirement started at 4pm … We had to pass over

---

50   TNA WO 95/1529: XXVII Brigade RFA, 24 August 1914.
51   TNA WO 95/1521: 5th Division Artillery, 24 August 1914.
52   TNA WO 95/1560: 14th Infantry Brigade, 24 August 1914.
53   TNA WO 95/1529: 120 Battery, XXVII Brigade RFA, 24 August 1914.

a railway crossing and up half a mile of road, which the Huns were shelling furiously, but we arrived under cover safe.'[54] Another battery was retiring at the same time. 'One shell pitched under one of [the] ammunition wagons, luckily without exploding the ammunition, and knocked off and wounded the gunners on the wagon and hit all the horses, but none were killed.'[55]

The 13th and 14th Infantry Brigades, with their artillery, were retiring by successive battalions from the left and right. The centre fell back still 'under very heavy fire'. Yet again, this fire did not significantly impede the retreat. By mid-afternoon the majority had made their way back to a line facing north at Blaugies, four miles south east of Dour.

4.9 Third German Infantry Advance

Brigadier General Headlam, that morning, had his reserve 25th Brigade RFA, in position just west of Dour, facing north and north-west. The advance of the German IV Corps to the west, was impeded only by the Cavalry Division. Lieutenant McLeod of the 80th Battery takes up the story:

> Rifle fire opened up on our left, and a trooper galloped up to me in the left section to say that the Germans were only a few hundred yards from us and that the cavalry would hold the farm 100 yards to our left to cover our withdrawal. Our rendezvous was Dour church, and while there a messenger arrived with orders for us to come under the orders of the 27th Brigade RFA.[56]

As previously described, this battery moved to just south of Wasmes, to reinforce the (eastern) right artillery group. The other two batteries of the brigade fell back in the first stage of the divisional retreat. The German infantry to the north-west threatening the western edge of Dour had supporting artillery. The 61st (Howitzer) Battery 'silenced [obliterated is probably a better word] a section of the enemy's guns', early that morning, and then retired south west with its sister 65th Battery to cover the left flank rear-guard.[57]

The 14th Infantry Brigade was first ordered to retire at 10.45, starting from the right. The refusal of the 2nd Manchester Regiment (on the far right) to move until the guns in their sector were safe delayed the whole operation, and the two battalions to their left moved before them. First, four guns of each supporting battery were sent back to take up positions to cover the retreat, leaving two guns to retire simultaneously

---

54 IWM 18429: Col. George papers, 24 August 1914.
55 RAM MD/1150: McLeod, Journal, 24 August 1914.
56 Ibid.
57 TNA, WO 95/1527: VIII Brigade RFA, 24 August 1914.

with the infantry. The 1st East Surrey Regiment formed the brigade rear-guard a mile south-east of Dour, and as the full brigade reached them, they all fell back to Blaugies to form the rear-guard to the 5th Division.[58]

Initially, on this front, the 28th Brigade RFA had little to do. 'Brigade is ready to open fire at dawn. Heavy firing. Brigade does not fire much.'[59] It took some time for the German infantry to make their way over the canal and other waterways and coordinate an attack, and the mere threat of the well sited British guns behind their embankment, with observation from it, was enough to prevent an early advance. Later however, and after the retirement had started, German forces started to arrive in strength near at hand. The 123rd Battery, 28th Brigade RFA, on the left of the 14th Infantry was in position:

> About midday, fire was opened on German infantry in close columns, succeeded by dense lines, which were first observed about 1000 yards away. Orders to retire reached the battery, so only some 60 rounds were fired at the infantry. The fire was believed to be very effective.[60]

They had to retire quickly because they were required to take up a rear-guard position, about 4000 yards south of Dour to cover over the heads of the infantry as they fell back. The German infantry to the north of Dour, unsurprisingly after this bombardment, did not follow up closely. The battery did not fire in its rear-guard position.

The enemy vanguard, consisting of six battalions, was never far behind. It was not an easy exercise, but as with all the other divisions, continuity of artillery cover was maintained at every stage of the retreat. The main body of the 5th Division reached the line west of Bavai at about 6 p.m.

4.10 Left Wing of the BEF

The main body of the 2nd Cavalry Brigade, which formed the rear-guard of General Allenby's Cavalry Division, was over 3 miles south-west of Dour by 11 a.m., though they had by then regained touch with the left flank

Major General Sir Edmund Allenby.

---

58 TNA WO 95/1560: 14th Infantry Brigade, 24 August 1914.
59 TNA WO 95/1532: XXVIII Brigade RFA, 24 August 1914.
60 TNA WO 95/1532: 123rd Batt, XXVIII Brigade RFA, 24 August 1914.

of the 5th Division.[61] The retirement of the 19th Infantry Brigade has already been described. The Royal Horse Artillery, attached to the cavalry, were not involved in this early phase of the rear-guard action. The VII Brigade RHA had arrived at Quievrain on the 23rd and fell back on the 24th, without firing a shot in the campaign.[62] Both batteries of III Brigade RHA had fired 'a few rounds' on patrol on the 22nd, out to the east of II Corps, having '2 horses cut', when counter-shelled by the enemy. On the 23rd they too had moved to Quievrain, remaining in billets for the 23rd.[63]

The right of the German IV Corps was advancing due south into the gap north of Elouges. According to the Official History:

> Hardly had the 13th and 14th Brigades begun their retreat, when Sir Charles Fergusson became aware that the withdrawal of the cavalry and the 19th Brigade had been premature, and that his left flank was seriously threatened by German forces of considerable strength.[64]

General Ferguson immediately sent his infantry reserve at Dour, the 1st Cheshire and 1st Norfolk Regiments of 15th Infantry Brigade, together with the 119th Battery RFA, one mile west to Elouges. The 2nd Cavalry Brigade, with supporting horse artillery, also advanced to Elouges. At 2 p.m., this force met up with the forward infantry of IV Corps. This was the Battle of Elouges, which started at about 2 p.m. It was the first of the retreat, and beyond the remit of this volume.

4.11 The Retirement of the 3rd Division Howitzers (Map 15)

Only one battery, the 130th, of the 30th (Howitzer) Brigade, 3rd Division, had arrived on the battlefield on the 23rd and they had taken up a position in front of Ciply, three miles south of Mons. They pulled back to billet at night-fall, but went back to this position at dawn to cover the retreating infantry. Lieutenant Colin Hutchison witnessed the withdrawal of the 7th Infantry Brigade from this rear-guard position:

> The next morning, we were ordered in to our position of the night before, and it was not long before columns of infantry, ambulances and transport began streaming past us. We eventually got the order to retire to a position on the left of the 3rd Division 60 pounders. … We passed through the village of Ciply and prepared for action in the middle of a turnip field.[65]

---

61 TNA WO 95/1110: 2nd Cavalry Brigade, 24 August 1914.
62 TNA WO 95/1103: VII Brigade RHA, 24 August 1914.
63 TNA WO 95/1123: III Brigade RHA, 24 August 1914.
64 Edmonds, *Military Operations France and Belgium 1914*, Vol. I, p.106.
65 Hutchison, *The Young Gunner*, p.10.

They fell back just before 9 a.m. to join the 129th Battery of the brigade which had just marched in, via Bavai, from Valenciennes rail station. The two howitzer batteries stayed in this forward position long after the rest of the 3rd Division had fallen back, presumably to provide a visible and close deterrent to the enemy infantry advance, though it is quite possible that they were just forgotten. (The 128th Battery, arriving slightly later, did fall back with the rest of the division):[66]

> We waited for about 2½ hours. Infantry went past us, the heavy battery retired, but 129th Battery and ourselves stuck on. Presently a cavalry patrol came past and asked what the deuce we were doing. All our infantry had gone past, and as far as they knew the Germans were not very far behind. However, the colonel was perfectly happy, so we remained another half hour.
>
> We then got a report from the wagon line that a German battery could be seen coming into action about 3000 yards from us. We got the order to 'prepare to advance'[sic]. The horses came up and we had just hooked in when over came four ranging rounds from the German battery. We got the order 'Column of sections, from the centre, dismount the gunners! Walk, march'! We had about ½ a mile of absolutely open ground to cover to reach the road and proceeded to do it at the walk. The next four rounds from the German battery (7.7 cm) got our line and was also pretty fair for range. We continued to walk out of action and did so under their fire, getting about 20 rounds in all into us. Two men were hit, one poor devil had to be left behind … We passed a line of infantry acting as rear guard. They were very surprised to see us, as they thought they were a long way the last. We arrived at last at the main road, only to see a never-ending column, all sorts of units mixed up, marching two columns deep.[67]

They were almost the last troops from the right wing of the army to leave the Mons battlefield, and they walked away under heavy fire. Yet again, not a horse or a man was killed. It illustrates, in one cameo moment, how the British escaped serious harm, if not annihilation at Mons.

66 TNA WO 95/1399 XXX Brigade RFA, 24 August 1914.
67 Hutchison, *The Young Gunner*, p.10, 11.

5

Consequences of Mons

5.1 Aftermath

The narrative in this volume differs materially from previous histories of the Battle of Mons. This is because most previous accounts depend heavily on the Official History, compiled by Brigadier General Edmonds in 1922. He took on the huge task of writing a military history of the War, partly to acknowledge those who had given all. He consulted widely with those still alive who 'remembered' the campaign, and produced a bland and non-judgemental account, which acknowledged success, and played down failure. He cannot be blamed for his many errors; but perhaps historians of later generations should have been less prepared to accept some of his assertions as fact. His inaccurate account has been widely quoted as an authoritative reference.

Since only the first four campaigning days by the BEF in a very long war are under consideration, one has to ask if this altered narrative is significant. It was certainly important to those who fought and died. And how the generals worked together, and what they learnt of each other in these first few days, had a disproportionate impact on future tactics and relationships. Field Marshal French, General Smith-Dorrien and General Haig were put to the test. How they performed is important. Like every other battle in France and Flanders over the next four years, Mons was an artillery battle. Their understanding of this fact, or lack of it, is supremely relevant.

5.2 Artillery Tactics at Mons

As has been emphasised throughout, the artillery was regarded as support to the infantry and cavalry divisions and was commanded and tactically deployed at that level. Neither French and GHQ, nor the diaries of either corps, refer at any time to the artillery as an entity. Though the senior generals were not aware of the tactical deployment of their own guns, they should have ensured their presence.

The elementary error of advancing without guns on 21 August was a GHQ aberration. It should never have happened. There is little doubt that General Grierson would have insisted that the advance be delayed by 24 hours in view of the shortage of guns and ammunition in his corps. If General Haig had taken this stance, he would have saved himself a lot of grief; and he probably should have done.

But once the guns did arrive, artillery positions were picked, at divisional level, with care and purpose. (No battery commander would set up for action without ascertaining his task. Suitable positions could not be selected without this knowledge.) The positions of the I Corps guns was certainly influenced by advice from Brigadier General Horne, CRA at Corps, but it was the divisional commanders who placed them. There is no evidence that General Horne consulted with General Haig and his staff. He seems to have been almost autonomous in his actions, when advising the divisions.

There are very few examples of batteries choosing open positions. Almost invariably, they selected 'covered' positions, meaning 'behind a crest' (which might be a railway embankment or slag heap), or 'on a reverse slope' saying the same thing. Forward observers, usually the commanding officer, selected an observation point and communicated by telephone, directing the fire of their battery. Several batteries enjoyed a double crest, their guns being behind the second. The German guns bombarded over the first crest, their fire then falling well short. Self-protection was the rule, not the exception.

The German light artillery, in contrast, at least initially, came into action in the open, often within range of rifle or machine guns, occasionally even of counter-batteries. It was a costly tactic, and their artillery (and infantry) units became much more circumspect during the course of the day. They learnt a sharp lesson.

The British never took up an offensive stance in this battle. The French in contrast had. It is fascinating to read what General Joffre, Commander in Chief of the French Armies, had to say after watching the general failure of his forces to stop the German advance on the 22nd August 1914. He issued the following instruction that day:

> It has been noticed in the information collected with regard to the actions which have so far taken place that attacks have been carried out, without close cooperation between infantry and artillery. Every combined operation includes a series of detailed actions aiming at the capture of the point d'appui.
>
> Each time it is necessary to capture a point d'appui, the attack must be prepared with artillery. The infantry must be held back, and not launched to the assault until the distance to be covered is so short that it is certain that the objective will be reached. Every time the infantry has been launched to the attack from too great a distance before the artillery has made its effect felt, the infantry has fallen under the fire of machine guns and suffered losses which might have been avoided. When a point d'appui has been captured, it must be organised immediately, and artillery must be bought up.[1]

---

1   Edmonds, *Military Operations France and Belgium 1914*, Vol. I, p. 44.

It is very difficult to imagine that any British general at GHQ could have written a sober assessment of artillery tactics after only twenty days of battle. But it seems likely that the German generals came to the same conclusions. He says two things. First is that infantry should not be allowed to attack enemy positions until they have been degraded by artillery. And second that once a position is captured, the artillery must immediately advance to take control of the gains made. In other words, all attacks should start and end with artillery planning, and the infantry must fall in with their capabilities.

It is striking that General Smith-Dorrien had made the same general point much more briefly in his analysis of the lessons to be learnt from the 1912 army manoeuvres discussed in the early chapters of this volume. But for the British, this was a battle of defence. Defensive tactics <u>did</u> begin and end with artillery planning, though this was not necessarily obvious at Corps and GHQ level, the latter, anyway, regarding Mons as an offensive battle. The divisional commanders did the work. They placed the guns; the infantry conformed under their protection. On withdrawal, half the guns fell back to create another line of protection, and the other half of the guns leap-frogged the first back to the next line of withdrawal. This was a well-rehearsed manoeuvre at brigade level. And at this brigade level, the artillery was not afraid to have a few guns forward, albeit always well dug in, but it was a few guns. Only sections of batteries were risked in this way, not whole batteries. Brigadier General Doran of the 8th Infantry Brigade, 3rd Division, was the only infantry officer who insisted on guns in close proximity to his infantry, and he can be forgiven, considering his perfectly justifiable anxiety at the exposed plight of his Middlesex Regiment on the canal at Obourg Bridge.

As anticipated, artillery batteries and brigades moved freely from Divisional Artillery to Infantry Brigade command, and back again, depending on circumstances. For instance, Brigadier General Headlam, commanding the 5th Division, was very pro-active, and not afraid to switch his batteries from brigade to group, and back again, with decisive effect on the second day, at Wasmes, according to the Dorset Regiment and the Yorkshire Light Infantry. The tactical task of almost every artillery brigade was constantly updated by all four divisional commanders, often resulting in a change in position. Mobility was key.

When transfers of command were made, they were very firmly observed. A battery of the 5th Division refused to fall back on orders from a brigadier: and two batteries of the 2nd Division refused to obey orders from their major general, both on the grounds they were on a different command pathway, assigned to a designated task. On both occasions, dispositions were changed to accommodate the refusal.

The tactical importance of these transfers of command is repeatedly illustrated as the British fell back. Batteries or brigades often moved to support other than their usual infantry formations. A single infantry brigade was the nominated rear-guard, but two artillery brigades were always involved, covering each other behind the infantry rear-guard. Every division benefited from this well-rehearsed teamwork. And it is clear that when the guns were in the right position, they were devastatingly effective. None of the German attacks got close to the infantry when they were targeted by a battery, and both artillery and infantry diaries record the 'effectiveness' of their contribution. Indeed, the surprise is how easily single batteries, or even sections of batteries, were able to deter vigorous enemy infantry attacks, even this early in the war.

The potential problem highlighted in the opening chapter on tactics, that of artillery selecting positions before being placed under infantry direction, occurred on a number of occasions in the ebb and flow of battle. It was a problem. The guns of neither half of the II Corps defence line were perfectly placed to support their nominated infantry brigades. The battery commanders of the 3rd Division had to guess from which direction the German threat would come. The battery commanders of the 5th Division had to guess where the infantry would stop to take up their defensive positions. Neither always got it right. But they adjusted.

Perhaps unsurprisingly, the use of light howitzers by both sides was less assured. Both the British and German armies kept their howitzers as a divisional resource. They were less used to working in close cooperation with the infantry. Their role in battle was as a second line of artillery attack. They were very effective when used, but they were not used as much perhaps as they should have been. It was late in the day before the Germans brought them into action at the canal, and only two British battalions – possibly also the Middlesex Regiment – significantly suffered from their attentions, another three the next day. The British used them only once against infantry, in defence, on the second day.

The Germans, becoming aware of the near futility of their light artillery fire, arguably learnt more from the battle in this respect than the British. The British light artillery was generally successful in achieving the necessary results. They worked far faster than the more ponderous howitzers, who on one occasion took a full six hours to come into action.

5.3 Impact of Field Service Regulations

Most of the contemporary Field Regulations were of course prescriptive, being the rules to be followed in the waging of war. GHQ spectacularly failed to follow Regulations, as they prepared Order 5 for the three-day advance starting on 21 August. The death of General Grierson is a footnote in history, but it probably contributed to the reason. He would have been French's prop and principal adviser. Grierson's unfortunate death was, as Field Marshal French observed a 'calamity'. Nobody is unaffected by deep personal grief. He forgot, and was allowed to forget, Field Service Regulations.

The tactical errors were pretty basic. Do not leave the artillery behind. Do not allow your forces to become separated. Do ensure a flank guard. Do not wheel without knowing the enemy lines of advance. Junior officers of all arms would have been chastised for any one of these elementary errors.

And, as a result of these errors, Field Marshal French immediately lost the confidence of his Corps and Division Commanders. General Smith-Dorrien decisively addressed the problems directly with French on the evening of the 21st. He was able to negotiate change, and subsequently communicate a clear plan to his troops. General Haig did not. He had an opportunity so to do, when he met French at the cavalry headquarters on the 21st. He did not take it, and subsequently transmitted his continuing lack of confidence in French to his staff and divisional commanders, resulting ultimately in uncertainty and disarray:

> It is necessary to train subordinates not only to work resolutely and intelligently in accordance with brief and very general instructions, but also to take on themselves, whenever it be necessary, the responsibility of departing from, or of varying the orders they may have received.[2]

This particular regulation was central to the way that the British fought the Battle of Mons. French issued 'brief and general' orders throughout the campaign, as did General Smith-Dorrien in that he allocated tasks, not specific positions to his units. General Haig was much more directive. He frequently concerned himself with the positions of individual battalions. Neither of his divisional generals were allowed much flexibility in their dispositions; and it is very possible that he took the 4th (Guards) Brigade under his personal control.

Variance of orders was almost the norm in the battle, and usually justifiably so. It was only a British victory because orders were varied. But disaster on the day was only narrowly avoided, and it is necessary to examine what went wrong.

There was a stated obligation on the officer who varies his order, to inform the officer who issued the order, what he was doing, and perhaps as importantly why.[3] In practice, this feedback usually occurred. But since a reply direct to the general was often impractical, it would fall on his staff to react. The fact that orders were varied was a fact of British army life. Generals therefore had an obligation to listen, as well as instruct. This is where an effective staff, and an easy relationship with those staff, became so important. If an order was varied, he needed to know. Junior staff had to pick up on the variance, and robustly inform their general. If the staff was very hierarchical, or dysfunctional, this did not necessarily happen.

Field Marshal French had dysfunctional staff. He was defeated by information overload, poor advisers and misinformation. His staff failed to pass on information about General Smith-Dorrien's battle plan, and more understandably, failed to pick up on General Haig's variances.

General Smith-Dorrien's staff were remarkably effective, in spite of, or perhaps because of, the short time they had been together. Both his II Corps staff and his divisions reacted to junior variances. General Haig's corps had the same ethos. The South Staffordshire Regiment moved to cover II Corps positions north of Harmignies

---

2 *Field Service Regulations*, 1912, p. 28.
3 Ibid., p. 32.

on the 23rd, and the Gloucestershire Regiment modified its orders for retirement on the 24th. The 2nd Division did not advance on the evening of the 22nd; and the Irish Guards ignored their sixth counter-order in 36 hours on the 24th, though arguably neither of these were true variances, using initiative. General Haig used his right of variance several times. But, when he cancelled the advance of the 2nd Division on the 22nd, and in revising the destinations of the 4th (Guards) on the 23rd, he inexplicably failed to tell those affected. It is almost as though he was ashamed of what he had done. But variance from the regulations, not the regulations themselves, was the problem with General Haig.

On a lighter note, there are at least two instances in II Corps records, where line officers justifiably 'varied' their orders by non-compliance, and gave their reasons. The relevant diaries, however, record that communications had failed. Variance, at a junior level, was all very well, but perhaps nobody wanted to draw too much attention to it.

Other issues pertaining to Field Regulations have been discussed. The difference between offensive and defensive 'outposts' is perhaps the most significant, but the issue of the weight of reserves behind an offensive line was also important. All the senior officers of II Corps knew, on the afternoon of the 23rd, that an offensive advance the next day was, at best, unlikely to succeed. One adjutant of an infantry brigade wrote out the dispositions of II Corps to emphasise this fact. Another prepared a detailed plan for a defensive withdrawal. One of the advantages, or disadvantages, of a professional army is that every officer is a potential general!

In a final observation, it will be remembered that British Field Regulations were not positive about artillery bombardment. 'By itself, bombardment should not succeed against a good garrison,' it says. If trench-lines are regarded as garrisons, which they effectively were, this had proved true of the I Corps lines. But the infantry commanders of II Corps who had endured howitzer fire on strongly held positions might have questioned this statement; and, when the time came for their units to be attacking, might have wanted artillery, particularly howitzer, support in the endeavour.

5.4 The Generals

Following the 1912 manoeuvres, the generals involved, the umpires and the director of proceedings all wrote reports. After the battle of Mons, Field Marshal French, General Smith-Dorrien and General Haig all left reports in one form or another, to justify their actions. It has done little favour to any of them that this became known as the battle of the memoires. All of their accounts left much unsaid. The various war diaries were of course retained in storage. The paucity of GHQ reports retained in the records is notable. They have been ruthlessly culled. The unique absence of the 4th (Guards) Brigade records, without explanation, is also notable. The doubtless accidental loss of these two sets of records must have occasioned considerable relief to more than one general. French was not one of them. The lack of records has not served him well. His performance in the battle was defined by his signing off, on

20 August, of Operation Order 5, the three-day advance into Belgium. It was a deeply flawed document. But he has not received the credit he deserves for rescuing the situation. His readiness to alter dispositions on the evening of the 21st, after discussion with General Smith-Dorrien, was admirable, arguably confirming the reliance that he would have placed on Grierson. In retrospect, he should have ordered I Corps to perform their enhanced advance on the 22nd much earlier in the day than he did. His reluctance to withdraw II Corps on the afternoon of the 22nd was perfectly understandable, given the French entreaties for him to remain forward, and the fact that he thought I Corps already on the march; and if I Corps had been where he thought they were at 6 a.m. on the 23rd, their presence would have eased the plight of the 3rd Division, and even that of the French on their right. He has been accused of being totally out of touch on the day, but that is unfair. He issued a series of 'brief and very general instructions', and there are none that can be criticised in isolation, on the information that he had available. He failed to listen to his Chief of Staff during the day of battle, but he acted decisively in ordering the withdrawal from Mons at midnight on the 23rd.

Smith-Dorrien maintained a dignified silence on his actions for many years; and in the event, his conduct in this battle was over-shadowed by events at Le Cateau. The very full records in the II Corps war diaries, tell the story. He says in his book that he was content to be judged on the account given in the Official History, and as far as II Corps is concerned, it is largely accurate. His very swift reading of the situation on the evening of the 21st, after only a few hours at his Corps headquarters, and his subsequent discussion with Field Marshal French, shaped the battle. He made an

Mons and Le Cateau, a German cartoon commentary: "The 'dear' cousin from England:" I came; I saw; I conquered. (*Kladderadatsch*, 6 September 1914)

equally swift and decisive assessment of his lines on the afternoon of the 22nd and planned the battle of extraction that he subsequently fought. That his outpost line was able to hold out long enough to enable his artillery to get into position and his second line prepared, was due to his very clear orders, and the sheer quality of the troops at his disposal, aided significantly by the failure of the German light artillery ordnance.

At no time did General Smith-Dorrien and his staff lose control. All seems purposeful. When significant decisions were made by General Smith-Dorrien, there was usually a pause, while his staff worked through the implications and issued orders. In none of the war diaries of II Corps, down to single battalions or batteries, is there confusion. There is occasional uncertainty at out-comes, or transient self-pity at severe losses, but no more than this. It is conceivable that if he had been facing less than two German Corps, he might even have been in a position to go on to the offensive on the morning of the 24th. The spotlight thus falls on General Haig. He sponsored the report of the battle, which is in I Corps records, and confirmed by his 'diaries'. From the afternoon of the 22nd, this retrospective account is not only inaccurate in detail, but misleading in overview.

It is difficult to be objective on the campaign he conducted in the light of this document. One should perhaps start by saying that he was mindful of General Kitchener's instructions to preserve the British Army. Probably intentionally, General Kitchener had chosen one cautious Corps commander and one aggressive, in General Grierson, replacing like with like, in General Smith-Dorrien. His extended advance on the morning of the 22nd to bring his forward 1st Division brigade north of Maubeuge, and closer in touch with II Corps, was well-conceived. Absenting himself from his headquarters on the afternoon of the 22nd was a disaster from which he never recovered. If he had been at his Headquarters, he could have robustly questioned Field Marshal French's order to advance I Corps. He might have persuaded French to change his mind; and recall II Corps to a line at Bavai, a logical and reasonable tactical option. As it was, he failed to stop the advance of his 1st Division; and it was a grave error to stop the 2nd Division as they were about to set off. Exhausted by order and counter order, they were immobilised for the next six hours. He could, and should, have allowed them to advance at least to a line which would have provided protection for the withdrawal of II Corps. The fact that he had (allegedly) formulated such a line, due north of Maubeuge, only a few hours before, make this failure all the more extraordinary.

Having halted the 2nd Division, he then failed to inform GHQ and II Corps. This was in defiance of Field Regulations. His staff did not coordinate an advance for the 2nd Division in the early hours of the 23rd, leaving him to order an urgent advance in an impossible time-scale at midnight. In an attempt to disguise his mistakes, he subsequently denied his presence at the 6 a.m. conference of the generals. He says that the meeting was at 10.30 a.m. This was the time that General Smith-Dorrien became aware of the failure of the 2nd Division to relieve his right flank and release much needed reserves. Haig stated that the changed disposition of his 4th (Guards) Brigade was agreed at this fictional meeting. By this time, he had already rescinded

GHQ orders for the 4th (Guards) to take up positions north of Harmignies. Again, he informed neither GHQ, nor those units affected by the decision. He had, of course, been told at 6 a.m. of the II Corps plan to fall back, sooner or later, to Harmignies. He expected sooner and, that morning, he wanted the 4th (Guards) in billets at Quevy, ideally placed, close to the main road, for a quick retreat. It is worth considering what would have been the reaction in Great Britain if an admiral, commanding a battle fleet, had ignored orders to advance his own ships to the support of another battle fleet under attack. There would have been a court martial. The consequences for the commander of the first fleet might well have been dire.

By 2 p.m., the reports emanating from Mons were alarming, and there is a more than a whiff of panic in his decision to send both reserve brigades of the 2nd Division to Harveng at the same time. He did not involve his staff in planning the detail of this concentration. General Monro had to personally sort out the resulting confusion; and arrange construction of the useless Haig line, which was dug to facilitate an expected withdrawal that afternoon. The 1st Division had already been ordered to prepare for withdrawal.

With indecision and near-panic in the air, the 4th (Guards) Brigade was particularly hard done-by. Exhausted units moved from task to task with bewildering rapidity. The Irish Guards, for instance, received six orders and counter orders in quick succession over thirty hours. The loss of the 4th Brigade records makes it hard to judge how avoidable this confusion was, and who was actually commanding them. There is a hint in the narrative that they were actually under I Corps control.

The speed with which Haig personally actioned GHQ orders to withdraw in the early hours of the 24th is unedifying. He did not involve his staff in the planning, and, despite orders to the contrary, arranged no early liaison with II Corps, or even with his own cavalry.

It is worth quoting in its entirety the I Corps staff diary entry for 24 August:

> 1st Army withdrawn from advanced positions covered by a rear-guard of the 1st Division, whose artillery were engaged with hostile artillery and other troops. Headquarters billeted for night at Vieux Mesnil. The retirement was covered by the rear-guard of the 1st Division and a special rear-guard of 4th (Guards) Brigade and 5th Cavalry Brigade and artillery under Brigadier General Horne. The troops were much fatigued by the days operations.[4]

In contrast, the war diary of II Corps consists of sixteen timed entries, many as long as this full day's report, recording in detail, and where necessary coordinating, the withdrawal of every part of the Corps from before 3 a.m. to the last entry at 10.25 p.m. Entries are referenced to orders issued, maps used and routes followed to final destinations.[5] It is striking that General Haig had not learnt from his experience in

---

4   TNA WO 95/588/1: I Corps staff, 24 August 1914.
5   TNA WO 95/630/1: II Corps staff, 24 August 1914.

the 1912 manoeuvres, when he was criticised for side-lining his staff.[6] Having fought a desperately unimpressive campaign, he then set about re-writing history. The inaccuracies in his report, and his private papers, are not simple mistakes, and his account deliberately conceals intentions, and blurs timelines. His report is a disgrace to the British Army, carefully drafted to protect and enhance his personal reputation.

There are other questions. There are carbon copies of just four letters, pertaining to the battle, in General Haig's private papers.[7] They are pages 3, 4, 6, 7, 8, 10 and 11 of the same notebook. These cannot be the originals. The question is whether they were copied out accurately after the events from his notes, amended in detail later, or fabricated. The first summarises his strategic vision for the 22nd, which he conspicuously failed to follow a few hours later. The second, to General Monro on the evening of the 22nd, is ambiguous, and, in the event, superfluous. The third, on the 23rd, is inaccurate in detail, and unbelievably optimistic. Against all the evidence, it informs General Smith-Dorrien that I Corps is looking to go onto the offensive. The fourth, again on the 23rd, tells General Monro to hold Point 93, a hill that was abandoned by mistake a few hours later. Two have unique misspellings of place names. All give rise to questions on timing, or content, or both. None can be cross-referenced, and the last two are challenged by entries in unit diaries. At best, their contemporaneous authenticity is severely in doubt; at worst, and this is a reasonable conclusion on the evidence, General Haig is guilty of forgery in an attempt to protect his reputation.

In contrast to his corps commander, the performance of Brigadier General Horne, CRA I Corps, was masterly. He calmly took responsibility for the 5th Cavalry Brigade, the 4th Brigade rear-guard and elements of his artillery, positioning his all-arms force to stabilise the retreat of the 3rd Division on his left, and the 2nd Division behind him. A sense of purpose returns to the accounts of the relevant units. I Corps records severely understate his achievement. That Haig's inept leadership and profound defeatism did not define the battle is a tribute to Smith-Dorrien, and Horne.

5.5 Potential Lessons of the Battle

The BEF escaped with remarkably few casualties from a defensive position of great peril. That they did so was largely due to the munitions failure of the German light artillery. The first effect of this was that the British cavalry was enabled to deploy effectively with minimal casualties. No British officer had any reason to challenge the assertion that the cavalry was a vital and equal offensive arm to the infantry, even in a continental war. There was no need to re-think the status quo.

The fact that Mons was a defensive battle also reinforced the status quo of the artillery. In defence and withdrawal, the artillery dictated the battle, but without appearing

---

6   Spencer Jones, *Stemming the Tide*, p. 146, ref. *Manchester Guardian*, 9 Sept. 1912.
7   NLS: Acc.3155/98: Douglas Haig Papers, p.80-82, 88-91.

to do so. They were simply carrying out their duty to protect the divisional infantry. The guns of both corps took up positions, and the infantry conformed to them. It was of advantage that the guns were commanded at sub-divisional level, liaising effectively with infantry units, firing from covered positions on targets of opportunity.

In Smith-Dorrien's case, the artillery dispositions were integral to the battle he fought. He issued 'brief and general' orders, but it was clear that he expected his artillery to take up positions from which they could act as the support on which his infantry could rely. He says in his book that 'even if I had personal knowledge of their several positions, it would take much space to describe them,' and that that their 'handling, initiative and courageous action… was something even for that courageous corps to be proud of'.[8] Only he, of three senior generals, leaves an impression that he believed the artillery was an arm as important, if not more important, than the infantry and cavalry. Not even the artillery officers realised it at this stage. They were taught to move tactically in support of infantry brigades, not strategically on corps objectives. They kept a subservient profile. It was not obvious to them, or to most generals, that battle was fought round an artillery backbone; and not round infantry muscle. But it was.

The relationship between the artillery and the cavalry was different. General Allenby, commanding the Cavalry Division, had two brigades of artillery at his disposal. The cavalry was fast ranging and mobile, engaged mainly in reconnaissance. At no stage during the run-up to the battle did their artillery make a significant contribution. Indeed, it is difficult to see how they could. And even when, on the day of battle, the cavalry dismounted and took up their positions on the canal east of Condé, the artillery stayed in billets. This is not a criticism. It is just that artillery was not integral to the success of the cavalry. A point made earlier in the book is that the generals of 1914 carried their early experience to this new continental war.

General Haig, like Field Marshal French, was a cavalry general. He was controlling, and seldom, if ever, consulted his staff in major decisions. Yet he allowed Brigadier General Horne exceptional freedom. Horne supervised the siting of I Corps artillery on the evening of the 22nd; took command of guns to position them according to his plan, not General Haig's, at Harveng on the 23rd; and then assumed command of the I Corps rear-guard, including the 5th Cavalry Brigade on the 24th. Of these, the Harveng episode is the most interesting. General Haig is massing two infantry brigades to make a defence line there. Yet General Horne is able to move most of the artillery to another tactical task, even taking two batteries under his own command.

The fact that General Horne was able to make a significant contribution to the campaign on all three days suggests that General Haig saw no threat from his activities, no invasion of his total control. Horne did not need to consult Haig – he was just responsible for the guns. Only three times does the I Corps summary of the battle

---

8   Smith-Dorrien, *Memories of Forty-Eight Years' Service*, p. 388.

specifically mention the artillery, once to record the partial disablement of one of the batteries, never to record their contribution.⁹

Available evidence suggests that Haig did not particularly concern himself with artillery dispositions. They were the support, a divisional responsibility. Unfortunately, the ineffectiveness of the German field artillery against the British would have reinforced this disinterest. In some senses, it was a tragedy to the future conduct of the war that the German field artillery was so ineffective at Mons.

Haig spent all the evening of the 23rd worrying about a heavy bombardment on his forces, which, in the event, caused almost no casualties. In future, he could, and would, be more sanguine about allowing his men to be bombarded. 'By itself, bombardment should not succeed against a good garrison.' He (and other senior officers) would have little reason to question this statement from the Field Regulations he had sponsored. Of course, those who had been bombarded by howitzers were not nearly so sanguine. II Corps had some experience of it. Five battalions lost significant casualties to them, but they were the exception, not the rule. Machine guns had been equally devastating when robustly handled. No II Corps battery had suffered. I Corps had had the reverse experience. Two of their batteries, both in the 2nd Division, had been bombarded by howitzers with significant effect. Every senior artillery officer in I Corps would have been wary of German howitzer fire-power, II Corps artillery perhaps less so over the next few days, and this may have influenced gun positions at Le Cateau a few days later. There was so little time to think.

One can only speculate on what the German generals made of the battle. Their artillery must have been dismayed at their lack of punch. It is worth repeating the words of General Erich von Falkenhayn, Chief of the General Staff of the German Field Army: 'Our men felt uncomfortably conscious of the inferiority, in terms of both range and effectiveness, of our field gun.'¹⁰ It was only when their howitzers came into action against the 'field fortifications' on the canal on the afternoon of the 23rd that their infantry made significant inroads into the British lines. Certainly, on the 24th, their howitzers were pushed forward much faster than the day before, to harry the British as they retired. So far as their field guns are concerned, an eye witness describes them still firing in shrapnel mode on the 25th but firing only in high explosive mode at Le Cateau on the 26th.¹¹

It remains necessary to address the issue of the relative casualties on the two sides during the battle. There is no way of calculating the figures. Even if records were available, they would be almost useless. A roll-call after the battle could, and did, reveal many men missing. It was no easy matter to find your way back to a unit on the march. Only for 2nd Royal Irish Regiment are there figures available for those

9   TNA WO 95/588/4: I Corps staff, 23 August 1914.
10   Herman Cron, *Imperial German Army 1914-18*, p.135
11   Hutchison, *The Young Gunner*, pp.13-16.

BEF prisoners, 1914.

re-joining, having been reported missing on the day, 87 out of 226, over a third. Some took a fortnight to re-join.[12]

Even those very trivially wounded were included in British statistics, since wounds in battle conferred more benefits than simple accidents on the march. Conversely, the Germans reported only the more severely wounded who were evacuated. The fate of prisoners was unknown for months. Meaningful comparative figures are impossible to obtain.

The Official History reports that I Corps had less than 40 casualties. This is an underestimate. About 60 are recorded in unit diaries. About 1600 total British casualties, including wounded and prisoners, is the figure generally accepted for the first day. It was probably slightly less than this for the first day, and slightly more, if the second day is included, but it is a not unreasonable educated guess, based on the references quoted.

Six German infantry divisions, with attached or supporting cavalry and artillery, (well over 100,000 men) vigorously attacked intact British lines over two days. If parallels are drawn with battles later in the war, a loss of 2,000 men per division is not excessive. German accounts describe 'bloody losses' to many units in all six divisions.[13] Artillery and cavalry casualties would have added very significantly to the figures. About 5,000 casualties is often quoted. This seems far too low. It was probably nearer 10,000, though, again, this can be no more than an educated guess.

12 Geoghegan, *Campaigns of the Royal Irish Regiment*, p. 29.
13 Reichsarchiv, *Die Schlacht bei Mons* quoted in Edmonds, *Military Operations France and Belgium 1914*, Vol. I, p. 94.

The Battle of Mons was the first battle of a very long war. For the British, the artillery was highly effective. It is relatively easy to identify the factors that contributed to that effectiveness.

The BEF at Mons was highly professional. Artillery batteries, commanded low-down in the army hierarchy, were aligned with the forward infantry; and well protected, both by their own efforts, and by those of the infantry. Obtaining for themselves good observation (not a simple task), they shot very straight. There were very few of them, but it did not need many, if the right targets were selected and hit.

A small, but nevertheless significant, point can be made. The British army of 1914 admitted mistakes. The Cavalry Division records two, I Corps and II Corps at least one each. No blame is assigned. They are admitted as part of a learning process. It takes impressive confidence in professionalism to do this.

This professionalism was the result of training, bolstered by initiative and liaison. Middle ranking officers, of both infantry and artillery, constantly adjusted their positions to provide mutual support and protection. But the very strong liaison required for this cooperation was not formalised. (Liaison is discussed in some detail in the 1913 lecture on infantry and artillery cooperation, reproduced in appendix IV. It is worth reading.) As the professional army of 1914 was depleted by casualties in 1914, and then swamped by the huge numbers recruited for the New Armies, the initiative required for this liaison, (and indeed the skills of self-protection and shooting straight), were largely lost. Furthermore, the British high command lost faith in variance of orders. It is easy from this account to understand why. Over the next year, 'brief and very general instructions' became a thing of the past. Detailed orders were issued, with almost no option of variance under Field Service Regulations. Initiative was increasingly discouraged, as the experience and competence of the officer corps, at both front-line and staff level, dwindled; and as officers unfamiliar with the regulations were drafted in to the upper echelons of command. The combination of decreasing liaison between infantry and artillery, and prescriptive orders from above had a devastating impact on the effectiveness of the guns.

It can be left to the reader to decide whether either Field Marshal French or General Haig, both cavalry generals content to leave artillery deployment to division, were capable of recognising why their artillery was increasingly failing to deliver. History might have been very different if the British high command had been dominated by an infantry mentality. It is beyond the remit of this book to discuss this issue further. Suffice it to say, that the conventional explanation for artillery failures through the war is that there was too little ammunition in mid-1915, too few guns later that year, and organisational difficulties in concentrating guns during 1916. Enormous energy was expended in addressing these issues. Front-line liaison between infantry and artillery almost disappeared in 1915 and was not robustly formalised in the British Army until late 1917.[14]

14 Hutchison, *The Young Gunner*, pp.228, 297-301, 413.

5.6 Postscript

Thanks to Field Marshal French, the battle was widely regarded as a defeat at the time with few military reputations enhanced. General Haig should, of course, have been sacked for incompetence. Brigadier General Horne has missed out on deserved recognition. His positioning of I Corps artillery and his handling of the withdrawal at the I Corps – II Corps interface was not only adept, but crucial to success on the day. He became a competent Corps Commander, notably at the Somme, when his was one of the few that made significant advances on the first day – thanks to his artillery preparation.

Major General Hamilton (3rd Division), Major General Lomax (1st Division), Brigadier General Wing (3rd Division artillery) and Brigadier General Findlay (1st Division artillery) were all killed within the year. Major General Monro (2nd Division) was promoted temporarily to full general in 1915, and confirmed in that rank in 1916. Major General Ferguson (5th Division) survived the war as a corps commander. Brigadier General Headlam (5th Division artillery) was promoted Major General by 1916. He went on to become a soldier politician assigned to foreign delegations. As for General Smith-Dorrien, he won the Battle of Mons. He was the only one of the three senior generals who recognised the importance of good artillery dispositions. He was the best general in the British Army. What else can one say? He knew of the early tactical errors of French. He knew of the severe deficiencies in General Haig's leadership. He had to go. It took eight months. But go he did. This book is written for him.

Appendix I

British Artillery Organisation, 1914

The smallest independent artillery unit was the battery, which consisted of six guns, although occasionally sections of one or two guns might be given independence away from the main body. Each battery had a wagon line of about 18 wagons, which carried all the equipment required to service the guns on a day to day basis, and all the food, water and equipment needed for the men and officers within the command. Two ammunition wagons, with 176 rounds per gun, were carried on active service, these being purpose-built limbers, with a wagon body and cellular construction to hold individual projectiles.

The full battery comprised about 200 men and 200 horses and was commanded by a major. He was supported by a captain, generally responsible for the management of the wagon line, but who was experienced enough to take over the battery and run it if necessary. Under the captain and the major, there would be about four subalterns, some 2nd lieutenants of less than two years' experience and some older 1st lieutenants. These junior officers, under training, rotated in their responsibilities, commanding two-gun sections at the battery, serving at the wagon line, caring for the horses, and one, again in rotation, seconded to their colonel for brigade duties as orderly officer.

Usually, but not invariably, there were three batteries to a brigade of artillery, commanded by a colonel. He commanded from a brigade office with secretarial NCOs, and the office was run by an adjutant, a captain in rank, who was responsible for all the routine paperwork pertaining to pay and provisions etc. On active service, the brigade office would also house the medical officer, and others. The colonel commanded not only his three horse-drawn batteries, but also a horse-drawn Brigade Ammunition Column (BAC), consisting in 1911:

> [O]f 18 ammunition wagons and 21 general service wagons loaded with gun ammunition. The column also carries rifle ammunition for the infantry, namely seven small-arm ammunition carts and nine GS wagons loaded with small-arm ammunition. There are also four store wagons. It is commanded by a captain

and has 3 subalterns. The duty of the column is to supply officers, men, horses, ammunition and stores to its own brigade, and to other brigades if called upon.[1]

In 1912, about half of this capacity was transferred to the Divisional Ammunition Column, though it continued to carry the same amount of artillery ammunition. It was still a significant unit with farriers, shoeing smiths, saddlers, wheelers, drivers and reserve personnel.

There were four such brigades of artillery in each division of about 18,000 men. Three of them were equipped with the 18-pounder field gun, and one with the 4.5-inch howitzer. In battle, it was assumed that each field gun brigade would support its allocated infantry brigade, there being three to a division. The howitzers would be held back, as a divisional resource. Each division also had a single battery of four horse-drawn 60 pounder guns, necessarily less mobile than the other batteries.

It is important not to confuse artillery brigades with infantry brigades. The infantry equivalent of an artillery brigade is the battalion, and each is commanded by a colonel. The four artillery brigades of a division were commanded by an artillery brigadier general. Four battalions made up an infantry brigade of 4000 men, also commanded by a brigadier general. There were three infantry brigades and four artillery brigades (three field-gun and one howitzer) to a division.

The artillery brigadier general had an artillery office at divisional headquarters. His office, later in the war, was run by a brigade major, supported by a staff captain, with other more junior officers attached with responsibility for intelligence, signals, liaison, etc. But in 1914, he had few staff and a very limited supply of communication equipment.[2]

He was responsible to the Major General commanding the infantry division, who was almost invariably an infantry officer, without specialist artillery experience.

1 Colonel H.A. Bethell, *Modern Artillery in the Field* (London: Macmillan, p. 219).
2 Marble, *The Infantry cannot do with a gun less.*

Appendix II

BEF Orders of Battle, August 1914

GHQ
C-in-C	Field-Marshal Sir John French
Chief of Staff	Lieutenant-General Sir A. Murray
Deputy Chief of Staff	Major-General H. Wilson.
Adjutant-General	Major-General Sir C. Macready
Commander Royal Artillery	Major-General W. Lindsay

Cavalry Division
GOC Major-General Edmund Allenby
1st Cavalry Brigade
    2nd Dragoon Guards (Queen's Bays)
    5th (Princess Charlotte of Wales's) Dragoon Guards
    11th (Prince Albert's Own) Hussars
2nd Cavalry Brigade
    4th (Royal Irish) Dragoon Guards
    9th (Queen's Royal) Lancers
    18th (Queen Mary's Own) Hussars
3rd Cavalry Brigade
    4th (Queen's Own) Hussars
    5th (Royal Irish) Lancers
    16th (The Queen's) Lancers
4th Cavalry Brigade
    Household Cavalry Composite Regiment
    6th Dragoon Guards (Carabiniers)
    3rd (King's Own) Hussars

Royal Horse Artillery	Brigadier-General B. Drake
III Brigade RHA	D and E Batteries
VII Brigade RHA	I and L Batteries

Independent 5th Cavalry Brigade
    2nd Dragoons (Royal Scots Greys)
    12th (Prince of Wales's Royal) Lancers
    20th Hussars
    J Battery, RHA

I Corps
GOC   Lieutenant-General Sir Douglas Haig
Chief of Staff   Brigadier-General J. E. Gough
Commander Royal Artillery   Brigadier-General H. S. Horne

1st Division
GOC   Major-General S. Lomax

1st (Guards) Brigade   GOC Brigadier-General F. Maxse
    1st Coldstream Guards
    1st Scots Guards
    1st The Black Watch (Royal Highlanders)
    2nd The Royal Munster Fusiliers
2nd Infantry Brigade   GOC Brigadier-General E. Bulfin
    2nd The Royal Sussex Regiment
    1st The Loyal North Lancashire Regiment
    1st The Northamptonshire Regiment
    2nd The King's Royal Rifle Corps
3rd Infantry Brigade   GOC Brigadier-General H. Landon
    1st The Queen's (Royal West Surrey Regiment)
    1st The South Wales Borderers
    1st The Gloucestershire Regiment
    2nd The Welch Regiment
Artillery   GOC Brigadier-General N. Findlay
    XXV Brigade RFA   113th, 114th and 115th Batteries
    XXVI Brigade RFA   116th, 117th and 118th Batteries
    XXXIX Brigade RFA   46th, 51st and 54th Batteries
    XLIII (Howitzer) Brigade RFA   30th, 40th and 57th Batteries
    26th Heavy Battery, RGA

2nd Division
GOC   Major-General C. Monro

4th (Guards) Brigade   GOC Brigadier-General R. Scott-Kerr
    2nd Grenadier Guards
    2nd Coldstream Guards
    3rd Coldstream Guards

    1st Irish Guards
5th Infantry Brigade   GOC Brigadier-General R. Haking
    2nd The Worcestershire Regiment
    2nd The Oxfordshire and Buckinghamshire Light Infantry
    2nd The Highland Light Infantry
    2nd The Connaught Rangers
6th Infantry Brigade   GOC Brigadier-General R. Davies
    1st The King's (Liverpool Regiment)
    2nd The South Staffordshire Regiment
    1st Princess Charlotte of Wales's (Royal Berkshire Regiment)
    1st The King's Royal Rifle Corps
Artillery   GOC Brigadier-General E. Perceval
    XXXIV Brigade RFA   22nd, 50th and 70th Batteries
    XXXVI Brigade RFA   15th, 48th and 7st1 Batteries
    XLI Brigade RFA   9th, 16th and 17th Batteries
    XLIV (Howitzer) Brigade RFA   47th, 56th and 60th Batteries
    35th Heavy Battery, RGA

II Corps
GOC   Lieutenant-General Horace
                                                         Smith-Dorrien
Chief of Staff   Brigadier-General G. Forestier-Walker
Commander Royal Artillery   Brigadier-General A. Short

3rd Division
GOC   Major-General H. Hamilton

7th Infantry Brigade   GOC Brigadier-General F. McCracken
    3rd The Worcestershire Regiment
    2nd Prince of Wales's Volunteers (South Lancashire Regiment)
    1st The Duke of Edinburgh's (Wiltshire Regiment)
    2nd The Royal Irish Rifles
8th Infantry Brigade   GOC Brigadier-General B. Doran
    2nd The Royal Scots (Lothian Regiment)
    2nd The Royal Irish Regiment
    4th The Duke of Cambridge's Own (Middlesex Regiment)
    1st The Gordon Highlanders
9th Infantry Brigade   GOC Brigadier-General F. Shaw
    1st The Northumberland Fusiliers
    4th The Royal Fusiliers (City of London Regiment)
    1st The Lincolnshire Regiment
    1st The Royal Scots Fusiliers
Artillery   GOC Brigadier-General F. Wing

XXIII Brigade RFA	107th, 108th and 109th Batteries
XL Brigade RFA	6th, 23rd and 49th Batteries
XLII Brigade RFA	29th, 41st and 45th Batteries
XXX (Howitzer) Brigade RFA	128th,129th and 130th Batteries

5th Division

GOC	Major-General Sir C. Fergusson
13th Infantry Brigade	GOC Brigadier-General G. Cuthbert

    2nd The King's Own Scottish Borderers
    2nd The Duke of Wellington's (West Riding Regiment)
    1st The Queen's Own (Royal West Kent Regiment)
    2nd The King's Own (Yorkshire Light Infantry)

14th Infantry Brigade	GOC Brigadier-General S. Rolt

    2nd The Suffolk Regiment
    1st The East Surrey Regiment
    1st The Duke of Cornwall's Light Infantry
    2nd The Manchester Regiment

15th Infantry Brigade	GOC Brigadier-General A. Count Gleichen

    1st The Norfolk Regiment
    1st The Bedfordshire Regiment
    1st The Cheshire Regiment
    1st The Dorsetshire Regiment

Artillery	GOC Brigadier-General J. Headlam
XV Brigade RFA	11th, 52nd and 80th Batteries
XXVII Brigade RFA	119th,120th and 121st Batteries
XXVIII Brigade RFA	122th, 123rd and 124th Batteries
VIII (Howitzer) Brigade RFA	37th, 61st and 65th Batteries
108th Heavy Battery, RGA	

19th Infantry Brigade (Independent)	GOC Major-General L.G. Drummond

    2nd Battalion, Royal Welch Fusiliers
    1st Battalion, Cameronians (Scottish Rifles)
    1st Battalion, Middlesex Regiment
    2nd Battalion, Argyll and Sutherland Highlanders

Appendix III

German Army General Structure, 1914[1]

The armed forces of the German Empire were largely unified under the command of Prussia. In 1871, an Army of the Realm (*Reichsheer*) had been created, the contingents of the Bavarian, Saxon and Württemberg kingdoms, together with the Grand Duchy of Baden, remaining semi-autonomous. By 1914, the German Army was organized into established Army Corps, most of which were commanded by the Prussian Army. Bavaria retained three Corps, Saxony two, and Württemberg and Baden one each. The Prussian Army maintained the Guard Corps, artillery, cavalry, and support units.

The entire army was under the command of the Kaiser, Wilhelm II, but, on mobilisation, he delegated authority to the Chief of the General Staff of the Field Army, Generaloberst von Moltke. The command structure was necessarily complex, and communications equally so. It is of interest that in the first days of the war, the commander of the German First Army, General von Kluck was under the command of General von Bülow of the Second Army, partly to try and simplify the transmission of orders.

German society was highly militarised, and a huge conscript force was maintained. There were four classifications of military service; Active, Reserve, Landwehr and Landsturm. At the age of 20, a man was conscripted into Active service for two years, or three years in the cavalry and field artillery. After that time, he would serve up to five years in the Reserve, undergoing two weeks training each year. After this period, he joined the Landwehr, translated literally as home guard, for the next 11 years. Following this, he was transferred for seven years to the Landsturm, the equivalent of the British Territorials. Also, within the Landsturm, boys between 17 and 20 might have been asked to serve. After the age of 45, a man was free from further military service. Both Reserve and Landwehr forces were called up on mobilisation.[2]

---

1 Cron, *Imperial German Army 1914-1918*.
2 General Staff, *The German Forces in the Field 1918*, 7th ed. (London: War Office, 1918).

On declaration of war, all the colourful individual uniforms of the different units were abolished and substituted with field grey. Officers sashes, and their red helmet designations were banned. All men had a green unit number on their helmet covers.

The forward echelons of the First Army approaching Mons were made up of the II, III, IV and IX Corps, supported by three cavalry divisions, which also covered the Second Army. The 2nd Cavalry Division had five Jäger battalions, crack infantry recruited in forestry areas, attached; the senior cavalry command had another three battalions available. Each cavalry division also deployed a horse artillery battalion, consisting of three batteries, and a machine gun section.

The nomenclature and command structure of the German army differed from the British, but each German infantry corps had two divisions, and each division had twelve infantry battalions, and twelve batteries of light artillery, one field howitzer battery for every three field gun batteries. This was an identical strength to a British division.

German formations also had eight 15cm (5.9 inch) schwere Feldhaubitze 13 field howitzers per division, in two batteries of four guns each, commanded at corps level. Each of these guns fired a shell weighing 93 pounds. For their part, the British had only four smaller 60 Pounder guns per division, commanded at that level.

Appendix IV

Lecture on Co-operation between Artillery and Infantry, August 1913[1]

Infantry has been, and always must be, the decisive arm, so it follows that the role of the artillery is to help the infantry maintain its mobility and offensive power by all the means at its disposal, and this must be the underlying principle of all artillery tactics.

Thus, it necessarily follows that the primary object of artillery fire should be:

1. To assist the movements of its own infantry
2. To prevent the movements of the enemy's infantry

Different phases of a battle would have to be discussed and details such as action of artillery in advanced guard, rear guard, main attack, encounter battle, in defence and counter attack etc. would have to be gone into, but as this would take too long to go thoroughly into, I propose to state very generally how best to ensure cooperation between the two arms.

There are two different methods employed to ensure cooperation and it is important that which method is to be adopted should be clearly defined, and the selection between the two methods will, as a rule, depend on the character of the ground.

As a guide as to which method should be adopted when a force is marching towards the enemy and an encounter is likely, the divisional artillery commander will detail officer's patrols to accompany the advanced troops. It is the duty of these patrols to rapidly reconnoitre the ground on which it appears probable that the force will deploy, and send, as soon as possible, to the divisional artillery commander information as to the nature and extent of artillery positions.

Should time be of importance and a rapid deployment necessary, there may be little or no opportunity for a detailed reconnaissance either by the divisional commander or by the artillery commander. Of course, if time permits it is advisable for the divisional artillery commander to make a personal reconnaissance and report the result to the

---

1   TNA WO 95/1510: 5th Div. War Diary, p. 45.

divisional commander before the manner of deployment is settled, stating how best, in his opinion, the artillery can be utilised to further the object in view.

If it is ascertained that the task assigned to the division can be carried out by the troops of the division acting in combination under the immediate control of the divisional commander, the method adopted will usually be that the whole of the control of the artillery will be left in the hands of the divisional artillery commander.

The divisional artillery commander would then either allot zones to the different brigades or units of artillery or allot tasks to them. By allotting zones is meant to divide the country into different areas and allotting each brigade or unit and area of country to watch, with orders to fire at any of the enemy who, in that area, are hampering the movements of our infantry.

By allotting task is meant allotting to each unit a definite job – such as keeping down the enemy's artillery fire, supporting a definite attack on the enemy's position, taking on a counter attack, etc.

Whether it is better to allot zones or tasks is a very vexed question and admits of considerable arguments, and of course much depends on the ground, but as a general rule, I think tasks are the best for attack, zones for the defence. But whichever course is adopted it will usually be best to keep a brigade of different batteries in reserve for dealing with unforeseen situations. Up to a short time ago, those in authority were of the opinion that though the fire of certain brigades and batteries should be kept in reserve, yet all the artillery should be, as a rule, bought into action. Now, and I am quite sure quite rightly, it thought that it is better instead of bringing all batteries into action, to keep some in positions of readiness which means that these batteries are not in action, but all preparations for their coming into action are made.

The second method is generally used if the country necessitates the employment of the division on more than one tactical operation, in such a manner that their efforts cannot be distinctly combined. In such cases the method of ensuing co-operation is that the artillery and infantry should be formed temporarily into what is called groups. As a rule, the units of the two arms thus brought together for a distinct tactical operation should have one commander. It is the duty of the divisional commander to organise these temporary groups. The Divisional artillery commander then conveys necessary orders to his subordinate artillery commanders, placing them at the disposal of the group commanders.

The artillery commander of a group would then act in exactly the same way in conjunction with the group commander, as the divisional artillery commander would act in conjunction with the divisional commander.

There is another method which is often adopted, and that is for the whole of the divisional artillery to be under the orders of the artillery divisional general and for subordinate artillery commanders to be given zones or tasks to help certain attacks or to assist different brigades in carrying out different objects. Personally, this method, which is in reality a combination of the other two methods, although often adopted, is as a rule, in my opinion, unsound and is very liable to lead to confusion. I think myself that if any unit of artillery is allotted a task which involves helping a certain brigade or force, that such artillery should always be put under the orders of the officer commanding that brigade or force. If it is not, the officer commanding the force cannot send [orders to] the officer commanding the artillery that is co-operating with his orders. He would have to send messages as to what he wanted from the artillery to the divisional commander, who would have to communicate them to the divisional artillery commander. He in his turn would have to communicate them to his subordinate artillery commander. There would be, of necessity, a great deal of delay, and by the time they reached him the opportunity of helping his infantry would in all probability have gone.

There was a time when artillery commanders thought that they should never be put under orders of the infantry commander, and though this is a thing that dies hard, I am sure that the majority of artillery officers now realise that it is an absolute necessity that the artillery, in order to co-operate properly with the infantry, must be under the orders of the officer who is carrying out the operations.

So much for the methods, but now the question comes how is the close co-operation that is so much needed between the two arms to be brought about.

After the Japanese War, there was a great craze for sending an artillery officer on with the infantry – practically into the firing line, this officer being told that it was his duty to keep the officer commanding the artillery informed as to how best to direct his fire so as to give the greatest possible assistance to the infantry. I have never thought that this was sound. Firstly, because it would be extremely difficult to spare an officer of the artillery for this purpose, though this difficulty might be overcome. Secondly, because he would very probably be shot before he was able to give any information of any value, and thirdly, because I do not see how, in ordinary circumstances, this officer is to send information back. He could not take a telephone; to use flags would in all probability only court disaster not only to himself but to the troops near. Dietz discs[2] have been suggested, these are very clumsy; probably the best method of communication would be butterfly discs like those invented by Colonel Stephenson; but to go practically into the firing line would be absurd and of little value. It would be possible of course to send an officer on some way in front to watch the movements of the infantry and to send back information re their movements etc. and in some cases this might certainly be advisable, but the all-important point seems to be that the officer commanding artillery must be in close touch with the officer commanding the operation, and it is, I think absolutely necessary that either the officer commanding the artillery or an officer detailed from the artillery must always be actually with the officer commanding the operations.

In order to ensure co-operation between the two arms, it is absolutely essential for infantry officers to acquaint themselves with what the artillery can do and what they cannot. Artillery are sometimes asked to fire at objects when it would be quite impossible to observe the fire.

---

2   A Dietz paraffin signal lantern, with a disc to block, or allow the light.

Effective artillery fire cannot be established in a moment on any given target. When under cover, especially, various arrangements have to be made, such as measuring angles of sight, lateral angles, laying correctly, setting fuses, loading &c.: so it follows that a frequent change of objective is to be avoided if possible.

In the earlier stages of an advance, when infantry begin to suffer from the fire of well-concealed or well-entrenched guns, we cannot guarantee to keep down this fire. If the guns are concealed, the only possibility is by a sustained searching fire, and we cannot afford the ammunition. In any case, it is largely a fluke.

We cannot at a moment's notice concentrate fire on a given point unless we have previous intimation. Some batteries will find it physically impossible without moving the guns, and all batteries require time to register before they can deliver effective fire. A really rapid rate of fire will exhaust the ammunition in the battery (not ammunition column) in half an hour.

If visible from anywhere within about 100 yards of the guns we can at very short notice absolutely prevent the movement of formed bodies of infantry within 5000 yards of our position. A column of fours appearing unexpectedly and visible for one minute, ought to suffer heavily. If it were appearing on a road where the guns were expecting it, the losses would be much greater; in two minutes in either case, they should be prohibitive.

If told exactly when and where it is required, and given time to register, a battery can for a short time (limited by ammunition) pour in such an intense fire over a length of 200 yards of trench that it should be very difficult for the defenders to lift their heads above the parapet. Good head cover of course lessons the effect. We can also on a fairly still day put such a cloud of smoke in front of the trench that the defenders will see nothing 50 yards in front of them.

The subject of communications is closely mixed up with the co-operation of artillery with infantry. For the purpose of directing and controlling the fire of artillery so as to best assist the infantry, it is of primary importance that the artillery should know:

1. Where exactly the infantry that he is supporting is.
2. What is its immediate objective?
3. Anything that is preventing it attaining its object.

The question naturally arises how these are to be communicated from the infantry to the artillery. Artillery communication involves two distinct ideas.

1. Communication between the divisional artillery commander and his subordinates
2. Between infantry commanders and artillery subordinate commanders.

Both must be kept in view and organised as far as possible. The means of communication are: 1) Staff or orderly officers, 2) Mounted orderlies, 3) Artillery Brigade telephone, 4) Visual signalling, 5) Divisional signal service.

Appendix IV

The telephone is primarily intended as a means of communication between the artillery brigade commander and his batteries. If the brigade commander is some distance from his batteries and the batteries are scattered, it is difficult to see how the telephone can be used as a means of communication whether between the brigade commander and the divisional artillery commander, or between the infantry and artillery subordinate commanders, though if the batteries are not scattered it would be possible to use it for the former purpose.

Signalling is apt to disclose positions and messages &c to the enemy, and in any case the number of signallers make it impossible to trust exclusively to this method of communication.

The divisional signal service is a useful alternative, and if the subordinate artillery commander is near the infantry brigadier with whom he is cooperating it might be possible for him to communicate with the divisional artillery commander by using the cable that connects divisional and infantry brigade headquarters; but it is extremely doubtful whether he would be often able to use this, as the line will nearly always be congested with messages between infantry brigadier and the divisional general. So, it would practically come to this – that the only available means of finding out what the infantry want would be that the artillery commander remains close to the infantry brigadier, who would inform him of how and in what manner the artillery can best help the infantry.

It would, I think, considerably help if the brigadier commanding the infantry would as far as possible stay near the guns under his command. In the same way, if a battery is told off to help a certain battalion, for the battalion commander to try and stay somewhere near the battery. If the brigade or battalion commander thinks it necessary to go away himself, if the headquarters station is left somewhat near the brigade or battery it will considerably help the cooperation.

It might be possible to send an artillery officer on with the advanced infantry with a signaller, and he might be able to supply information of the three headings mentioned. This has often been tried, but I cannot say with any great success, as it has always been found to be extremely difficult to get any information back in sufficient time to be of any value.

In open country, cooperation between the two arms is extremely difficult, but when it come to a closely enclosed country, the difficulties are considerably increased. I am inclined to think that the only method to adopt is to push sections forward with the infantry, with orders to assist the infantry in every way possible, as it may be possible to get a section up to a position, when it would be quite impossible to get a battery. The section commanders of the sections pushed forward must of course be in close touch with the infantry commanders whom they are assisting.

The co-operation between the artillery and infantry at a decisive part of an action has been of late greatly discussed. It has been argued that at this stage artillery should be pushed forward as far as possible, and that unless they advance and come into action at short ranges, they are not affording the infantry the moral support that they should.

There can of course be little doubt that as the attack is about to be pushed home that it will be probably be necessary and advantageous to push forward some of the artillery to positions where it will have a clearer view of the infantry fight, and thus be able to afford to the infantry more effective support, but it must be remembered that artillery on the move is a very vulnerable target, and it is practically impossible for a unit of artillery to move in the open under a heavy artillery fire without completely losing its mobility, and I think personally that the tendency there was a short time ago, to argue that in order to give moral support to the infantry that batteries should be pushed forward close to the infantry firing line was a great mistake, unless such batteries could get there more or less under cover.

A battery that could afford close support to the infantry from a position where it was more or less immune from infantry fire would, I think, in reality, afford far greater moral support to the infantry, than a battery that was pushed forward under heavy fire with result of heavy losses to men and horses, and even if it managed to some of its guns into position, it would be a sorry sight to behold and its mobility would be gone. It must also be remembered that if artillery is pushed too far forward it will be unable often to shoot at all.

At ranges under 1500 yards on the level, it would be dangerous to fire over friendly troops at all; at longer ranges infantry would be in ordinary cases be safe at 500 yards from the guns or from the target. It also has to be remembered that at very close ranges, difficulties come in clearing the crest in front.

The difficulties of clearing the crest at short ranges has led to it being thought that field howitzers should be used for close attack and defence instead of field guns, and undoubtedly, they would be of great value for this purpose, but at the same time it must be remembered that they would have the same difficulty of getting there as the field artillery have.

In conclusion, there can be little doubt that in order to ensure really good and effective cooperation between the two arms, it is absolutely necessary that the two arms must be constantly practised in combination, and that the better the both arms get to know each other's needs and capabilities both by a personal exchange of views and by working together in training and manoeuvres, the better the cooperation will become.

Bibliography

The bibliography is organised as follows:
1. Archival Sources
    1.1 National Archives of the United Kingdom
        1.1.1 War Diaries
        1.1.2 Papers & reports
    1.2 National Library of Scotland
    1.3 Royal Artillery Museum, Larkhill
    1.4 Imperial War Museum

2. Published Sources
    2.1 Articles in Scholarly Journals
    2.2 Memoires Based on Diaries & Letters
    2.3 General Works & Special Studies
    2.4 Official History
    2.5 Regimental Histories
    2.6 Reference Works
    2.7 War Office publications

1. ARCHIVAL SOURCES

1.1 National Archives of the United Kingdom: Public Record Office, Kew

1.1.1 War diaries:

WO 95/1/2	General Staff
WO 95/588	I Corps staff
WO 95/629	II Corps staff intelligence
WO 95/630	II Corps staff
WO 95/646	II Corps Signal Co. RE
WO 95/1096	1st Cavalry Division
WO 95/1103	VII Brigade RHA
WO 95/1110	2nd Cavalry Brigade
WO 95/1123	III Brigade RHA

WO 95/1133	D Battery RHA
WO 95/1135	J Battery RHA
WO 95/1138	5th Cavalry Brigade
WO 95/1139	E Battery RHA
WO 95/1139	Scots Greys
WO 95/1227	1st Division
WO 95/1239	1st Division Artillery
WO 95/1248	XXV Brigade RFA
WO 95/1249	XXXIX Brigade RFA
WO 95/1250	XXVI Brigade RFA
WO 95/1250	XLIII Brigade RFA
WO 95/1261	1st Infantry Brigade
WO 95/1267	2nd Infantry Brigade
WO 95/1274	3rd Infantry Brigade
WO 95/1283	2nd Division
WO 95/1313	2nd Division Artillery
WO 95/1324	XXXIV Brigade RFA
WO 95/1325	XXXVI Brigade RFA
WO 95/1326	XLI Brigade RFA
WO 95/1327	XLIV Brigade RFA
WO 95/481	XXXV Heavy Battery
WO 95/1341	4th (Guards) Brigade
WO 95/1342	1st Irish Guards
WO 95/1342	2nd Grenadier Guards
WO 95/1342	2nd Coldstream Guards
WO 95/1342	3rd Coldstream Guards
WO 95/1343	5th Infantry Brigade
WO 95/1352	6th Infantry Brigade
WO 95/1364	19th Infantry Brigade
WO 95/1365	2nd Argyll & Sutherland Highlanders
WO 95/1375	3rd Division
WO 95/1390	3rd Division Artillery
WO 95/1395	RAMC, 3 Division
WO 95/1399	XXIII Brigade RFA
WO 95/1399	XXX Brigade RFA
WO 95/1400	XL Brigade RFA
WO 95/1401	XLII Brigade RFA
WO 95/1413	7th Infantry Brigade
WO 95/1414	2nd Prince of Wales (South Lancashire)
WO 95/1415	1st Duke of Edinburgh's (Wiltshire Regiment)
WO 95/1415	2nd Royal Irish Rifles
WO 95/1415	3rd Worcestershire Regiment

WO 95/1416	8th Infantry Brigade
WO 95/1421	1st Gordon Highlanders
WO 95/1421	2nd Royal Irish Regiment
WO 95/1422	4th Duke of Cambridge (Middlesex Regiment)
WO 95/1423	2nd Royal Scots (Lothian Regiment)
WO 95/1425	9th Infantry Brigade
WO 95/1429	1st Lincolnshire Regiment
WO 95/1430	1st Northumberland Fusiliers
WO 95/1431	4th Royal Fusiliers, (City of London)
WO 95/1432	1st Royal Scots Fusiliers
WO 95/1510	5th Division
WO 95/1521	5th Division Artillery
WO95/1527	VIII Brigade RFA
WO 95/1528	XV Brigade RFA
WO 95/1529	XXVII Brigade RFA
WO 95/1532	XXVIII Brigade RFA
WO 95/1548	13th Infantry Brigade
WO 95/1552	2nd Duke of Wellington's (West Riding Regiment)
WO 95/1552	2nd King's Own Scottish Borderers
WO 95/1553	1st Queen's Own (Royal West Kent)
WO 95/1558	2nd King's Own (Yorkshire Light Infantry)
WO 95/1560	14th Infantry Brigade
WO 95/1424	2nd Suffolk Regiment
WO 95/1563	1st East Surrey Regiment
WO 95/1564	2nd Manchester Regiment
WO 95/1564	1st Duke of Cornwall's Light Infantry
WO 95/1566	15th Infantry Brigade
WO 95/1570	1st Bedfordshire Regiment
WO 95/1571	1st Cheshire Regiment
WO 95/1572	1st Dorsetshire Regiment

1.1.2 Papers & reports

WO 159/23	Creedy papers
WO 279/47	Army Manoeuvres 1912
WO 27/508	Inspector General of Forces, 1912

1.2 National Library of Scotland

Acc. 3155/96	Douglas Haig Papers
Acc. 3155/98	Douglas Haig Papers

1.3 Royal Artillery Museum, Larkhill

MD/425	Lt E Schreiber, XXV brigade RFA, Journal
MD/657	Sergeant William Collins RAMC, Letter
MD/1150	Lieutenant (later Colonel) Roderick McLeod, Journal
MD/2960	Robert Francis Foljambe MC, 120th Battery RFA, Diary

1.4 Imperial War Museum

87/47/10	Smith-Dorrien papers
Document 15384	Lt Francis Henry Le Breton, private papers
Document 18429	Col. Albert Cyril Laurence George, private papers.

2. PUBLISHED SOURCES

2.1 Articles in Scholarly Journals

Hall, Maj Darrell, Guns in South Africa 1899-1902, Part 3, *South African Military History Society Journal*, Vol. 2, No 2, December 1971.

Hutchison, D., The Effectiveness of German Field Artillery at Mons and during the Retreat in August 1914, *Journal for the Society of Army Historical Research*, Vol 95, Winter 2017.

2.2 Memoires Based on Diaries & Letters

Charteris, John, *Field Marshal Earl Haig* (London: Cassell & Company, 1929)

French, Sir John, *1914* (London, Constable & Co. Ltd., 1919)

Hutchison, Colin, Journals and letters. Ref. D Hutchison, *The Young Gunner: The Royal Field Artillery in the Great War*, (Kibworth Beauchamp, Troubador Press 2016)

Smith-Dorrien, Sir Horace, *Memories of Forty-Eight Years' Service* (New York, E.P. Dutton and Company, 1925)

Spears, E.L., *Liaison 1914, a Narrative of the Great Retreat* (London, Heinemann, 1930)

2.3 General Works & Special Studies

Cooper, Duff, *Haig* (London, Faber & Faber, 1935)

Beckett, I.F.W. & Corvi, S.J. (eds.), *Haig's Generals* (Barnsley: Pen & Sword, 2006)

Bethell, H.A., *Modern Artillery in the Field: A Description of the Artillery of the Field Army, and the Principles and Methods of its Employment* (London, Macmillan, 1911)

Hamilton, Ernest, *The First Seven Divisions, Being a Detailed Account of the Fighting from Mons to Ypres*, (Lavergne, Tennessee, 2017, first published 1916)

Hutton, John, *The Gunners of 1914, Baptism of Fire* (Barnsley, Pen and Sword Books Ltd, 2014)

Jones, Spencer (ed.), *Stemming the Tide: Officers and Leadership in the British Expeditionary Force 1914* (Solihull, Helion & Co., 2013)

Marble, Sanders, *The Infantry cannot do with a gun less: The Place of the Artillery in the British Expeditionary Force, 1914-1918* (Gutenberg-E, 2013)

Terraine, J., *Mons, the Retreat to Victory* (London, B.T. Batsford Ltd, 1960)

Zuber, Terrence, *British and German Cavalry*, <http://terencezuber.com/ BritishandGermanCavalry.pdf>, (undated) Accessed December 2018.

2.4 Official Histories

Edmonds, J.E., History of the Great War, *Military Operations France & Belgium 1914, Vol. I* (London, Imperial War Museum and Nashville, Battery Press Inc.1922, revised 1933, reprinted 1996)

2.5 Regimental Histories

Geoghegan, Brig. Gen. S., *The Campaigns and History of the Royal Irish Regiment, Vol II* (Edinburgh, William Blackwood and Sons Ltd, 1927)

Jones, James A., *A History of the South Staffordshire Regiment (1705-1923)* (Wolverhampton, Whitehead Bros, 1923)

Kingsford, Charles, *The Story of the Duke of Cambridge's Own (Middlesex Regiment)* (London, Country Life, 1916)

O'Neill, H.C., *The Royal Fusiliers in the Great War* (London, William Heinemann, 1922)

Simpson Maj. Gen. C. R. (ed.), *The History of The Lincolnshire Regiment, 1914-1918, Compiled from War Diaries, Dispatches, Officers' Notes and Other Sources* (London, The Medici Society, Ltd, 1931)

The Worcestershire Regiment <http://www.worcestershireregiment.com/bat_2_1914.php>

2.6 Reference Works

Cron, Herman, *Imperial German Army 1914-18* (Solihull, Helion & Company Ltd, 2001)

Jäger, Herbert, *German Artillery of World War One* (Marlborough, Crowood Press, 2001)

Hogg & Thurston, *British Artillery Weapons and Ammunition 1914-1918* (Shepperton, Ian Allan Ltd, 1972)

Ralph Reiley, *The Organization of the German Army, August 1914* <http://www.worldwar1.com/sfgarmy.htm>. accessed December 2017

Tucker, Dr Spencer (ed.), *World War One: A Student Encyclopedia,* (Santa Barbara, California, ABC-CLIO Inc., 2006)

2.7 War Office

War Office, *Field Service Regulations, 1909, reprinted with amendments 1912*, (London, HMSO, 1914)

—— *Notes from the Front, collated by the General Staff,* (London: HMSO, 1914)

—— *The German Forces in the Field; 7th Revision, 1918.* (London: HMSO, 1918)

Index

PEOPLE

Allenby, Major General Sir Edmund vi, x-xi, 46-48, 65-68, 72, 104, 108-109, 114, 125, 138, 145

Breton, Lieutenant Le 97, 112
Bulfin, Brigadier General E. 108, 146

Chapman, Lieutenant 120-121
Collins, William 89, 160
Cuthbert, Brigadier General G. 51-52, 148

Davies, Brigadier General R. 81, 108, 147
Doran, Brigadier General B. 77, 96, 115, 130, 147

Edmonds, Brigadier General 50, 66, 128

Falkenhayn, General Erich von 20, 139
Fergusson, Sir Charles 28, 42, 70, 109-110, 126, 142, 104, 115, 126, 148
Findlay, Brigadier General 62, 90, 142, 146
French, Field Marshal Sir John ix-xi, 17, 21, 23-24, 27, 29, 33, 35-40, 42-49, 54-59, 61, 64-69, 100, 107-109, 111, 128-129, 131-135, 138, 141-142, 145, 160

Gough, Brigadier General J.E. 107, 146
Grierson, Lieutenant General ix, 23-24, 29-30, 33, 39, 42, 44, 48, 128, 131, 134-135

Haig, Lieutenant General Sir Douglas ix, 22-24, 29-30, 33, 41, 43-46, 48-49, 54-63, 65-70, 83-84, 92-95, 97, 100-102, 105-108, 110, 112, 128-129, 132-133, 135-139, 141-142, 146, 159-160
Haking, Brigadier General R. 100, 147
Hamilton, Major General Hubert vi, 68, 78, 91-93, 99-100, 102-103, 115, 142, 147, 161

Headlam, Brigadier General 51-53, 70-71, 87-88, 120, 121, 124, 130, 142 148
Horne, Brigadier General Henry xi, 56, 60, 62-63, 89, 94, 99, 101-102, 108, 112-114, 119, 129, 136-138, 142, 146

Joffre, General 37, 39, 129

Kitchener, Field Marshal Lord 20, 38, 40, 44, 65, 135
Kluck, General von 74, 109-110, 149

Lanrezac, General 39, 65
Lindsay, Major General W.F.L. 29, 41, 145
Lomax, Major General S. 23, 47, 92, 104-105, 142, 146

Mas-Latrie, General de 55-56
McCracken, Brigadier General F. 119, 147
McLeod, Lieutenant Rory 28, 70-71, 121, 124
Monro, Major General C. 59, 94, 101-102, 105-106, 108, 136-137, 142, 146
Murray, Sir Archibald x, 66-68, 92, 100, 104, 106, 145

Percival, Brigadier General 62, 90, 94, 147

Schreiber, Lieutenant 77, 98, 112
Scott-Kerr, Brigadier General 101-102, 105, 146
Short, Brigadier General A. 42, 147
Smith-Dorrien, Sir Horace ix-xi, 23-24, 30, 44-51, 53-54, 58, 61, 64-70, 72, 83, 88, 91, 96, 99-104, 106, 108-110, 115, 128, 130-135, 137-138, 142, 147, 160

Wing, Brigadier General 53, 72, 77-79, 87, 142, 147

163

PLACES

Aisne River 39, 87
Aldershot 33, 35
Amiens 35, 45
Ath 44, 54

Bavai x, 42-43, 45, 53, 56, 58, 61-62, 67-68, 71, 82, 84, 90, 100, 102, 107, 111-113, 125, 127, 135
Belgium ix, 31-32, 34-40, 42, 45-46, 50, 55, 57, 69, 75, 79, 85, 87, 96, 103, 107-108, 110, 116, 126, 129, 134, 140, 161
Binche 36, 42, 59, 101, 111
Blaugies 124-125
Bois la Haut 51, 53, 59, 63, 68, 73, 77-78, 80-83, 90-91, 95-96, 106
Bonnet 100-101
Bougnies 90-94, 100, 105, 112-114, 119
Boussu 67, 70-71, 106
Bray 57, 63
Brussels 36, 42, 44, 46

Charleroi 43, 83
Ciply 64, 68, 72-73, 83, 95, 113, 116-117, 119, 126
Condé 49, 108, 138
Conde Canal 45, 66

Dour 51, 53, 67-68, 70-71, 88, 109, 116, 121-122, 124-126

Fort des Sars 44, 48, 49, 59
Frameries 67, 72-73, 99, 101, 103, 116-118, 122

Genly 67, 83, 90-92, 113, 115
Givry 46-49, 51, 59, 63-64, 90, 94-95, 97-98, 101, 108, 111-114

Haine River 51, 88, 103-104
Harmignies 47, 51, 55, 59, 63-64, 67-69, 72, 78, 81-84, 90-91, 93-97, 99-103, 105, 112-115, 118-119, 132, 136
Harveng x-xi, 83, 90, 92-95, 98, 100-103, 105, 108, 113, 136, 138
Havre 33-36
Hill 93 51, 84, 93, 95, 100, 103, 105, 112, 115, 137

Ireland 28, 31-32

Jamappes 69, 85, 116

Landrecies 36, 45, 108
Le Cateau 39, 45, 52, 107-108, 134, 139
Liège 36, 42
Liverpool 34, 147

Mariette 49, 79, 85, 103
Maubeuge 36-37, 40, 43-44, 48-49, 54-56, 59, 110-111, 113, 135

Namur 36, 42
Nimy 47, 49, 65, 67, 74-76, 78-79, 81
Noirchain 73, 102, 117
Nouvelles 73, 95, 105

Obourg Bridge 63, 78, 130

Paris 39, 85
Paturages x, 72, 91, 100, 102-104, 111, 113, 119-120, 123
Péronnes 57, 59, 83, 96
Pommeroeul 49, 69, 88

Quevy 82-84, 90-92, 95, 113-114, 136

Rouen 34-36, 40, 42, 53
Rouveroy 55, 89-90, 104, 108, 111-112

Sars-la-Bruyère 55, 64-65, 101, 103, 108, 115, 119
South Africa 15, 17, 30, 160
Southampton 31, 34-35
St Ghislain 51, 59, 71, 85, 87, 116, 120

Thulin 45, 47, 71

Valenciennes 61, 65, 67, 89, 127
Vellereille-le-Sec 55, 57, 89-90, 96-97, 113

Wasmes 70-72, 88, 99, 103-104, 120-122, 124, 130
Woolwich 14, 29

York 35

INDEX OF MILITARY FORMATIONS & UNITS

Belgian Army 36-37
British Army 13-15, 20, 23-24, 30-31, 44-45, 66, 132, 135, 137, 141-142
British Expeditionary Force (BEF) 17, 21, 23, 29, 33, 36-38, 40, 43-44, 64, 106, 125, 128, 137, 140-141, 145, 161
French Fifth Army 36-37, 39, 42-45, 107, 109
German First Army 37, 74, 149-150
Indian Army 13, 15

I Corps ix-xi, 33, 36, 40-41, 43-46, 48, 54-57, 59, 61-63, 65, 67-68, 72, 75, 83-84, 89, 91-97, 99-102, 104, 106-108, 111-112, 114-115, 119, 123, 129, 133, 135-136, 139, 141-142, 146
II Corps ix-xi, 20, 33, 36-37, 39-49, 54-64, 67-69, 71-76, 78, 83-84, 89, 91-92, 99-109, 113-115, 118-119, 126, 131-133, 135-136, 139, 141-142, 147, 150

German
II Cavalry Corps 107, 109
III Corps 37, 74, 75, 85, 87, 107, 110-111, 150
IV Corps 37, 88-89, 107, 110, 115, 124, 126, 150
IX Corps 37, 74, 75, 78, 85, 87, 91, 107, 110, 150
VII Corps 66, 96, 107

1st Division x, 33, 36, 41, 44, 47-48, 55-58, 59, 60, 62, 68, 82, 89-90, 92, 94, 98, 101, 104, 108, 111-114, 135-136, 142, 146, 158
2nd Division x, 33, 36, 41, 55-65, 68, 73, 77-78, 81-84, 89-98, 101-102, 104-105, 108, 111-113, 115, 119, 122, 130, 133, 135-137, 139, 142, 146, 158
3rd Division x-xi, 20, 32-34, 36, 41-43, 47, 49, 53, 55, 59-60, 63, 67-68, 72, 74, 77-78, 82, 85, 87, 90-96, 99-106, 110, 112-116, 118-119, 122, 126-127, 130-131, 134, 137, 142, 147, 158
4th Division 50, 66
5th Division xi, 15, 26, 28, 32-33, 36, 41-42, 47, 49, 51-53, 66-67, 69-72, 74, 77, 85, 87-88, 99, 101-104, 106, 109-110, 115-116, 120-123, 125-126, 130-131, 142, 148, 159

Cavalry Division 20, 33, 35-36, 39-40, 42, 46-48, 54, 56-57, 61, 64-67, 71-72, 74-75, 89, 108-109, 124-125, 138, 141, 145, 150, 157

German
17th Division 78, 91, 96
18th Division 74, 78, 80

1st (Guards) Infantry Brigade 89, 146
2nd Infantry Brigade 90, 112, 146, 158
3rd Infantry Brigade 35, 44, 47-48, 54, 56, 59, 89, 92, 98, 104-105, 111-112, 146, 158
4th Infantry Brigade 93, 95, 100, 111, 136-137
4th (Guards) Infantry Brigade 31, 82-83, 93, 95, 105
5th Infantry Brigade 35, 56, 60, 83, 90-94, 101-102, 104, 113, 119, 123, 147, 158
6th Infantry Brigade 60, 81-84, 89-91, 93-94, 96-97, 99, 101, 105, 111-112, 147, 158
7th Infantry Brigade 47, 63, 72-73, 89, 91, 95-96, 104-105, 116, 118-119, 126, 147, 158
8th Infantry Brigade 31-32, 63-64, 72-74, 76-79, 81, 88, 96, 101, 105, 115-116, 118-119, 130, 147, 159
9th Infantry Brigade 47, 53, 73, 76, 78-79, 85, 99, 103, 114, 116, 119, 147, 159
13th Infantry Brigade 49, 52, 71, 85, 87-88, 99, 103-104, 120-123, 148, 159
14th Infantry Brigade 49, 53, 71, 87-88, 104, 109, 123-125, 148, 159
15th Infantry Brigade 49, 70, 99, 104, 120-122, 126, 148, 159
19th Infantry Brigade 61, 67, 72, 89, 104, 108-110, 126, 148, 158
Cavalry Brigade 42, 48, 56-58, 84, 97, 108-109, 112-113, 119, 125-126, 136-138, 145-146, 157-158

Bedfordshire Regiment 103-104, 120, 122, 148, 159
Coldstream Guards 82-83, 92, 146, 158
Dorsetshire Regiment 99-100, 103-104, 120, 122, 130, 148, 159
Dragoon Guards 145, 146
Duke of Cornwall's Light Infantry 69, 148, 159

Duke of Wellington's 122, 148, 159
East Surrey Regiment 53, 87, 125, 148, 159
Gloucestershire Regiment (Glosters) 104, 111, 133, 146
Gordon Highlanders 78, 81, 95-96, 147, 159
Grenadier Guards 82-83, 95, 99, 101, 105, 146, 158
Highland Light Infantry 102, 147
Irish Guards 60, 82, 84, 94-95, 101, 105, 111, 133, 136, 147, 158
Irish Rifles 47, 64, 72, 95, 105, 147, 158
King's Own Yorkshire Light Infantry (KYOLI) 121-123, 130, 148, 159
King's Royal Rifle Corps 146-147
Lincolnshire Regiment 79, 116-118, 147, 159, 161
Lothian Regiment 147, 159
Manchester Regiment, 123-124, 148, 159
Middlesex Regiment 63, 76-78, 81, 95, 130-131, 147-148, 159, 161
Norfolk Regiment 49, 148
Northumberland Fusiliers 76, 92, 147
Prince Albert's Own Hussars 57, 145, 146
Queen's Own Hussars 145, 148, 159
Royal Berkshire Regiment 97, 147
Royal Field Artillery 14, 20-22, 24, 76-77, 160
Royal Fusiliers 75-76, 78-79, 99, 146-148, 159, 161
Royal Horse Artillery 14, 24, 28, 126, 145
Royal Irish Regiment 63, 73, 78, 80-81, 95, 139-140, 145, 147, 159, 161
Royal Irish Rifles 47, 64, 72, 95, 158
Royal Scots 63, 72, 78, 81, 95, 105, 146-147, 159
Royal West Surrey 111, 146
Scots Greys 66, 146, 158
South Lancashire Regiment 64, 116-118, 147
South Staffordshire Regiment 81, 82, 91, 95, 97, 132, 147, 161
South Wales Borderers 111, 146
Welch Regiment 111, 146
West Kent Regiment 76, 85, 92, 148
West Riding Regiment 122, 148, 159
Wiltshire Regiment 72, 147, 158
Worcestershire Regiment 72, 111, 118-119, 147, 158

III Brigade RHA 126, 145, 157
VII Brigade RHA 72, 89, 126, 145, 157
15th Brigade RFA 28, 46, 70-71, 88, 148, 159
23rd Brigade RFA 32, 42, 53, 73, 79, 117-119, 148, 158
25th Brigade RFA 77, 89, 98, 112, 124, 146, 158, 160
26th Brigade RFA 89, 146, 158
27th Brigade RFA 52-53, 71, 85-86, 88, 104, 120-121, 123-124, 148, 159
28th Brigade RFA 32, 71, 88, 125, 148, 159
34th Brigade RFA   90, 98, 147, 158
36th Brigade RFA 90, 93-94, 112-113, 147, 158
39th Brigade RFA 90, 112, 146, 158
40th Brigade RFA 32, 42, 53, 73, 77-78, 81, 95, 118, 148, 158
41st Brigade RFA 82-83, 90, 92, 94, 97, 99, 101, 105, 112-114, 147, 158
42nd Brigade RFA 32, 42, 73, 119, 148, 158
119th Brigade RFA 87-88, 126, 148
121st Brigade RFA 87-88, 126, 148

8th (Howitzer) Brigade 71, 88, 148
30th (Howitzer) Brigade RFA 32, 73, 119, 126, 148
43rd Howitzer Brigade RFA 89 146
44th (Howitzer) Brigade RFA 94, 147
47th (Howitzer) Battery 94, 98

6th Battery 78 81, 96, 14
9th Battery 90, 97, 111, 114, 147
15th Battery 28, 53
16th Battery 82, 90, 94, 99, 105, 114, 147
17th Battery 82, 90, 94, 99, 105, 114, 147
22nd Battery 90, 147
23rd Battery 78, 80-81, 95, 148
30th Battery 32, 42, 73, 119, 126, 146
35th Heavy Battery RGA 93, 147
37th Battery 71, 88, 122, 148
40th Battery 32, 42, 73, 119, 126, 146
47th Battery 94, 98-99, 147
49th Battery 78, 81, 148
50th Battery 90, 97, 98, 111, 112, 147
57th Battery 32, 42, 73, 119, 126, 146
61st Battery 71, 88, 122, 148
56th Battery 94, 98-99, 147
60th Battery 94, 98-99, 147
65th Battery 71, 88, 122, 148
70th Battery 90, 98, 111, 147
71st Battery 93, 147
80th Battery 70, 121, 124, 148
107th Battery 78, 117-118, 148

Index   167

108th Battery 71, 88, 118, 148
109th Battery 79, 117
115th Battery 111-112, 146
116th Battery 111-112, 146
117th Battery 111-112, 146
118th Battery 111-112, 146
120th Battery 52, 71, 85-87, 104, 121, 123, 148, 160
121st Battery 120, 123

123rd Battery 32, 125, 148
130th Battery 32, 126, 148

'J' Battery RHA 112-114, 119, 146, 158

Brigade Ammunition Column 14-15, 25, 32, 41-42, 73, 80, 143
Divisional Ammunition Column 15, 34, 42, 44, 62, 73, 119, 144